Shakespeare Only

Shakespeare Only

JEFFREY KNAPP

The University of Chicago Press ✸ *Chicago and London*

JEFFREY KNAPP is
chancellor's professor of
English at the University
of California, Berkeley. He
is the author of two books,
*An Empire Nowhere:
England, America, and
Literature from* Utopia
to The Tempest (1994),
and *Shakespeare's Tribe:
Church, Nation, and Theater
in Renaissance England*
(2002), published by the
University of Chicago
Press and winner of the
Bainton Prize of the
Sixteenth-Century Stud-
ies conference, the Book
of the Year Award of the
Conference on Christian-
ity and Literature, and the
Best Book in Literature
and Language Award of
the Professional/Scholarly
Publishing Division of the
Association of American
Publishers.

The University of Chicago Press, Chicago 60637
The University of Chicago Press, Ltd., London
© 2009 by The University of Chicago
All rights reserved. Published 2009
Printed in the United States of America
18 17 16 15 14 13 12 11 10 09   1 2 3 4 5
ISBN-13: 978-0-226-44571-7 (cloth)
ISBN-10: 0-226-44571-2 (cloth)

Library of Congress Cataloging-in-Publication Data
Knapp, Jeffrey.
    Shakespeare only / Jeffrey Knapp.
        p.   cm.
    Includes bibliographical references and index.
    ISBN-13: 978-0-226-44571-7 (cloth : alk. paper)
    ISBN-10: 0-226-44571-2 (cloth : alk. paper)   1. Shake-
speare, William, 1564–1616—Authorship.   2. Shakespeare, William, 1564–1616—Criticism and interpretation.
3. English drama—Early modern and Elizabethan, 1500–
1600—History and criticism.   4. English drama—17th
century—History and criticism.   I. Title.
    PR2937 .K59 2009
    822.3′3—dc22   2009006781

∞ The paper used in this publication meets the
minimum requirements of the American National
Standard for Information Sciences—Permanence
of Paper for Printed Library Materials,
ANSI Z39.48–1992.

To Maddie and Dori

He is himself alone,
To answer all the city.

CORIOLANUS

Contents

Preface

Several decades ago, widespread interest in the presumed historicity of the self led many scholars to question whether a self as we understood it even existed during the English Renaissance. Some traced the origins of modern subjectivity, interiority, and individuality to the Renaissance stage, particularly to Shakespeare. Others came to offer more focused and conditional versions of the broader historical claim. They argued that the *author* did not exist before 1600, or that no dramatic authors existed—in the commercial theaters, anyway. For these scholars, too, Shakespeare seemed a pivotal figure. But whether he was associated with one historical development or the other, the change was always understood to be for the worse. Both selfhood and authorship were characterized as ideologies, illusions that subjected and confined energies otherwise communal and free.[1]

Shakespeare Only belongs to a different time and a different critical movement, which a recent issue of *Shakespeare Studies* has plausibly titled "The Return of the Author." Like all polemical labels, however, this one fails to capture the organic continuity of new projects with the work that has preceded them. The idea of a return implies that for the past few decades the author and his followers have been wandering in the wilderness and are only now getting back to the critical perspectives that matter: back to formalism, say, instead of feminism or poststructuralism or cultural studies or historicism. *Shakespeare Only* does indeed take issue with recent historicist work on the Renaissance theater, but it also stems directly from that work. My goal in this book is to help write the history of authorship that earlier Renaissance scholars first called for and then barred themselves from pursuing, when they insisted that there were no authors in Shakespeare's world. In my view, this project requires a historical approach that allows change to be more complex than an epistemic break with the past, and the individual to be more complex than a breaker of community, as it also resists an utopian identification of the good with any one of these terms—with the past, with change, with the individual, or with community.

What I chiefly draw from earlier theater historians is the insight that Shakespeare's conception of himself as an author was shaped by a distinctly new development in English culture toward the end of the sixteenth century: the *institutionalization* of drama as mass entertainment. A few years after Shakespeare was born, the first new permanent theaters in Europe since Roman times opened on the outskirts of London, and these playhouses "capable of many thousands" offered writers "the first direct and regular contact with a large and committed crowd of hearers that poets in England had ever enjoyed."[2] The prospects for ambitious dramatists seemed so great that by the end of the century the satirist Joseph Hall (1597) could expect his readers to believe that some inebriated hack was at that very moment fantasizing he could equal the spectacular success of a contemporary play like *Tamburlaine:*

> Then weeneth he his base drink-drownéd sprite,
> Rapt to the threefold loft of heaven's height,
> When he conceives upon his fainéd stage
> The stalking steps of his great personage,
> Gracéd with huff-cap terms and thund'ring threats
> That his poor hearers' hair quite upright sets.

"His great personage": thanks to the proven force of words in the new theaters, Hall could imagine a writer who imagined himself *as* his "thund'ring" character, exercising one and the same power to tyrannize over audiences.[3]

With this unprecedented reach in the theaters, however, came unprecedented risks. The first was failure on a grand scale. When Shakespeare's first editors maintained in 1623 that his plays had "had their *trial* already" on the stage, they were using no mere figure of speech.[4] In 1630 the dramatist Philip Massinger mocked coterie poets for "not daring to endure the public test" of commercial playwriting. Flaunting his bravery, the playwright Thomas Dekker began his 1612 work *If This Be Not a Good Play, The Devil Is In It* with the wish "that at all New-plays / *The Makers* sat o'th *Stage*, either with *Bays* / To have their *Works Crown'd*, or beaten in with *Hissing*." Not all dramatists were so stoical about the public trials they had to endure. "How is't possible to suffice / So many Ears, so many Eyes?" bemoaned the prologue to Thomas Middleton's *No {Wit Help} Like a Womans* (1611), while the prologue to John Day's *Isle of Gulls* (1606) bitterly complained that "neither quick mirth, invective, nor high state, / Can content all: such is the boundless hate / Of a confuséd Audience."[5] Failing to please could place more than an author's pride in danger. If a dramatist should "strike at abuse, or ope the vein of sin," the prologue to the *Isle* continues, "he is straight inform'd against for libeling"—and Day learned soon enough that he was right to be worried: thanks to its satire, *The Isle of Gulls* caused "sundry" of the actors and possibly Day himself to be "committed to Bridewell."[6]

A more common fate for playwrights was debtor's prison. From the "loft" of his delusion, Hall's "high-aspiring" poetaster overlooks the crucial practical intermediary between his words and his audience: the actors, whose companies made the lion's share of any profits from plays. One of these companies, the Admiral's Men, employed stables of writers such as Robert Daborne, whose surviving correspondence with the company's banker and landlord Philip Henslowe shows a dramatist constantly in financial straits, begging for advances on the plays he was helping to write, and offering to fix "any other book" Henslowe might have in his possession. Why, Samuel Rowlands asked in 1600, were poets "spending" their "invention's treasure" to enrich "Stage parrots" and not themselves? So too, John Donne ridiculed the poet who "gives idiot actors means/(Starving himself) to live by his labor'd scenes."[7]

But Shakespeare was no starving poet: he was an actor in the king's own theater company, an immensely popular playwright, and a moneymaker to boot. Unlike any other English dramatist before him, he came to own part of the acting company and theater for which he wrote and therefore earned a larger than normal share of the profit from his labors. What's more, his unusual position as an author, actor, and investor almost certainly gave him greater control over the enactment of his scripts than most or perhaps any other commercial playwrights enjoyed. But it also tied him more closely than other playwrights to the interests of a single company. Daborne, though poor, could at least move "freely from one theater to another": in his study of Henslowe's business diary, Neil Carson concludes that "the majority of the playwrights mentioned in the diary were independent agents selling their talents wherever they could."[8] For all his distinctive good fortune, Shakespeare's exclusive attachment to one company must have exerted considerable pressure on him to see his authorship as part of a group endeavor.

But then no playwright for the new arena theaters could escape the even heavier group pressure of the theaters' mass audiences, who were as heterogeneous in class as in taste. Against the hack's visions of glory, Hall sets the vulgar actuality of the "base" playgoer with "clumsy fist" and "teeth in double rotten-row" who purchased standing room in the theaters for a penny. What true poet, Hall demands, could "bide to pen some hungry *Scene*/For thick-skin ears, and undiscerning eyne?" And how could pleasing this herd result in anything but humiliation? "Shame," Hall calls it: "Shame that the Muses should be bought and sold,/For every peasant's Brass, on each scaffold."[9]

Such conflicting potentialities for liberation and restriction, triumph and disgrace make any modern pronouncements about the communal or else self-aggrandizing nature of Renaissance playwriting seem airily detached from the fundamental complexity of the author's position in Renaissance English theater culture. If any author could have overcome the obstacles facing commercial dramatists, we might guess, it would have been the chief dramatist of the most prestigious acting company in England, the man who subsequently became the most famous playwright in the world. But Shakespeare, I will argue throughout this book, did not want to overcome the obstacles—he wanted to *absorb* them; and his singular combination of professional roles and responsibilities both encouraged and facilitated that project. Revealingly, the conquering hero that Shakespeare fashioned for the stage launches his brilliant career by *descending* to the tavern from which Hall's poetaster dreams of arising. Rather than terrorize his poor hearers with thundering words, moreover, Prince Hal chooses to sound "the very base-string of humility," learning among other things how to "drink with any tinker in his own language." The prince intends to reform, of course, and expects that the very shamefulness of his beginning will help make him a wonder in the end. Shakespeare, like Hall's hack, may have shared the ambitions of his high-aspiring character, but he never ceased to remind himself that he lacked the princely title Hal depends upon to shake off "vulgar company." Differentiating himself from both the playwright and the poet as Hall imagined them, Shakespeare embraced the paradoxical and yet thoroughly professional theory that a commercial dramatist could achieve "rareness" and "glory" only by aspiring to seem "common" too.[10]

Acknowledgments

Richard Helgerson, Stephen Orgel, and Stephen Greenblatt were the guiding lights of this project. I don't know what I could have written without them, or without the aid of Joel Altman, Oliver Arnold, Deirdre D'Albertis, Lorna Hutson, Victoria Kahn, Steven Knapp, Sharon Marcus, Samuel Otter, Nancy Ruttenburg, and James Schamus. Also essential to me was the practical and moral support of Milena Edwards, Paul and Suzy Billings, Maria Mavroudi and Panos Papadopoulos, Xanthippe Philips, and Donna Grethen and Paul Tong. Marisa Libbon was a superb researcher, as were Gertrude Obi and Matthew Seidel. Through two books now I have drawn liberally from the wells of E. K. Chambers and G. E. Bentley, whose achievements boggle me even more now than when I first encountered them.

I'm deeply grateful to the University of California, Berkeley, for the time and money that underwrote this project. I particularly want to thank three chairs—Janet Adelman, Cathy Gallagher, and Ian Duncan—as well as two deans—Ralph Hexter and Janet Broughton. My thanks go also to the audiences at Berkeley, Harvard, Columbia, Bard, Vanderbilt, Salt Lake City, Munich, Waterloo, and Sydney who commented on earlier drafts of this book, and to my colleagues on the board of *Representations* who helped me conceive of the book *as* a book. Patrick Cheney, David

Landreth, Walter Benn Michaels, Gail Kern Paster, and Brian Vickers also advised me on early drafts, and my two readers at Chicago, Katherine Maus and an anonymous colleague, gave me valuable feedback on the entire manuscript. As before, my editor at Chicago, Alan Thomas, has been wonderfully supportive, and my copyeditor, Lys Ann Weiss, wonderfully thorough. The first installment of this project appeared as "What Is a Co-Author?" in *Representations* 89 (2005): 1–29; an early version of chapter 3 appeared as "Religious Pluralization and Single Authorship in Shakespeare's Histories" in *Representing Religious Pluralization in Early Modern Europe,* edited by Andreas Höfele et al. (Berlin: Lit-Verlag, 2007), 153–73; and a portion of chapter 4 appeared in *Shakespeare Studies* 36 (2008): 49-59 as "Shakespeare as Coauthor."

It has taken me too long to thank my parents Arthur and Betty Knapp for giving me the freedom to pursue literary studies. What can I say to Dorothy Hale and Madeline Hale? Only that I love you both.

Introduction

Our Author submits his labors to you, as the Authors of all the content he hath within this circumference.

« PROLOGUE TO THOMAS HEYWOOD, *The Foure Prentises of London* (acted c. 1594) »

Where my previous book *Shakespeare's Tribe* asked how Shakespeare's thinking was shaped by the religious, political, and especially professional groups to which he belonged, *Shakespeare Only* asks whether Shakespeare and his contemporaries ever thought of him as one of a kind.

At first glance, these two projects might seem antithetical to one another, divided along the polemical lines of the past four decades in Shakespeare scholarship. On one side of the controversy are the Shakespeare lovers, the bardolatrists, whose boldest spokesperson Harold Bloom has denounced recent historicist scholarship on the Renaissance theater for its denial of "Shakespeare's unique eminence" as an author: "Shakespeare criticism," writes Bloom in *The Western Canon* (1994), "is in full flight from his aesthetic supremacy and works at reducing him to the 'social energies' of the English Renaissance."[1] On the other side of the debate are the historicists who view Shakespeare's greatness as a *post facto* construction with no substantial relevance to the historical person and his writings. According to Michael

Dobson, for instance, Shakespeare's supremacy as an author was first elaborated in the eighteenth century to buttress English claims of national unity and greatness. Margreta de Grazia traces the origins of Shakespeare's singularity to the great eighteenth-century editions of Shakespeare's works, which depicted most of the playscripts attributed to Shakespeare as stemming from the coherent intentions of one incomparable mind; others, such as Leah Marcus and David Kastan, trace this bibliographical fabrication of "a transcendent Shakespeare" to the very first edition of his collected works, the First Folio of 1623. But the most widespread and influential critique of bardolatry has arisen from the attempts of scholars such as Stephen Orgel, Peter Stallybrass, Richard Helgerson, Jeffrey Masten, and Lukas Erne to demystify the study of Shakespeare by placing him in the historical context of his profession in particular.[2] How, these scholars ask, can we speak of Shakespeare as a solitary eminence when he worked in mass entertainment, writing and acting for a theater company that staged plays before thousands of spectators? For these critics, the bardolatrous emphasis on Shakespeare only is itself a form of denial that blinds us to the inescapably social nature of drama. If we want to see the Renaissance theater for the communal and collaborative institution it really was, writes the boldest of the historicists, it is indeed over Shakespeare's "dead authorial body/corpus that we have the most to learn."[3]

But why must the individualizing and the institutionalizing perspectives on Shakespeare be opposed to one another?[4] Bloom attacks historicists for "reducing [Shakespeare] to his contexts," but placing Shakespeare in his own time would of necessity reduce him only if his value depended on his *difference* from that context, which Bloom himself does not believe.[5] A bardolatrous ban on historicism would in any case be hard to take seriously because it would amount to claiming that we appreciate Shakespeare more when we know less about him. Conversely, Bloom seems right to insist that the historical context alone cannot explain why the works of Shakespeare have received such extraordinary attention. "If it is arbitrary that Shakespeare centers the

Canon," Bloom asks, then why was Shakespeare "rather than, say, Ben Jonson" selected "for that arbitrary role"? "How much simpler," Bloom concludes, "to admit that there is a *qualitative* difference"?[6]

The problem for Bloom is that most historicists of the Renaissance theater *do* admit the difference. What they resist is the claim that *Shakespeare in particular,* or any other single author, wrote the astonishing plays that we now ascribe to him. As Orgel argues at the start of his foundational essay "What Is a Text?" (1981), "the creation of a play" during the English Renaissance was in fact "a collaborative process, with the author by no means at the center of the collaboration. The company commissioned the play, usually stipulated the subject, often provided the plot, often parceled it out, scene by scene, to several playwrights. The text thus produced was a working model, which the company then revised as seemed appropriate." Orgel repeats these influential claims at the start of his more recent *Imagining Shakespeare* (2003): "in most cases in Shakespeare's time," he maintains, "the playwright was not at all at the center" of the "collaboration" that generated plays; "he was an employee of the company, and once he delivered the script his interest in it, and his authority over it, was ended."[7]

In subsequent work by Orgel and by others he has inspired, this provocative depreciation of authorship has been elaborated into a richly detailed and also comprehensive historiographical vision of a theater where authors figured only marginally or not at all. It is hard not to notice how neatly the vision matches the method that generated it: having concentrated on a nexus of theatrical practices, on the theater as an institution, Orgel and his fellow historicists decide that the institution is the key. But this is not a necessary outcome of their method. While *Shakespeare Only* springs from the recent historiography of authorship and is profoundly indebted to the work of Orgel, Helgerson, and Erne in particular, I join other theater historians, such as Stephen Greenblatt, Robert Weimann, and Patrick Cheney, in arguing that an institutional analysis of Renaissance drama can and indeed must keep authors squarely in the picture.

Before I begin this task, however, I must first look more closely at the reasons why historicists as formidably learned and intelligent as Orgel believe they should steer Renaissance theater scholarship away from authors. The case they've made deserves sustained analysis on several grounds. First, the arguments of Orgel and others could not be so widely accepted if they were not also powerfully compelling. Second, the assumption of a fundamental contrariety between authorship and mass entertainment has taken several ostensibly different forms—that the author is elitist, or individualist, or antitheatrical—and I want to show how these variations share a common theme. Third, the counterposing of authorship to mass entertainment has been defended by many subsidiary arguments that seem to stand independent of the claim when they in fact derive from it, and I want to trace these arguments back to their conceptual origins. Finally, by insisting that dramatic authorship be understood *in relation* to mass entertainment, historicist scholarship has paradoxically done more than any previous scholarship to highlight just how deeply authorship shaped mass entertainment in Renaissance England and mass entertainment shaped authorship.

The Case against Authors

As Orgel stresses in "What Is a Text?" the authors of most commercial Renaissance plays had considerably less power over their scripts than we might now assume. Not only were they subject to their employers, the acting companies, but they also lacked modern legal protections such as copyright laws to enforce ownership of the scripts they sold. Those scripts were probably always revised, to a lesser or greater extent, by the companies that performed them, as well as by the publishers that printed them, leaving what Orgel rightly calls "a hard core of uncertainty" about who wrote what in the surviving scripts, and why. Yet none of these factors justifies Orgel's blanket assertion that the dramatic author was "by no means at the center of the collaboration" that generated Renaissance playscripts. While we may be uncertain about the attribution of scripts written four hundred years ago, it does not follow that their attribution was always uncertain—that scripts arose from a bewildering "whirlwind of activity," as one historicist imagines.[8] What's more, uncertainty about attribution cuts both ways: if we cannot be sure that individual playwrights were the primary producers of these scripts, neither can we be sure that they were not. Orgel elides this problem by presenting the author's delivery of his script to the company as an absolute rupture between the writer and his writing: once the company took possession, in Orgel's account, the author lost not only his "authority" over the script but his "interest" in it as well. Yet what do "interest" and "authority" mean in this context? Even under modern copyright laws, an author must eventually lose any *legal* interest in and authority over her writing, but this does not stop her from being considered the author still. Why should a loss of control over a script (if playwrights did indeed lose control as completely as Orgel assumes) amount to a loss of authorship?[9] Angered by the staging of *The Isle of Dogs* in 1597, the Queen's Privy Council sought to arrest the playwright Thomas Nashe and searched the "papers" in his "lodgings": why would they have done so if they believed that the author was largely irrelevant to the play as performed?[10]

These questions grow in relation to the best recent critical anthology on the Renaissance theater, *A New History of Early English Drama* (1997), whose editors declare their aim "to dislodge authors and scripts from the center of dramatic history." For John Cox and David Kastan, it is so important *not* to focus on authors that they offer the sheer lack of such a focus as their anthology's major achievement. "No essays about individual authors will be found" in the *New History,* Cox and Kastan declare: "To some, no doubt, this will seem a major drawback of the volume; to others—to most, we hope—it will be the volume's principal strength." In older theater histories, Cox and Kastan imply, dramatists played the part that rulers did in older political histories: they took more credit for events than they deserved and in the process drastically simplified the story. By removing playwrights "from the center of dramatic history," Cox and Kastan believe they can restore other relevant issues, such as staging, financing, and censorship, to their "proper place and dignity in a narrative" where they have "too long suffered neglect."[11] The bardolatrist might counter that these matters first became interesting to scholars *because of* the authors and scripts they illuminated. But Cox and Kastan are not concerned to highlight one feature of early English drama over another: instead, they want to show that the real historical picture has no defining center at all.

In his foreword to the *New History*, Stephen Greenblatt similarly urges theater scholars "to attend to the peripheries as well as the center," when he compares early English drama to the "amazingly complex" scene of a Brueghel painting, *Children's Games* (1560): "So many and various are the figures, so fragmentary and multifaceted the represented actions," Greenblatt writes, "that it would be virtually impossible to give a single, coherent account of what is happening. The swirling confusion of distinct groups and diverse motives seems to defy a unitary order, a resolution of the scene into a narrative or a set of stable, interlocking propositions." Cox and Kastan see Renaissance theater history the way Greenblatt sees the drama itself: as a "fragmentary and multifaceted" story of "many and various" figures, not of "single" individuals such as authors. To displace the author from the center of dramatic history means, for Cox and Kastan, "to restore drama to the rich field of its social origins."[12]

But society and authorship are not at odds in Greenblatt's understanding of history: he attributes the complex scene in *Children's Games* to Brueghel, "the artist." Why do Cox and Kastan think of the author and society as locked in struggle? By emphasizing the "richness" of the social field that generated Renaissance drama, Cox and Kastan belie the strict economy that they impose on artistic production. In their account, creative capital is so limited that it must be taken from authors if it is to be distributed to society generally. "Authors and plays are recognized within the *determining* contexts in which plays were written,"

Cox and Kastan declare. While conceding that "playwrights are of course essential to playmaking," Cox and Kastan nevertheless insist that dramatists "write always and only within specific conditions of possibility, both institutional and imaginative, connecting the individual talent to preexisting modes of thought, linguistic constructions, literary conventions, social codes, legal restraints, material practices, and commercial conditions of production." Kastan repeats the point in his introduction to a later critical anthology, his *Companion to Shakespeare* (1999): "However seductive is a romantic notion of artistic genius, solitary and sovereign, untouched by the world, all artists work within a web of engagements with the world, work always and only within the set of imaginative, material, and institutional possibilities that are available to them."[13] But these formulations have a tautological ring to them: after all, artists cannot work within possibilities that are *not* available to them. What's more, our "connection" to "social codes," "commercial conditions," and "preexisting modes of thought" is so basic a part of our existence that it has no special relevance to artists: it cannot qualify our notion of them in any way that it does not also qualify our notion of any other human agent. And the mere fact that artists "work within a web of engagements with the world" tells us nothing about the force or forces that *determine* plays.[14] While we can (for instance) identify cultural trends or biases that might influence artists, how can we know for certain that these predispositions determined the artist's choices instead of suggesting possibilities that the artist *invented* and thus *added to* the culture?

More than a general theory of history commits Cox and Kastan to "shifting the emphasis from drama as the timeless achievement of sovereign authorship to drama as collective activity." In their account, drama is so intrinsically social an art form that it must "always" be "radically collaborative," too: "to restore drama to the rich field of its social origins" must also mean "to restore the collaborative sense of early English dramatic activity." One immediate problem with this line of argument is that not all Renaissance drama was *staged* drama. Closet drama also flourished throughout the period: as Peter Blayney notes elsewhere in the *New History*, "the professional stage produced only a single play—*Mucedorus* [c.1590]—capable of outselling" Samuel Daniel's closet drama *Cleopatra* (1594), which ran to eight editions in its first eighteen years.[15] A greater problem with Cox and Kastan's account of drama as inherently social and therefore inherently collaborative is that the social and the collaborative represent two different forms of "collective activity," operating at two different levels of generality: one on the level of society at large, the other on the level of the theatrical profession. "Social origins" have such comprehensive power in the *New History* because they allow Cox and Kastan to collapse diverse concepts into one.

The very formulation of drama as "collective activity" supports a further conflation of separate issues, insofar as it blurs the distinction between the acting of plays and the writing of them. If historical events are social, and if theatrical performances are social, then, Cox and Kastan assume, playwriting must be social too; otherwise, it would not fit the model of production they invoke at every other level of their analysis and would therefore, in their strict economy, figure as a repudiation of that model. To emphasize single authorship would amount, in their eyes, to privileging "elite terms of cultural value over the popular," which would deny Renaissance drama its true historical status as mass entertainment. Instead, Cox and Kastan assimilate authorship to the collective process of performance: "Plays inevitably register multiple intentions, often conflicting intentions, as actors, annotators, revisers, collaborators, scribes, printers, and proofreaders, in addition to the playwright, all have a hand in shaping the text."[16] Few would now dispute that the surviving texts of Renaissance plays attributed to single authors such as Shakespeare frequently record word choices, stage directions, act divisions, even whole characters, scenes, and plots that someone other than the attributed author must have added to the text. But the question is *how much* others added, and how often these additions make it impossible to view the attributed author as the primary writer of the text we have. Like many or perhaps most other theater scholars, Cox and Kastan straddle the polemical divide with which I began, finding themselves torn between a common-sense notion of theater as socially produced and an equally common-sense notion of plays as singly authored. While they argue, for instance, that the collaborativeness of performance makes drama, "of all the literary forms," "the least respectful of its author's intentions," Cox and Kastan nevertheless speak of drama as emanating from an "author." And, while they credit actors, annotators, and all the other groups of workers they mention with "a hand" in shaping the playtext, Cox and Kastan nevertheless imagine these groups as working "in addition to" a single "playwright."[17]

Other historicists have tried to resolve Cox and Kastan's ambivalence about the social or authorial origins of Renaissance plays by radicalizing Orgel's vision of playwrights on the margins and erasing the author from the historical picture altogether. A major inspiration for these scholars is Roland Barthes, whose essay on "The Death of the Author" (1968) challenges any "image of literature" that "is tyrannically centered on the author" by treating the author not as a given but rather as a "modern figure," a historical construct of "capitalist ideology." Yet Barthes's essay presents two stumbling-blocks for historians of authorship. First, like Cox and Kastan, Barthes repeatedly lapses into the language of authorship he is criticizing—for instance, when he claims that "Mallarmé was doubtless the first to see and to foresee in its full extent the necessity to substitute language itself for the person who until then had been supposed to be its owner." More problematic for historicists is Barthes's association of the decentered literary "field" with language rather than with history. Once we look past the author, Barthes argues, we can see how the "hand" of the writer traces "a field without origin—or which, at least, has no other origin than language itself, language which ceaselessly calls into question all origins." Cox and Kastan oppose their anthology not only to the "idealist criticism" that centers on authors but also to the "mystifications" of "poststructuralist theory" such as Barthes's, where "playmaking" disappears "into the assumed priority of the linguistic order itself."[18]

Theater scholars have found a more straightforwardly historical critique of authorship in Michel Foucault's "What Is an Author?" (1969), which famously expands upon the historiographical claims of Barthes by asserting that "in our civilization" (the West?), "there was a time when the texts that we today call 'literary' (narratives, stories, epics, tragedies, comedies) were accepted, put into circulation, and valorized without any question about the identity of their author." Only "in the seventeenth or eighteenth century," Foucault contends, did literary texts come to require "attribution to an author," and that requirement grew in importance "at the end of the eighteenth and the beginning of the nineteenth century," "once strict rules concerning author's rights, author-publisher relations, rights of reproduction, and related matters were enacted."[19] Foucault's bracing conjunction of modern literary authorship with copyright law has done much to energize the historiography of authorship.[20] But Foucault cites no evidence to support his claim that modern copyrighted authorship is the only kind of literary authorship "our civilization" has ever known. Like Barthes, he relies instead on a highly conventional and hence unexamined assumption about the difference between medieval and Renaissance mentalities. During the Middle Ages, Jacob Burckhardt maintained as long ago as 1860, "man was conscious of himself only as a member of a race, people, party, family, or corporation—only through some general category." But for Burckhardt the Renaissance brought something new, and Barthes and Foucault agree: the author arose when "our society . . . emerging from the Middle Ages . . . discovered the prestige of the individual."[21]

Counter-evidence to this supposedly definitive link between literary authorship and modern individualism seems easy enough to come by. For an early English example, take *The Canterbury Tales,* attributed to Chaucer in medieval manuscripts and printed as *The Boke of Chaucer Named Caunterbury Tales* in 1498, with a character named "Chaucer" who claims to have compiled the book. For an example closer to Shakespeare, consider this oft-quoted passage from the *Palladis Tamia* of Francis Meres, published in 1598: "As the Greek tongue is made famous and eloquent by *Homer, Hesiod, Euripedes, Aeschylus, Sophocles, Pindarus, Phocylides* and *Aristophanes;* and the Latin tongue by *Virgil, Ovid, Horace, Silius Italicus, Lucanus, Lucretius, Ausonius* and *Claudianus:* so the English tongue is mightily enriched, and gorgeously invested in rare ornaments and resplendent habiliments by Sir *Philip Sidney, Spenser, Daniel, Drayton, Warner, Shakespeare, Marlowe* and *Chapman.*"[22]

Some theater historians have tried to refine Foucault's manifesto on authorship by limiting their own arguments for the most part to the historical "construction of *dramatic* authorship" in Renaissance England. In an essay for Cox and Kastan's *New History* and in a monograph, *Textual Intercourse,* published that same year, Jeffrey Masten (1997) maintained that single and collective playwriting were not merely practical or theoretical alternatives in the Renaissance theater; they represented distinct historical phases in the development of English drama. "Collaboration," Masten asserts, "was the Renaissance English theater's dominant mode of textual production." "Eventually," he argues, such "plural" writing was "displaced" as standard theatrical practice "by the mode of singular authorship with which we are more familiar"; so, too, a theoretical "paradigm of collaboration" gave way to "one of singular authorship." But the new authorial paradigm "emerged tentatively" in the period, only "gradually" becoming "attached to playtexts over the course of the seventeenth century." Thus, Masten concludes, not just an emphasis on the author but the very "idea" of the author is an "anachronistic" imposition on Renaissance drama.[23]

This absolute displacement of authors from the center of Renaissance theater history has achieved a remarkable currency among theater scholars. Perhaps the most revealing evidence of its pervasiveness is the matter-of-fact appearance of similar claims in other critical anthologies besides the *New History.* "By the time Shakespeare retired from the theater, in about 1612," declares Scott McMillin in Kastan's *Companion to Shakespeare,* for example, "the modern sense of 'authorship' in the theater was beginning to flicker into existence." Philip McGuire, writing in Arthur Kinney's *Companion to Renaissance Drama* (2002), seconds Masten's description of "collaboration" as the dominant mode of playwriting in England until the seventeenth century and agrees with him that "collaboratively written plays precede, elude, and resist 'categories of singular authorship.'"[24] What has made Masten's radical dismissal of authors so swiftly orthodox? In large part, the way seems to have been paved by the two widely held assumptions I have already underscored: that drama is fundamentally social and that premodern society was fundamentally communal. In Peter Stallybrass's own ascription of Renaissance playwriting to "a network of collaborative relations" rather than to "a single author," for example, Stallybrass acknowledges his desire "to celebrate collaboration *in the moment before the individual.*"[25] Unlike Foucault's claims in "What Is an Author," however, Masten's contention that a theater without authors preceded a theater with authors also depends upon two seemingly weighty and well-documented sets of historical evidence: first, the high rate of collective playwriting in the commercial theaters of Renaissance England; and second, the lack of authorial attributions on the title pages of early printed plays from those theaters.

Masten bases his account of Renaissance playwriting as "predominantly collaborative" on G. E. Bentley's educated guess that "as many as half of the plays by professional dramatists in the period incorporated the writing at some date of more than one man."[26] But if half of English Renaissance drama was co-authored, then half must have been single-authored, which suggests that neither form of playwriting dominated theatrical practice.[27] Other theater historians, including McGuire, address this problem by rejecting Bentley's estimates on collaborative writing as too conservative. As Bentley himself notes, "nearly two-thirds" of the plays mentioned in the business diary of the theatrical impresario Philip Henslowe "are the work of more than one man." Taking Henslowe's diary "as the nearest indication there is of typical practice" in the commercial theaters, Andrew Gurr concludes that commercial playwriting "was chiefly a collective enterprise." But why should the practice of one theater company be generalized into the pattern for all? Even in Henslowe's diary, the proportion of single to collective authorship varies considerably from year to year. Theater historians often cite Neil Carson's estimates from the diary that "collaborated plays accounted for 60 per cent of the plays completed in Fall–Winter 1598, and an astonishing 82 per cent in Spring–Summer 1598." Yet Carson's estimates for the next two half-seasons in Henslowe's diary show collaborated plays dropping to 50 percent and then 37 percent of completed plays, well under half the plays for that year.[28] Whatever the proportion of collectively written to single-authored plays, neither Henslowe's diaries nor any other theatrical records for the period indicate that collectively written plays *preceded* single-authored ones, as Masten, McGuire, and McMillin all claim.

Paradoxically, the stronger evidence for the historical priority of collective playwriting appears outside the theater, in the publication record of Renaissance plays. Before Shakespeare's professional career began, plays written for the new permanent theaters were more often than not printed without attributions to authors. As Kastan notes in his *Shakespeare and the Book* (2001), "title pages usually advertised their plays as the records of performance rather than as the registers of a literary intention." This picture changed during the 1590s. Of the "sixteen plays performed before paying audiences" that "were published between 1584 and 1593," Lukas Erne observes in his *Shakespeare as Literary Dramatist* (2003), "only one . . . indicates the playwright's full name, not on the title page, but at the end of the text." In 1594, however, when eighteen commercial plays were printed, seven cited the playwright's full name, and authorial attributions continued to rise throughout the rest of the period: "Between 1601 and 1616, there is not a single year in which the majority of printed playbooks failed to attribute the plays to their authors. By the second decade of the seventeenth century, playbooks published without any indication of authorship had become exceedingly rare, totaling less than 10 percent." Joseph Loewenstein (2002) persuasively cites these changing numbers as evidence of a sudden, striking "increase in authorial prestige" and "authorial self-promotion" around the turn of the century.[29] But Erne goes further. He takes the early scarcity of authorial attributions as proof that a "concept" of authorship "would not have applied to the text of a public stage play in 1590," when contemporaries would have assumed that the script had been "collaboratively produced." For Erne, indeed, authorship was so foreign to the theater that it had to be imposed from without: "The first people who had a vested interest in the rise of dramatic authorship were not the playwrights themselves but the London printers, publishers, and booksellers eager to render respectable and commercially profitable what was initially an enterprise with little or no prestige." Thus, Erne contends, "the creation of the dramatic author in early printed playbooks preceded the creation of the dramatic author in the playhouse."[30]

There is, however, something strangely literal-minded about the assumption that Renaissance readers lacked any concept of dramatic authorship until Renaissance publishers decided to advertise the names of playwrights. It seems particularly surprising for historians of popular culture to focus so exclusively on print as a means of disseminating and even formulating knowledge. According to Masten, for instance, the writers of plays "were not known" until their names "appeared in print." Yet Meres's *Palladia Tamia* attributes twelve plays to Shakespeare, only three of which had been published by 1598 with Shakespeare's name attached to them.[31] Although actors were probably always more famous than dramatists, dramatists, too, were the objects of public scrutiny and gossip. One notorious record of the taste for inside information about dramatists is the playwright Robert Greene's attack on Shakespeare in his 1592 *Greenes Groats-worth of Witte*—which, it might as well be said, puts the author's name not just on the title page but in the title.[32] Addressing "those Gentlemen his Quondam acquaintance, that spend their wits in making plays," Greene advised his fellow authors no longer to trust the play-ers "that spake from our mouths," "for there is an upstart Crow, beautified with our feathers, that with his *Tiger's heart wrapt in a Player's hide*, supposes he is as well able to bombast out a blank verse as the best of you: and being an absolute *Johannes fac totum*, is in his own conceit the only Shake-scene in a country." This famous insult disproves the thesis that dramatic authorship came late to Renaissance England not only by deriding Shakespeare for his failure to approach an authorial ideal that preceded him but also by presuming that clues alone will enable at least some readers to identify Shakespeare as the hack in question. One of these clues is the parodic misquotation of a line from the third part of Shakespeare's *Henry VI*, "O tiger's heart wrapp'd in a woman's hide!"[33] Without a general notion of authorship and the specific knowledge that Shakespeare authored the line Greene parodies, no contemporary could ever have gotten Greene's joke, and Greene would never have thought to make it. (I'll have more to say about Greene's attack on Shakespeare in later chapters.)

The wave of authorial attributions in the 1590s was in any case not the first time that Renaissance English publishers singled out dramatists in print. The names of classical dramatists had long been common knowledge to the reading public.[34] Terence and Plautus were regularly taught in Elizabethan grammar schools, and their names were always cited in English editions of their plays. The *Comoediae* of Terence, for instance, first published in England in 1497, appeared again in 1575 and in three other edi-tions before 1600; an English translation of Terence's *Andria* was published in 1588, while an English translation of the complete plays, *Terence in English*, was printed in 1598.[35] The author was considerably more than a nominal presence in these texts: some editions of Terence included Suetonius's life of the dramatist, while nearly all of them preserved Terence's prologues, which speak autobiographically about the playwright and his hated rivals.

Nor were authorial attributions before the 1590s confined to classical drama. By the time Ben Jonson chose to model his 1616 *Workes* on the lines of a classical *Opera,* the names of single authors had been attached to printed English plays for over a century. To cite only a few instances, the title pages of *Fulgens and Lucrece,* published c. 1512, and of *Nature,* published c. 1534, attribute the two plays to Henry Medwall; John Heywood's name appears on the 1533, 1544, 1560, and 1573 title pages of *The Play of the Wether;* while both the 1571 and 1582 title pages of *Damon and Pithias* declare that play to have been "made by Master Edwards."[36] References to the "author" were common *within* pre–seventeenth-century plays as well, beginning with the epilogue to *Fulgens and Lucrece,* which may have been performed as early as 1490. At least twenty-four English plays printed before 1600 speak of their "author," "poet," or "writer" in a prologue or epilogue.[37] In the 1577 edition of John Bale's *Chiefe Promises of God Unto Man,* the author simply *is* the prologue, "Baleus Prolocutor."[38] Theater historians rarely cite any of these internal references; the earliest one Masten mentions appears in the 1623 Folio version of Shakespeare's *Henry V.* But, as its predecessors show, the epilogue to *Henry V* is not striking out in the direction of a radically new episteme when it invokes "our bending author" with his "all-unable pen"; it is rather following long-established theatrical procedure.[39]

Just as historicists try to salvage Foucault's argument about the invention of authorship by limiting their case to dramatic authorship, so they often hedge their accounts of dramatic authorship. "If we consider the suddenness and the frequency with which Shakespeare's name appears on title pages of printed playbooks from 1598 to 1600," writes Erne, "it is no exaggeration to say that *in one sense,* 'Shakespeare', author of dramatic texts, *was born* in the space of two or three years at the end of the sixteenth century."[40] Masten offers a similarly bold yet tentative argument: "the more frequent appearance of playwrights' names on quarto title pages and the publication of dramatic folios organized around author-figures signals *in some sense 'the birth of the author*.'" But in what sense exactly *was* an author "born"? Like Cox and Kastan when they conflate special and general senses of *collaboration*, historicists tend to waver between special and general senses of *authorship*: not only authorship and dramatic authorship, but also authorship and modern authorship, authorship and commercial authorship, authorship and published authorship, authorship and celebrated or prestigious authorship. In an essay for Kastan's *Companion to Shakespeare*, Thomas Berger and Jesse Lander exemplify this wavering when they speak of "the collaborative nature of the theatrical venture and the non-authorial status that Shakespeare, a playmaker among other playmakers, merited early in his career." By "non-authorial status," do Berger and Lander mean the strong claim that Shakespeare worked solely as a member of a collective and not as an author, or do they mean the weaker claim that as an author for the theater Shakespeare was simply not accorded the status granted to authors working in other environments?[41]

Erne tries to limit his own argument not merely to dramatic authorship but also to dramatic authorship *in the commercial theaters*. "From very early on," Erne concedes, "certain kinds of dramatic publications acknowledged the writers' identity," but these were amateur products of the university, the closet, the Inns of Court, not "plays of the commercial stage"; they were "associated neither with the disreputable acting profession nor with the stigma of commerce." (Since Terence and Plautus were commercial dramatists, Erne is tacitly imposing the further argumentative restriction that the drama in question be modern and English as well as commercial.) Yet while most of the plays that Erne categorizes as amateur may not have been staged in the new arena theaters, some at least were performed commercially.[42] More important, the attribution of authorship in these plays, as in Renaissance editions of classical drama, attests to an implicit cultural understanding of dramatic authorship that spectators can scarcely be thought to have left at the doors of commercial theaters. Erne himself compares "sixteenth-century playwrights" to "modern screenwriters" who "are known by insiders and experts but ignored by the multitude. There is a general awareness that they exist, but little curiosity about their specific contribution to the final product." This "lack of interest in playwrights" seems quite different from the lack of a "concept" that Erne elsewhere alleges.[43]

In 1581, the existence of commercial dramatists was acknowledged by no less a figure than Queen Elizabeth herself, when she issued a patent to her Master of Revels giving him authority over all the "playmakers" as well as "players" in her realm. And well before the first title-page attribution to Shakespeare, a common-sense assumption that commercial plays were authored also manifested itself in the last place that one would look for the promotion of playwrights: in the antitheatrical literature of the period. One section of Anthony Munday's *Third Blast of Retrait from Plaies and Theaters* (1580), for instance, is entitled "Against Authors of plays." In his *Playes Confuted in Five Actions* (1582), Stephen Gosson more specifically reprehends "the drift of him that wrote the play termed *the three Ladies of London*," "the writer of the play called *London against the three Ladies*," and especially "the Author of the *Play of plays* shown at the Theater, the three and twentieth of February last," who seems to have intended his entertainment as a riposte to Gosson's earlier attacks. Gosson even goes so far as to name one of the dramatists he deplores— the now-remorseful figure of Gosson himself.[44]

Models of Dramatic Authorship

The polemical drive of historicists to broaden our vision of play-writing during the English Renaissance has itself distorted the historical picture. It has prevented theater scholars from recognizing that paradigms of single authorship not only significantly predated Shakespeare but also dominated his contemporaries' sense of how plays were written. By opposing authorship to collaboration, moreover, historicists have foreclosed the historiographical analysis of authorship and even of coauthorship as integral features of the professional Renaissance theater. And, rather than open our eyes to the variety of authorial paradigms that were operative during the Renaissance, the historicist emphasis on the difference between Renaissance and modern theories of authorship has reduced Renaissance playwriting to a single, collaborative paradigm defined in opposition to the modern.

Above all, the antibardolatrist thrust of recent theater scholarship has blinded us to the historical specificities of Shakespeare's professional career as a playwright. In his own time, Shakespeare was distinctive on many counts. More published plays were attributed to him in his lifetime than to any other living dramatist.[45] Financially, he was far and away the most successful dramatist of his day. He was, again, the only playwright in his lifetime who also acted professionally and owned a share in his theater as well as his acting company.[46] No other Renaissance dramatist wrote exclusively for one company for as long as Shakespeare did.[47] Shakespeare appears to have been the first dramatist for the arena theaters to write a cycle of plays—indeed, to write a sequence of more than two plays.[48] And in print as well as in the minds of many contemporaries, he achieved a success across dramatic genres that no other playwright at the time or in the past could match.

My goal in pursuing a historiographical analysis of Shakespeare's dramatic authorship is to ask and answer three sets of questions about his extraordinary career. How was dramatic authorship actually conceived during the Renaissance? How did Shakespeare's contemporaries, and Shakespeare himself, understand his authorship in particular? Most important, how did the authorial paradigms of Shakespeare and his contemporaries shape his plays? These models of authorship lent far more than incidental color to his work. Many of Shakespeare's most popular plays in his own time, including the *Henry IV* plays, *Hamlet,* and *The Tempest,* would have been unthinkable without Shakespeare's consciousness of himself as a dramatic author at their core. Throughout *Shakespeare Only,* therefore, I combine an extensive survey of contemporaneous cultural frames for thinking about dramatic authorship with an intensive focus on Shakespeare's writings. Just as the individual and the institutional informed one another during the English Renaissance, so did plays and their contexts.

A glimpse into the variety of authorial models that were available to Shakespeare and his fellow playwrights can be provided by a comedy, *Histrio-Mastix* (c. 1599), that was written and published during Shakespeare's career and that has been ascribed, with some uncertainty, to Shakespeare's younger contemporary John Marston. *Histrio-Mastix* is especially interesting as an example of authorial styles or concepts during the Renaissance because it has recently been cited as evidence of dramatic authorship's defining itself in opposition to theatrical collaboration: according to Robert Weimann (2000), *Histrio-Mastix* "clearly marks a new virulence in the rapidly shifting relations between a learned author's pen and common players' bodies and voices." But this dichotomizing account of the play glosses over the presence of *two* dramatists in *Histrio-Mastix:* a common author, Posthaste, as well as a learned one, Chrisoganus. Of the two, Chrisoganus the scholar is clearly the more respectable figure. He is granted numerous long speeches throughout the play; toward the end he serves as a kind of chorus to the action; and in the final act he rises to become what Philip Finkelpearl calls the "moral and intellectual mentor" of the aristocracy. Posthaste, by contrast, is a talentless drunkard who convinces some fellow lowlifes to form "a company of Players," with himself as "the Poet." By the end of the play, the company's fortunes have sunk so low that both poet and players are shipped out of the realm as sturdy vagabonds, to be "set ashore no man / Knows where."[49]

Yet even with the success of Chrisoganus and the failure of Posthaste as guides, the choice between the two dramatists is not so simple as it appears. Although Finkelpearl claims that Chrisoganus is a "totally admirable figure" in the play, *Histrio-Mastix* consistently presents him as an elitist with a violent antipathy to that "common beast the multitude." *Histrio-Mastix* begins with the allegorical figures of Peace and the Arts promising to spread their "bounties" throughout the commonwealth; Grammar, for instance, declares her power "to make the rudest brain both speak and write." But when we first encounter the scholar Chrisoganus, he promises several visitors to his study that they "shall meet with projects ... *remov'd*/From vulgar apprehension." Chrisoganus does eventually write a play that he considers selling to Posthaste's vulgar company, but the players balk at his high asking price, one of them wondering aloud in frustration, "Will not our own stuff serve the multitude?" The question enrages Chrisoganus: "Write on, cry on, yawl to the common sort/Of thickskinn'd auditors," he roars; "load the Stage with stuff,/Rak'd from the rotten embers of stall jests:/Which basest lines best please the vulgar sense[.]/Make truest rapture lose preeminence." While this breakdown in negotiations helps Chrisoganus avoid the humiliation of having his raptures debased by Posthaste and company, it also means that Chrisoganus remains a dramatist in name only, the author of a play we never witness.[50]

Other critics such as James Bednarz have acknowledged that *Histrio-Mastix* adopts a partially critical stance toward Chrisoganus, yet in characterizing the play's attitude toward Posthaste as "*entirely* sarcastic," Bednarz simplifies the comedy in another direction. Even Posthaste's company admit that his writing is dreadful, but at least we get to see some of it enacted, in a comic scene clearly borrowed from *A Midsummer Night's Dream.* "No more, no more," cries the aristocrat in whose house the entertainment has been staged, and yet Posthaste blithely continues in Bottom-like doggerel, "My Lords/of your accords,/some better pleasure for to bring,/if you a theme affords,/you shall know it,/that I *Post-haste* the Poet,/extempore can sing." Indisputably, the entertainment is crude, but *Histrio-Mastix* cautions us to temper our judgment by having an Italian lord denounce the proceedings in the same elitist terms that Chrisoganus will later employ: "Most ugly lines and base-brown-paper-stuff/Thus to abuse our heavenly poesy." This foreign derision allows Posthaste's baseness to be prized along patriotic lines: "England is

plain," an English lady proudly proclaims. In a play that presents
factiousness as the greatest threat to a commonwealth, the very
impulse of Posthaste to organize his friends into a company positively distinguishes him from the often solitary and soliloquiz-
ing Chrisoganus. Although a self-confessed "knot of Knaves,"
the common playwright and his players are also merry "good-
fellows" who, in their vulgar way, espouse the solidly communal
virtues of good fellowship.[51]

By thus presenting Chrisoganus as less than entirely admirable and Posthaste as less than entirely degenerate, *Histrio-Mastix*
keeps each model of a playwright alive as an alternative to the
other. And this balancing act accomplishes more. It implicitly
recommends the actual author or authors of *Histrio-Mastix* as
modeling a third style of playwrighting, with the flexibility to
steer between the extremes of elitist Latinate study and popular
vernacular extemporaneity that Chrisoganus "*solus*" and Posthaste
the good-fellow separately exemplify.[52] This dramaturgical range
goes hand in hand with the social inclusivity of *Histrio-Mastix*,
the willingness of the play's actual author or authors to engage
both high and low. Revealingly, Chrisoganus gains a pedagogical
authority over the aristocracy only when he climbs down from
his high perch, submitting himself to poverty and staging himself as "the poorest slave in show." Posthaste, by contrast, fades
away because he fails to broaden his initial appeal: his plays never
succeed at pleasing "the gentlemen." And he increasingly loses
touch with his lowly roots, too. From the start, his conception
of himself as a dramatist had encouraged some preening: when
one character met the newly contracted company and demanded
to know "what saucy knaves are these," Posthaste had replied,
"'A speaks to you *players;* I am the *poet.*"[53] Once Peace gives way
to Plenty and then to Pride, Envy, and War, such airs become
more than a pose. The nature of Posthaste's company changes:
we now hear that it is divided hierarchically between "master-
sharers" and "hired men," with Posthaste as one of the sharers,
eating dinners at "six pence a piece" while "the hirelings" dine for
a penny.[54] The actual dramatist or dramatists of *Histrio-Mastix*

stay detached from such class divisions, remaining as free in the drama to enter the study or the palace as the alehouse.

In later plays that are more solidly attributable to Marston, he advertises his own virtues more directly, offering himself as a flexible alternative to the extremes of playwrighting in *Histrio-Mastix* by conspicuously adopting an urbane posture of humility. "Our poor author," the prologue to *Parasitaster* (c. 1604) calls him, while the prologue to *The Dutch Courtesan* (c. 1604) apologizes for his "slight hasty labors": "his best's too bad," asserts the prologue to *What You Will* (1601), "A silly subject too too simply clad." The front and end matter to *Parasitaster* links this modesty with inclusivity. Professing his humble wish "to kill envy," Marston assures other dramatists who "affect to be the only Minion of *Phoebus*" that "I am not so blushlessly ambitious as to hope to gain any the least supreme eminency among you. . . . Nor do I labor to be held the only spirit, whose Poems may be thought worthy to be kept in Cedar chests."[55] Instead, Marston maintains from first to last, "I have ever more endeavored . . . to be unpartially beloved of all, than factiously to be admired of a few."[56]

The difference, or ostensible difference, between Marston and Chrisoganus could hardly be clearer—and not coincidentally, the likeness between Chrisoganus and a particular "ambitious" rival of Marston becomes clearer, too. The prizing of one's own drama as heavenly rapture and the denigration of other drama as trash; disdain for the common herd, and the factious wish to be admired of a few; the desire for supremacy and the dream of being held the only playwright who matters: these are the hallmarks of Ben Jonson. The envy that Marston disclaims at the start of *Parasitaster* was Jonson's obsessive theme. In Jonson's 1601 *Poetaster*, for instance, "invidia" is everywhere: as the final word of the prefatory poem "Ad Lectorem"; as the allegorical character Envy who begins the play, "arising in the midst of the stage"; in Horace's central meditation on "envy and detraction,/ Moods only proper to base groveling minds"; in the couplet of Caesar's on "envy" that closes the action; and finally as the very last word of the play.[57] Although Jonson's famous ode to Shakespeare begins by insisting that he has no wish "to draw . . . envy" on Shakespeare's "name," the disavowal would not have persuaded many of Jonson's contemporaries. So irresistibly did the thought of envy arise for Jonson whenever he considered other writers that he admitted to envying the dramatist Francis Beaumont for writing eloquently in praise of Jonson.[58] The view of Jonson recorded by Nicholas Rowe in 1709 was already conventional during his lifetime: that "*Ben* was naturally Proud and Insolent, and in the Days of his Reputation did so far take upon him the Supremacy of Wit, that he could not but look with an evil Eye upon any one that seem'd to stand in Competition with him."[59] In *Parasitaster*, Marston places this pretension to supremacy at the heart of the authorial identity he rejects. And just as *Parasitaster* links envy with the ambition to be regarded as supremely great, so *Histrio-Mastix* depicts an obsession with envy as a projection of such ambition. The first line of Chrisoganus's first soliloquy is a quotation of Ovid's maxim that "summa petit livor, perflant altissima venti [envy attacks the greatest; the winds howl around the highest peaks]." And yet Chrisoganus admits that the envious winds wail at him him only in his fantasy: "Then poor *Chrisoganus*, who'll envy thee,/Whose dusky fortune hath no shining gloss/That *Envy's* breath can blast? O I could curse/This idiot world!"[60]

When Marston forswears any desire for supremacy "among you," however, he clearly has more rivals than Jonson in mind. Recent accounts of Renaissance drama as essentially collaborative make it difficult to think of competitiveness in the Renaissance theater as anything but antitheatrical. This is a view that *Histrio-Mastix* itself appears to promote when it gives the only soliloquies in the play to the envious closet dramatist Chrisoganus and to Envy herself, "whose nature is to work alone,/As hating any Agent but her self." Yet, like the other allegorical figures in the play who take turns presiding over the commonwealth, Envy becomes a systemic force in *Histrio-Mastix*, breathing her poison on "all the Actors."[61] As the vanity of both Chrisoganus and Posthaste suggests, the drive to be seen as "the only Minion of *Phoebus*" cannot be ascribed to the Jonsonian model of author-ship alone. In *Parasitaster*, Marston's very attack on the envy of other dramatists is itself competitive, with humility as Marston's perceived edge in the rivalry. Undeniably, Jonson labored to set himself apart as a dramatist, but in our time as in his, his fierce ambition has made him seem to personify and therefore absorb an envious competitiveness that actually pervaded the Renais-sance English theater.[62]

There were several powerful catalysts for the urge to be re-garded as the best, the supreme, the only scene-shaker around. One was a deep cultural investment in the idea of the clas-sics, which made the search for corresponding modern para-gons inevitable. "As *Plautus* and *Seneca* are accounted the best for Comedy and Tragedy among the Latins," wrote Meres in 1598, "so *Shakespeare* among the English is the most excellent in both kinds for the stage." Fixated as he was on such superla-tives, Jonson in his ode to Shakespeare went further than Meres and actively promoted Shakespeare *above* the greatest classical comic playwrights, but this was nothing more than what George Turberville had done for the Elizabethan dramatist Richard Ed-wards half a century earlier. Not only was Edwards "chiefest" amongst English dramatists, Turberville declared in 1567, but "all the learned *Greeks*/And *Romans* would repine/If they did live again, to view/His Verse with scornful eyne."[63] The very notion of outdoing the classics was itself classical: "Step aside, Roman writers, step aside, Greeks!" Propertius exclaimed in his praise of Virgil.[64] And the quest for modern exemplars of such incom-parability in the theater was not limited to playwrights. Just as Thomas Nashe proclaimed the dramatist George Peele "the *Atlas* of Poetry, and *primus verborum Artifex*," so he insisted that "not *Roscius* nor *Aesop*, those admired tragedians that have lived ever since before Christ was born, could ever perform more in action than famous *Ned Alleyn*."[65]

A second source of pressure for singling out the "chiefest" of playwrights was the example of a rigidly hierarchical society ruled by a king.[66] Jonson routinely thought of himself in royal terms, as in the epilogue to *The New Inn* (1631), which ended by claiming that "A King's, or Poet's birth do ask an age."[67] But such comparisons came easily to many other contemporaries, too, habituated as they were to distinguishing aristocrats from commoners, the better sort from the worse, and the monarch from everyone else. When George Puttenham, writing in the early 1580s, offered his connoisseur's list of the finest dramatists, he chose from among "courtly makers" exclusively, either noblemen or gentlemen-servants of the crown: for tragedy, "the Lord of Buckhurst" and "Master Edward Ferrers," who "gave the king so much good recreation"; for comedy, "the Earl of Oxford and Master Edwardes of her Majesty's Chapel."[68] Commercial theater people had economic as well as ideological reasons for thinking about their profession in courtly terms. Thanks to Elizabethan statutes on vagabondage that withdrew from "the knight or plain gentleman" the right to patronize a company of traveling players, "practically all the companies of professional players which appeared in London during Elizabeth's reign were noblemen's servants." Shakespeare wrote most of his drama for the Lord Chamberlain's Men; in 1603, they became the King's Men. Shakespeare's high standing among his contemporaries seems difficult to separate from the lofty patronage that helped bring his company more court performances "in his lifetime . . . than all rival companies put together."[69]

This patronage meant more than prestige. Inevitably, the desire to be the best or to be named the best gathers momentum whenever there is real fame and fortune at stake, as was the case for Renaissance dramatists once the permanent theaters were built.[70] Indeed, competition for the social and financial capital to be gained from public as well as court performances lent greater weight to the hierarchical ranking of Renaissance playwrights than it had ever possessed before in English literary or theatrical circles. But this commercial incentive for excellence sat uneasily with the elitist connoisseurship predicated on the classics and the court. Puttenham, for instance, made no mention of commercial playwrights, even when he spoke of the best dramatists as those who "deserve the highest price." Other commentators noted the paradox of a drama divided in its allegiance between aristocratic patrons, on the one hand, and popular audiences, on the other. London city officials (c. 1584) expressed their astonishment that commercial actors should be allowed to "present before her majesty such plays as have been before commonly played in open stages before all the basest assemblies in London and Middlesex." According to the satirist Joseph Hall (1597), the mere fact of a dramatist's writing for a mass audience rendered any claim to authorial distinction null and void: "Too popular is *Tragic Poesy,* / Straining his tip-toes for a farthing fee."[71]

Surprisingly, recent theater historians tend to share Hall's views on the popular stage: they too find it impossible to reconcile the high standards of elitist connoisseurship with the low standards of mass entertainment. But in *Histrio-Mastix,* writing high as well as low is what distinguishes the play's actual dramatist or dramatists from the pedantic Chrisoganus and the vulgar Posthaste. Thanks in large part to the complexity of its market, the commercial London theater set a premium on such versatility[72]— a premium that, in the fiction of one popular play at least, even a classicizing courtier could appreciate. Polonius calls the visiting "Tragedians of the City" in *Hamlet* "the best actors in the world, either for Tragedy, Comedy, History, Pastoral, Pastoral Comical, Historical Pastoral, scene individable, or Poem unlimited. *Seneca* cannot be too heavy, nor *Plautus* too light[,] for the law of writ, and the liberty: these are the only men."[73] From the perspective that Shakespeare gives Polonius, neither flexibility nor inclusivity can be opposed to competitive envy as Marston suggests they can, because it is precisely the ability of the professional actors to play anything and everything that makes them uniquely great— "the only men."

Shakespeare himself exemplified the desired range of the theatrical professional in ways that Marston proved incapable of matching. Like Posthaste, Shakespeare was an actor as well as author, and, like the players of *Hamlet,* he was thought to have excelled in every genre he attempted, becoming the first English playwright to be credited with the authorship of comedies, histories, and tragedies on one title page.[74] In combination with this collaborativeness and adaptability, the popularity of Shakespeare made him so compelling a foil to Jonson's Chrisoganean brand of authorship that contemporary writers dichotomously ascribed other Posthastean attributes to him as well: a lack of learning, for instance, and a genius for extemporizing.[75] Yet Shakespeare himself generally resisted this polarizing opposition—not because it drew him into competition with Jonson, but rather because it reduced his authorship to a single mode, when his competitive edge lay in versatility instead.

Not even Jonson was consistently Jonsonian in the ways that the contrast with Shakespeare made him appear. The commercial ideal of range was powerful enough at the time that Jonson, too, strove to embody it. In a commendatory poem to Jonson's *Volpone* (1607) that echoes Meres's praise of Shakespeare as excellent "in both kinds" of drama, Edmund Bolton declared that where "the ancient dramatists were content to win glory either in tragedy or in comedy," "this man, the sun of the stage, handles tragedy and comedy with equal skill."[76] Jonson advertised this breadth of achievement on the frontispiece of his own First Folio, where the title of the volume is flanked by the statues of "Tragœdia" and "Comœdia," with statues representing Satire, Pastoral, and Tragicomedy on the frame above them. After Jonson's death, Edmund Waller (1638) went so far as to extol him for the sort of characterological adaptability that we now tend to identify with Shakespeare exclusively: "For as thou couldst all *characters* impart,/ So none can render thine, who still escapes,/ Like Proteus in variety of shapes,/ Who was nor this nor that, but all we find,/ And all we can imagine in mankind."[77]

If Shakespeare aimed at rehearsing a variety of authorial styles and self-conceptions to match his protean versatility as a dramatist, there was nevertheless a deep consistency to his experimentations. Throughout his playwriting career, and even in such literary projects as his sonnets, Shakespeare worked to develop specifically *theatrical* paradigms of authorship that would better reflect his professional engagement with his fellow actors and his mass audience.[78] This is perhaps the most important feature of Shakespeare's playwriting that recent theater scholarship has tended to overlook. Historicists have portrayed the dramatic author as a high-handed misappropriator of communal funds who strove to detach himself from his audience as well as his coworkers. As Stallybrass and White put it in their *Politics and Poetics of Transgression* (1986), "the symbolic domain of 'authorship' as it emerged in the late sixteenth century was produced *over against* the popular, as embodied in . . . the popular drama."[79] Yet the notion that authorship and mass entertainment were opposites by definition during the Renaissance is no more sustainable than the assertion of a historical dividing line between a theater with authors and a theater without. Rather than abstract playwriting from the stage, Shakespeare helped infuse playwriting with the multifarious desires and agencies of commercial English drama. It was the intensity of his *immersion* in the theater that created the effect of his singularity even in his own day.

The Structure of This Book

Shakespeare Only has two parts. The first two chapters treat works of Shakespeare that not only raise the question of authorship expressly, but also directly incorporate the figure of an author into their narratives. In the sonnets, the subject of my first chapter, the speaker repeatedly refers to himself as a poet, while in *Hamlet*, the subject of my second chapter, the protagonist is shown to have written letters, poetry, and part of a tragedy. Authorship is also manifestly an issue in the plays to which I devote the last two chapters of *Shakespeare Only:* the second tetralogy of history plays, and the late tragicomedies *Pericles* and *Two Noble Kinsmen*. But here the figure of the author seems less consequential a presence than in the sonnets or *Hamlet*. Though invoked and in one case even embodied on the stage, the author or authors in these plays appear to be confined to prologues and epilogues, never directly participating in the action. As I hope to demonstrate, however, the histories and tragicomedies reflect on authorship almost as intensively as the sonnets and *Hamlet* do: that is, Shakespeare's understanding of himself as an author shapes the dramatic material in these plays, just as their dramatic material shapes his understanding of his authorship. The greater implicitness of Shakespeare's views on authorship in the histories and tragicomedies makes my readings of these plays necessarily more speculative than the analyses in the first half of my book. Yet I try to show how this implicitness enabled Shakespeare to be speculative as well, freeing him to a degree from convention in conceptualizing the author within and through the dramatic action.

In short, the organizing principle of *Shakespeare Only* is not the chronology of Shakespeare's writings, but rather their relative openness in deliberating on his authorship. I have chosen to *avoid* a chronological structure because I believe it would foster the misleading impression that I am tracing a development in Shakespeare's views on authorship, when I am instead trying to show how Shakespeare experimented with various styles and theories of authorship throughout his career. Each chapter of *Shakespeare Only* also highlights a different aspect of Shakespeare's relationship to the commercial theater, in order to show how Shakespeare adjusted his authorship—both his theory and his practice of it—to address these various facets of his working life. In chapter 1, I examine Shakespeare's career as a mass entertainer from the literary perspective of his sonnets; in chapter 2, I consider his ties to his fellow players; in chapter 3, his ties to his audience; and in chapter 4, I focus on Shakespeare's collaborations with fellow dramatists. For all this emphasis on the contingencies of Shakespeare's authorial self-consciousness, however, I do argue that toward the end of his career Shakespeare focused with increasing obsessiveness on the relation between his authorship and his aging.

My first chapter takes its title from Shakespeare's Marston-like account of himself in the epilogue to *2 Henry IV,* which invokes "our humble author." But the chapter begins by examining Shakespeare's quite different contemporary reputation as a *commanding* writer. I show how celebrations of Shakespeare as a sovereign poet were complicated by the very popularity of his work for the stage, and how Shakespeare himself emphasized this complication in his *Sonnets* (1609). The first portion of the sonnets, which portrays the speaker's love for a lordly young man, expresses at times a supreme confidence in the speaker's literary power: "Not marble nor the gilded monuments / Of princes shall outlive this pow'rful rhyme." Yet once the later sonnets allude to Shakespeare's acting, which they present as shamefully degrading, the speaker never again celebrates his talent as a poet. The narrative of the sonnets thus seems to reverse the Foucaldian story line: it seems to begin with authorship and to end somewhere else. Where it ends is "the wide world's common place," the speaker's characterization of the promiscuous dark lady who replaces the lordly young man in the speaker's attentions. The dark-lady sonnets tilt the speaker toward a public, heterogeneous, and conflictual identity whose primary components are either a perverse desire to seek out shame or a penitential desire to confess shame. Surprisingly, however, these sonnets are also the first to name Shakespeare as their author. The speaker calls himself "*Will*," as if he personified the base appetite of "the world," and yet this exemplarity also differentiates him from others less wholly degraded, "the world" that condemns the dark lady he perversely loves.[80] Although authorship ceases to be a sufficient description of the speaker in the later sonnets, a strangely base kind of sovereignty becomes more prominent there, as the high-mindedly ambitious poet metamorphoses into a singularly vulgar mass entertainer.

Chapter 2, "The Author Staged," turns from the sonnets to Shakespeare's dramatizations of his authorship in his plays. For recent theater historians, the appearance of authorial proxies in Renaissance drama was an ominous development: an "intrusion," even a "colonization of the previously improvisatory and collaborative theater" by "an emerging figure . . . that would eventually

eclipse the popular stage."[81] According to the polarizing logic
of such accounts, theatrical celebrity was the exclusive property
of actors, and consequently any author who achieved celebrity
must have stolen it from actors. Indeed, he must have stolen it
from the theater generally, because authors (by this view) were
essentially literary creatures, whose growing fame transformed
artisanal and communitarian performances into elitist scripts. In
chapter 2, I acknowledge the inescapable potentiality for tension
between actors and authors, but I also show how Renaissance
drama treated this tension innovatively, by attempting to *theatricalize* the author. The two major figures in this enterprise,
Jonson and Shakespeare, were not coincidentally actors as well
as authors. In the first half of the chapter, I trace Jonson's simul-
taneously self-aggrandizing and self-degrading efforts to incorporate the heterogeneous agencies of mass entertainment into
the figure of the master poet, and then in the second half of the
chapter I turn to Shakespeare's strangely tragicomic staging of a
dramatist in *Hamlet*. Through the instability of its genre as well
as its title character, *Hamlet* transforms the author from a literary
figure modeled on a king who issues "prescripts" to a histrionic
prince who is pulled in irreconcilably diverse directions by his
"distraction."

Chapter 3, "The Author Sacrificed," focuses on Shakespeare's
sense of the losses that an author incurred by his theatricalization: the loss of dignity to a profane and degenerate popular medium; the loss of authority to the autonomous forces of actors
and audiences. In certain plays, notably *Julius Caesar* and *Henry V,*
Shakespeare tried to embrace these losses by thinking about
them in christological terms, as sacrifices. I begin the chapter by
underscoring the connection between Shakespeare's cycle of history plays and the cycles of medieval plays on the life of Christ
that Elizabethan authorities had suppressed. Scholars have generally assumed that Shakespeare meant to secularize the medieval cycles, but the theory of secularization that underwrites this
assumption exaggerates the difference between sacred and profane in Shakespeare's plays, just as Renaissance theater-haters

exaggerated that difference in their attacks on the commercial stage.[82] I go on to explore a vein of surprisingly deep concern in Shakespeare's culture about the feigning of death and resurrection on commercial stages, and then I show how Shakespeare's second tetralogy makes the Passion the essential frame of reference for any conceptualization of loss, real or feigned.

In my fourth chapter, "The Author Revived," I examine Shakespeare's return at the end of his career to the coauthorial playwriting he seems to have practiced when his professional life began. Although historicists claim that Shakespeare's contemporaries thought of playwriting as a collective labor before they came to see it as authorial, the surviving record shows that single authorship was far easier to conceptualize during the Renaissance than coauthorship ever was. Yet Shakespeare's commitment to devising a specifically theatrical conception of authorship impelled him toward a dramaturgy that could make room for the diverse forces of other authors, as well as players and audiences, even if this process entailed some sacrifice of the sovereignty that a literary author was presumed to exercise over his work. I argue that Shakespeare drew upon contemporary acknowledgments of collective writing in the histories, anthologies, continuations, controversies, and commentaries of his day to help him build a notion of coauthorial playwriting *within* the single-author paradigm that dominated his professional life as a dramatist. In *Pericles,* which he cowrote with George Wilkins, Shakespeare conceived of himself as the *heir* to another man's writing. But in *Two Noble Kinsmen,* which he cowrote with John Fletcher, Shakespeare seems to have been torn between thoughts of bequeathing his power to another dramatist and keeping the inheritance for himself—as if he were his own heir. Throughout his career as a mass entertainer, whether writing singly or with others, Shakespeare felt the need to see himself and be seen as many in one.

Our Humble Author

What can mine own praise to mine own self bring?
« SHAKESPEARE, *Sonnet 39* »

In her foreword to a recent neuroscientific appreciation of Shakespeare entitled *The Bard on the Brain* (2003), the writer Diane Ackerman affirms "the simple, universally accepted truth" that in terms of "artistic genius" Shakespeare "stands alone." "There's Shakespeare," she explains, "followed by a very large gap, and then all the other English writers who have ever lived." The many theater scholars who would regard such praise of Shakespeare as exaggeration or mystification—as bardolatry—might cite several grounds for disputing Ackerman's appraisal. First, they might argue, Ackerman has not read all the other English writers who have ever lived and so is not in a good position to pass judgment on all of them. Second, ranking Shakespeare above Chaucer, Milton, or Dickens, say, might seem like comparing apples to oranges. Shakespeare wrote no collection of tales, no epic, no novel. He did publish two long erotic poems, *Venus and Adonis* and *The Rape of Lucrece*, but neither is regularly considered to be better "by a very large gap" than Marlowe's *Hero and Leander*. The same might be said of Shakespeare's lyric poetry in comparison to Donne's, or Keats's, or Wordsworth's. Only as a playwright, theater scholars might concede, does Shakespeare appear to outstrip his rivals. But even this was not always thought to be the case. Comparing the record of allusions to Shakespeare and to Jonson in the seventeenth century, particularly the references to each dramatist "as a standard of poetic or dramatic greatness," G. E. Bentley found that "the evidence of Jonson's preeminence in the estimates of the time is overwhelming. In every single decade of the century he is praised more often than Shakespeare," and the total number of allusions to him throughout the century, by Bentley's count, "is nearly three times as great" as the total number of allusions to Shakespeare.[1] According to the statistics Bentley compiles, it was Jonson, not Shakespeare, who was the Shakespeare of his day.

Jonson himself thought otherwise. In his elegy "To the memory of my beloved, The AUTHOR Mr. William Shakespeare: And what he hath left us," which appeared in the first edition of Shakespeare's collected plays, the First Folio, in 1623, Jonson set the standard of adoration for all future Shakespeare lovers:

> Soul of the Age!
> The applause! delight! the wonder of our Stage!
> My *Shakespeare,* rise; I will not lodge thee by
> *Chaucer,* or *Spenser,* or bid *Beaumont* lie
> A little further, to make thee a room:
> Thou art a Moniment, without a tomb,
> And art alive still, while thy Book doth live,
> And we have wits to read, and praise to give.
> . . . .
> And though thou hadst small *Latin,* and less *Greek,*
> From thence to honor thee, I would not seek
> For names; but call forth thund'ring *Aeschylus,*
> *Euripedes,* and *Sophocles* to us,
> *Paccuvius, Accius,* him of *Cordova* dead,
> To life again, to hear thy Buskin tread,
> And shake a Stage: Or, when thy Socks were on,
> Leave thee alone, for the comparison
> Of all, that insolent *Greece,* or haughty *Rome*
> Sent forth, or since did from their ashes come.

Triumph, my *Britain,* thou hast one to show,
To whom all Scenes of *Europe* homage owe.
He was not of an age, but for all time! [2]

Even Jonson finds it difficult to compare Shakespeare to nondramatic authors, abandoning the effort in the same line of verse in
which he gets it under way: after the poets Chaucer and Spenser
comes the playwright Beaumont, and then it's nothing but playwrights for the rest of the poem. But the more Jonson evaluates
Shakespeare in relation to other dramatists, the more his enthu-
siasm for him grows. First Shakespeare is the "Soul of the Age,"
then he is "for all time." Rising from the tomb of past English
worthies, he takes the stage "alone" before the greatest classical
playwrights and then ascends to the heavens as the "Star of *Poets,*" the "one" "to whom all Scenes of *Europe* homage owe." Bardolatrous seems the right term for praise that treats Shakespeare
as a kind of Christ.

Such extravagant tribute from the man whom Bentley identifies as Shakespeare's chief dramatic rival in the seventeenth century would appear to weaken Bentley's historicizing claim that
Shakespeare's contemporaries thought less of him than we do.[3]
But recent historicists have actually intensified Bentley's critique
of Shakespeare's preeminence as a dramatist. Where Bentley
turned to the historical record for proof that the modern percep-
tion of Shakespeare's incomparability should be seen as relative,
theater scholars now appeal to that record for proof that the very
notion of an incomparable dramatist should be seen as relative,
and, what's more, as anachronistic when applied to Shakespeare.
Their basic claim, as I explained in my introduction, is that commercial Renaissance plays were generated by acting companies,
not authors—and if the author was a later development for these
historicists, even more so was the author who stands alone. In
the introduction to his *Companion to Shakespeare* (1999), for instance, David Kastan distances his volume from "the enormous
culture investment in the idea of [Shakespeare's] unique genius"
by arguing that the "concept" was "virtually invented for" Shakespeare after his death. As Kastan explains at greater length in

Shakespeare and the Book (2001), the process of invention began with the First Folio, which "might be said to be the creator of Shakespeare." In his own lifetime, Kastan claims, Shakespeare never "actively sought" the "role" of "author," let alone the title of "genius." On the contrary, he "was largely indifferent to such individuation, comfortably working in the collaborative ethos of the theater." Not until Jonson and the First Folio fabricated a literary rather than theatrical conception of Shakespeare, Kastan maintains, did Shakespeare begin to emerge "as the towering figure of individual genius" he now represents in our culture, "never . . . having sought his greatness but having it thrust upon him seven years after he died."[4]

For Kastan, in other words, the notion of unique genius is worse than anachronistic as a description of Shakespeare the theatrical collaborator: it is antithetical to that professional identity and therefore ultimately antitheatrical as well. But the concept had already been applied to Shakespeare thirty years before Jonson's poem, in the earliest surviving reference to Shakespeare as a working dramatist. Where Jonson praised Shakespeare for transcending his professional milieu, Robert Greene in his 1592 *Groats-Worth of Witte* lambasted Shakespeare as a stage-bound "*Johannes fac totum,*" a Johnny-do-all laboring under the absurd delusion that he could emulate real poets. And yet Greene ascribed to Shakespeare the same desire for exclusive mastery that Jonson supposedly foisted upon Shakespeare in his elegy: according to Greene, Shakespeare was "in his own conceit the only Shake-scene in a country."[5]

The ambition itself was not what bothered Greene. Earlier in the *Groats-worth,* he had described himself as "an Arch-play-making-poet," and he later reminded his fellow dramatists that the players had relied on "none of you" so much as they had on "me." But Shakespeare and his fellow actors had forced Greene out of the picture, and within two decades Shakespeare's purported dream of himself as the only "Shake-scene" would in certain irrefutable respects come true. Unlike every other playwright of the period, as I emphasized in my introduction, Shakespeare would make a fortune from his theater work, become by far the most published dramatist of his day, and own a share in both his acting company and the theaters where he played. For Bentley, the sheer range of Shakespeare's professional responsibilities made him "the most complete man of the theater in his time," but for Greene such multitasking proved that Shakespeare was worse than a hack: he was also a grasping monopolist with no sense of obligation to his collaborators. Although the players had once depended on Greene so mightily, Shakespeare's ability to write as well as act meant they could now cast off Greene, and Greene warned his fellow dramatists that, no matter how "beholding" the players might be to them, these other playwrights would soon find themselves "forsaken," too.[6]

Greene's caustic appraisal of Shakespeare as someone who thought he could do it all and do it better than anyone else leads me to the questions I hope to answer in this chapter about how Shakespeare actually saw himself as an author. Historicists such as Kastan have crucially highlighted the strangeness of bardolatrous attempts to abstract Shakespeare from the world of mass entertainment in which and for which he wrote his plays. But their corrective emphasis on mass entertainment has also misled these historicists into claiming that a model of singular authorship postdated Shakespeare, when it was in fact the conventional view of playwriting throughout the Renaissance, as Shakespeare well knew. The most distinguished apologist for the stage in Shakespeare's time—Alberico Gentili, Regius Professor of Civil Law at Oxford—begins his 1593 defense of dramatists by importing the figure of the master poet into the theater: "When Vergil entered the theater," Gentili writes, "the whole [universus] Roman people rose to its feet, revering him as if he were Augustus." Rather than lose himself among the theater's masses, Virgil as Gentili imagines him turns the masses into one, "universus," in their universal admiration for his literary supremacy. But Virgil was no playwright: as soon as Gentili begins to discuss theatrical poets specifically, he is forced to admit that Roman law attached "the mark of infamy" to their profession. And then the playwright's dependence on actors—"vile" actors, Gentili calls them—further disrupts the exclusive identification of the theatrical scene with the imperial figure of the dramatist. Yet the actors also provide the dramatist a convenient scapegoat for the theatrical infamy that would otherwise taint him: "poets can be held in honor," Gentili argues, "although the actor, their voice and mouthpiece [vox, et os], may remain unhonored. Agents are servile [servilia]; so we use the mind to command, the body to serve. And indeed, the authors supply the mind, the actors the body."[7]

As both author and actor, Shakespeare was in no position to profit from such stigmatization of actors. But he could—however incompletely—embody a unity among the different agencies at work in a play that Gentili never even considers. I will argue in this chapter that, just as Shakespeare bent his stage identity to the conventional model of the kingly poet, so he also bent that literary model to the actuality of his "vile" stage work. Shakespeare, in other words, theatricalized the idea of the poet, and to show how he did it I will turn to the writings of his that most plainly adopt an autobiographical as well as literary pose: his sonnets. Shakespeare's self-portrait in the sonnets has long been recognized as unconventional, both in the homoerotic young-man sonnets at the start and the misogynistic dark-lady sonnets at the end. The dark-lady sonnets in particular strive for a singularity of effect that, as I shall maintain, more nearly approaches Greene's conception of Shakespeare than Ackerman's: in these sonnets, Shakespeare seems to believe that he can achieve a kind of uniqueness as a theatrical professional only when he can imagine and portray himself as the very principle of the theater's vulgarity and commonness.

Prince of Poets

Echoing Jonson's celebration of Shakespeare as the star of poets, another commender in the First Folio, Hugh Holland, calls Shakespeare the "*Poets*' King." This royal figure of speech for Shakespeare's incomparability was no innovative trope of praise:

Petrarch had been crowned with laurel nearly three centuries earlier. And naturally, the notion of a literary monarch was encouraged by the political monarchism of the day, gaining a special currency from the literary ambitions of the only two English monarchs Shakespeare ever knew: Elizabeth I, whom Spenser in 1591 proclaimed "most peerless Prince, most peerless Poëtress," and James I, whom Michael Drayton in 1600 hailed as "Of Kings a Poet, and the Poets' King."[8] *Homer Prince of Poets* was the title that George Chapman gave his partial translation of *The Iliad* in 1609, just as Abraham Fleming had named Virgil the *Prince of All Latine Poets* in the title of his 1589 translation of *The Eclogues* and *The Georgics*. Such honors were not limited to the classics or to actual kings. During Shakespeare's lifetime, the literary crown was passed back and forth among many of his contemporaries: Sidney, Spenser, Marlowe, William Warner, George Buchanan, Samuel Daniel.[9] Jonson repeatedly tried to crown himself: in the 1601 prologue to *Cynthia's Revels,* for instance, he asked the discerning spectator and reader to "cast" the "piercing rays" of their judgment around his poetry "as a crown" that the poet would consider more meritorious than "honor'd Bays." Jonson's disciples heard and obeyed: in a 1638 collection of memorial verses for him, they hailed him as "th'only *Genius* of the *Times,*" "*Poet* of princes, Prince of *Poets,*" "Great **Jonson** King of *English Poetry.*" Perhaps John Taylor (1612) said it best to Jonson during Jonson's and Shakespeare's lifetimes: "all the Worthies of this worthy Land,/Admires thy wondrous all-admired worth."[10]

Bentley may be right that Jonson was more often compared to a king in the seventeenth century than Shakespeare was, but he does not adequately acknowledge the incompleteness or partiality of such praise as a measure of "poetic or dramatic greatness." Almost inevitably, the royal trope distances the poet's value from any popular judgment on it. Having declared James "a God of Poets, and a King of Men," Sir William Alexander imagined his monarch as "ravish'd still above the vulgar sort."[11] So Spenser envisioned Elizabeth as the "one only" who could rescue poetry from the clutches of "the base vulgar." And that is how Jonson understood his literary kingship in *Cynthia's Revels:* "loath to prostitute" his talent "to every vulgar, and adulterate brain," he denounced "popular applause" as the "foamy praise, that drops from common jaws." In lines from Horace that Jonson borrowed for the epigraph to his own first folio in 1616, Jonson reminded himself not to "labor so that the mob [*turba*] may wonder at you" but rather to "be content with few readers."[12] Facing this epigraph was a portrait of Jonson crowned with laurels.

Luckily, Jonson's plays were often unpopular enough to grant him just the rarefied audience he preferred. After the failure of *Sejanus* in 1605, Edmund Bolton expressed his "indignation" at "the People's beastly rage" against Jonson; when *Catiline* failed in 1611, Francis Beaumont congratulated Jonson for not having "itched after the wild applause / Of common people"; and when *The New Inn* failed in 1629, Thomas Carew exhorted Jonson to "let others glut on the extorted praise / Of vulgar breath"—"their hiss," Thomas Randolph added, "is thy applause." Not all contemporary critics agreed, however, that pleasing the few was the best measure of dramatic success. Calling *Sejanus* "irksome" and *Catiline* "tedious," Leonard Digges in the 1640 edition of Shakespeare's *Poems* (1640) admitted that *Volpone* and *The Alchemist* had justly won Jonson "a crown of Bays": "Yet these sometimes, even at a friend's desire / Acted, have scarce defrayed the Seacoal fire / And door-keepers: when let but *Falstaff* come, / *Hal, Poins,* the rest[,] you scarce shall have a room / All is so pester'd." Jonson himself acknowledged the force of Shakespeare's popularity. Having asserted that Shakespeare's "writings" are "such, / As neither *Man,* nor *Muse,* can praise too much," Jonson insisted "'tis true, and all men's suffrage." But for his own more rebarbative writings Jonson prized the measure of the one over the all, as in his epistle to *Volpone* (1607), where he scorned those who try to "make themselves a name with the Multitude."[13]

If Shakespeare's popularity thus distinguished him from Jonson, it did not necessarily prevent him from sharing Jonson's elitism. In the dedication to Shakespeare's earliest publication, *Venus and Adonis,* which was also the work of his that was most often reprinted during his lifetime, Shakespeare, too, seems to prefer the one reader to the many, assuring the Earl of Southhampton that "only if your Honor seem but pleased" will Shakespeare "account" himself "highly praised" for his poetry. The epigraph to *Venus and Adonis,* a quotation from Ovid's *Amores* that is prominently displayed on the title page of every contemporary edition of Shakespeare's poem, sounds no less dismissive of the multitude than Jonson's epigraph to his *Works.* "Vilia miretur vulgus: mihi flavus Apollo/Pocula Castalia plena ministret aqua": let the *vulgus* (the vulgar-minded, the common people) admire vile things, writes the poet; may golden Apollo serve me full cups of Castalian inspiration instead. Facing each other across the divide of a colon, *vulgus* and *mihi* define each other adversarially. And the vulgar sort are by implication not the only social group who fall below the poet's estimation of his own high calling: in the poem from which Shakespeare quotes, Ovid enjoins even "kings and kingly triumphs [reges regumque triumphi]" to give way to his songs.[14]

A year after *Venus and Adonis,* Shakespeare published a second long poem, *Lucrece,* which he once again dedicated to the Earl of Southhampton as to the only reader who mattered: "What I have done is yours, what I have to do is yours, being part in all I have, devoted yours." Yet both poems appeared while the commercial theaters were closed because of plague. After the theaters reopened, Shakespeare returned to the stage and never dedicated another publication to anyone. Most recent critics treat this change as evidence that Shakespeare renounced the elitist singularity of poet and patron for the communitarian ethos of acting company and theater audience. Yet the earliest surviving account of Shakespeare's acting, an epigram published in 1611 by John Davies of Hereford, suggests that even after Shakespeare got down to business in the theater, he continued to imagine himself in kingly, or perhaps more accurately *counter*-kingly terms:

> Some say (good *Will*) which I, in sport, do sing,
> Hadst thou not played some Kingly parts in sport,
> Thou hadst been a companion for a *King;*
> And, been a King among the meaner sort.[15]

In one respect, it would be hard to imagine higher praise for a mere commoner: Davies implies that Shakespeare can act like a king because he *is* one, effectively. But Davies also emphasizes that he speaks, as Shakespeare has acted, "in sport." By pretending to be a king, Shakespeare has actually rendered himself unfit for princely company. From Davies's perspective, the very medium that royalizes Shakespeare has also disgraced him.

In an earlier poem on Shakespeare, Davies put the paradox this way: "though the *stage* doth stain pure gentle *blood*, / yet generous ye are in *mind* and *mood*." The stain, for Davies as for nearly every other contemporary commentator on the theater, came from writing and playing to please the meaner sort, "the vulgar opinion," "the rude multitude." "For what mind can be pure and whole among such a rabblement, and not spotted with any lust," one Elizabethan theater hater asked, where actors "may say and do what they list, be it never so filthy and fleshly, and yet are suffered and heard with laughing and clapping of hands." Again and again throughout the period, a playwright would agree and turn away from his mass audience in disgust: at the end of his long poem *Scillaes Metamorphosis* (1589), for instance, the erstwhile dramatist Thomas Lodge vowed "to write no more, of that whence shame doth grow: / Or tie my pen to *Penny-knaves'* delight." Davies shared Lodge's dismay that a poet should subject himself to a mass audience, yet at the same time—both because of and despite Shakespeare's popularity—Davies's epigram also credits Shakespeare with "a reigning wit." Contrary to the antitheatricalist's or the historicist's view of dramatic authorship, a sense of Shakespeare as a king of poets crops up again and again in the earliest references to him: first satirically in Greene; then encomiastically in "the first extant poem addressed" to Shakespeare, a 1599 epigram by John Weever that imagines "thousands" of readers and spectators vowing "subjective duty" to Shakespeare's fictions; then both satirically and encomiastically in Davies's epigrams. Davies's double vision of Shakespeare as at once royally singular and vulgarly common, as a king among the meaner sort, also figures prominently in the earliest surviving anecdote on Shakespeare's theatrical life, from a 1602 entry in the diary of a law student, John Manningham:

> Upon a time when Burbage played Rich. 3. there was a citizen grew so far in liking with him, that before she went from the play she appointed him to come that night unto her by the name of Ri: the 3. Shakespeare overhearing their conclusion went before, was entertained, and at his game ere Burbage came. Then message being brought that Rich. the 3.d was at the door, Shakespeare caused return to be made that William the Conqueror was before Rich. the 3.[16]

In Manningham's anecdote, Shakespeare wins a royal crown not by transcending the vulgar, but rather by embracing it.

A King among the Meaner Sort

Shakespeare did publish one more book of poetry after his return to the theater: *Shake-Speares Sonnets* in 1609.[17] The notion of an incomparable individual is, of course, a conventional feature of Renaissance sonnet sequences, and in Shakespeare's sonnets that ideal crops up primarily in the praise of the fair young man, a "king" of "beauties" who exercises a kind of creative mastery over appearances: he has "all hues in his controlling" and, though "but one, can every shadow lend."[18] The speaker of the sonnets loves the young man, "my sovereign," "Lord of my love," and feels himself ennobled by the young man's love in return: where some men "glory" in such "particulars" as their birth or skill or wealth, the speaker believes that "All these I better in one general best," "For thy sweet love remember'd such wealth brings,/That then I scorn to change my state with kings." Indeed, the speaker credits the young man with a magisterial power over his poetry as well as his affections. "Thou art all my art," the speaker declares, and by reproducing the beauties of the young man, the speaker hopes that his poetry will, like Ovid's, "outlive" the "gilded monuments/Of princes": "So long as men can breathe or eyes can see,/So long lives this, and this gives life to thee."[19]

Yet the very comprehensiveness of the young man's virtues, his being "all" in "one," also weakens the confidence of the speaker in his own self-sufficiency. "O'ercharg'd" with admiration for the "most high deserts" of the young man, the speaker recurs again and again to the thought of his own "blots" and "defects." So plenteous are the "gifts" and "graces" of his beloved, moreover, that they continually betray the speaker's "poverty" in praising him, "dulling my lines, and doing me disgrace." Only by imagining himself as "sufficed" in the "abundance" of the young man can the speaker entertain the fantasy that "I all other in all worths surmount." "Having thee," he claims, "of all men's pride I boast," but he quickly admits that the young man might "take / All this away, and me most wretched make."[20] The later sonnets in the young-man sequence set forth the speaker's fears of the young man's possible infidelity, of other poets who might more winningly praise the young man, and finally of the speaker's own, barely suppressed desire to liberate himself from the young man's overwhelming attractiveness. In sonnet 109, where the speaker once again professes to the young man that "thou art my all" and yet also confesses to the perversity of having "rang'd" from him, the speaker for the first time imagines himself, hypothetically, as the "all" of something other than worthiness:

> Never believe, though in my nature reign'd
> All frailties that besiege all kinds of blood,
> That it could so preposterously be stain'd,
> To leave for nothing all thy sum of good.

If the young man is one general best, then the speaker can achieve a similarly supreme fullness on his own, sonnet 109 suggests, only by perceiving himself as one general worst.

Such strangely boastful self-loathing becomes the keynote of the remaining sonnets, in which the speaker does indeed "preposterously" transfer his affections from the fair young man to a whorish dark lady and thus throws not only his fidelity but his very judgment into question: "In my mind thy worst all best exceeds," he proclaims to the lady, "For I have sworn thee fair, and

thought thee bright,/Who art as black as hell, as dark as night."
But first the vision of himself in sonnet 109 as the sum of "all
frailties" leads the speaker to confess a shameful particular about
his life that he had not previously acknowledged. In the three
sonnets that follow 109, the speaker's disgraceful ranging from
the lord of his love is redefined as his ignominious wandering
by profession: "Alas, 'tis true, I have gone here and there/And
made myself a motley to the view."[21] What the speaker now confesses, in other words, is that he is an actor as well as a poet: his
sum of bad now appears as the degrading "motley" of a clown.
And his very insufficiency, he insists, is what has forced him to
debase himself this way: "O, for my sake do you with Fortune
chide,/The guilty goddess of my harmful deeds,/That did not
better for my life provide/Than public means which public manners breeds." Far from the comfortably collaborative environment
that Kastan envisions, the theater in these sonnets is presented
as inimical to the speaker, threatening to overwrite him with the
publicity to which he feels disgracefully exposed. Only the en-
nobling "love and pity" of the young man, the speaker declares,
can "fill" "th'impression" that "vulgar scandal" has "stamped upon
my brow."[22]

But now the speaker's acknowledgment of his professional
vulgarity appears to weaken his devotion to the fair young man.
After the theater sonnets, he never again presents himself as
the poet of the young man's worthiness. In fact, he never again
presents himself as an active poet. Although more than a third
of the sonnets before sonnet 110 had made some reference to
the speaker's writing lines or rhymes or verses, the only remaining references after sonnet 112 sound like recantations. "Those
lines that I before have writ do lie," begins sonnet 115, and the
following sonnet ends, "If this be error and upon me proved,/I
never writ, nor no man ever loved." In sonnet 122, the speaker
apologizes for having given away a writing-tablet he received
from the young man without ever writing on it.[23] This is not
to say, of course, that the speaker has stopped being a poet: he
continues to generate sonnets about his degraded position. But

he now seems to feel that the role of poet is no longer sufficient to account for the motley *range* of an individual who in sonnet 116 can declare his love for the young man to be "an ever-fixed mark" and then in the very next sonnet admit to the "willfulness" of having wandered from him.[24] This is an individual, moreover, who acts as well as writes, and whose continual association of his poetry with the young man's sovereign beauties seems to make it impossible for him to link his identity as a poet with his vulgarity as an actor.[25] After the theater sonnets, the speaker no longer merely refers to his frailties and to the "disgrace" he suffers "in men's eyes." He now *performs* that disgrace, in his perverse love for the dark lady's "insufficiency" and in the increasing vulgarity of his actions as well as language. Where the speaker had earlier claimed that the young man inspired his verse and thus was able to "advance / As high as learning my rude ignorance," he now maintains that the dark lady elevates an obscenely literal part of him, the "flesh" that, "rising at thy name, doth point out thee / As his triumphant prize."[26]

Paradoxically, it is at this low point in the sonnets, when the speaker insists on his degradation most emphatically, that he also stakes his claim for the kingly status of "one only" most emphatically:

Whoever hath her wish, thou hast thy *Will*,
And *Will* to boot, and *Will* in overplus;
More than enough am I that vex thee still,
To thy sweet will making addition thus.
Wilt thou, whose will is large and spacious,
Not once vouchsafe to hide my will in thine?
Shall will in others seem right gracious,
And in my will no fair acceptance shine?
The sea, all water, yet receives rain still,
And in abundance addeth to his store.
So thou being rich in *Will* add to thy *Will*
One will of mine to make thy large *Will* more.
   Let no unkind, no fair beseechers kill;
   Think all but one, and me in that one *Will*.[27]

Now the speaker adds a further particularity to the picture he had earlier drawn of himself as a poet and an actor: he tells us for the first time that his first name is Will.[28] Not William, as in the Manningham anecdote, but the common nickname Davies uses, more appropriate to a boon companion than to a conqueror.[29] Two decades after Shakespeare's death, his fellow dramatist Thomas Heywood ruefully observed that where "past Ages did the ancient Poets grace" by adding place names to "their swelling styles," "our modern Poets to that pass are driven,/Those names are curtail'd which they first had given." He proceeds to list fifteen modern poets—all of them commercial playwrights—for whom "we scarcely can afford . . . half" the sound of their first names: among them, "Robin" Greene, "Kit" Marlowe, "Frank" Beaumont, "Ben" Jonson, and "melifluous *Shake-speare,* whose enchanting Quill/Commanded Mirth or Passion," yet never could command a name more respectful than "*Will.*"[30] According to Heywood, in other words, the name that Shakespeare made for himself with the multitude was "Will." But even the full Christian name "William" would hardly seem as distinctive as the proper name that Greene had felt compelled to belittle with "Shakescene" or that Jonson chose to magnify when he claimed that "in each" of Shakespeare's "lines" "he seems to shake a Lance,/As brandish'd at the eyes of Ignorance."[31] William, indeed, was the *least* distinctive name a man could have in Renaissance England: according to the parish records of the time, it belonged to nearly a quarter of all Shakespeare's male contemporaries.[32]

In both of the Will sonnets, the speaker wryly acknowledges the commonness of his name, admitting that the dark lady might be attracted to other lovers named Will—the "Will" that "in others" might "seem right gracious"—and asking that she simply "add" him to "the number." At the same time, however, the speaker also urges the dark lady to regard him as the only Will who counts: "Think all but one, and me in that one *Will.*" This all-in-one sufficiency had previously been the sovereign property, of course, of the young man, but the speaker now hopes that he can fill the "defect" of the dark lady as the young man had once made the disgraced speaker feel "replete" with him. "More than enough am I," declares the speaker, in the next sonnet stuffing his verse with the sound of his common name: "*Will* will fulfill the treasure of your love,/ Ay, fill it full of wills, and my will one."[33] But the transfer of sovereign singularity from the gracious young man to the degraded speaker comes at a cost to the ideal of sovereignty in the sonnets, as well as to the good name of the speaker. The Will sonnets insist on correlating the speaker's first or Christian name with *will* as a vulgar term for genitals, both male and female, which the speaker hopes will mingle and which do become one in the one word *will*. These sonnets also turn the speaker's name into a byword for the libertinism that would induce him to joke about his name as a double entendre, have sex with a woman he goes on to call "the wide world's common place," and then proclaim that sex publicly, thus underscoring his infidelity to the young man. Perversely abandoning the ideal of sunlike "sacred majesty" that had been exemplified by the young man, the speaker presents himself instead as the masculine personification of indiscriminate debauchery, as Will itself: "my name is *Will*."[34]

By 1609 such vulgarity was of course nothing new in Shakespeare's writing. A younger contemporary favorably compared Fletcher to Shakespeare on this score, applauding Fletcher for having a "vein" as "free" as Shakespeare's "but without his scurrility," "Bawdry," or "obsceneness."[35] Bardolatrists regularly defend the profanity in Shakespeare by treating it as evidence of his supreme imaginative range as a writer, the "*myriad-minded*" comprehensiveness that established Shakespeare, in Coleridge's eyes, as "the greatest genius, that perhaps human nature has yet produced." According to Keats, the "poetical Character" of Shakespeare "has as much delight in conceiving an Iago as an Imogen" because "it has no self—it is everything and nothing." But Shakespeare's account of his art and scope in the sonnets more closely resembles the antitheatricalist's view than the bardolatrist's. When the Elizabethan clergyman Thomas Beard

(1597) described Christopher Marlowe, "a play-maker, and a Poet of scurrility," as "giving too large a swinge [i.e., a swing and a sway] to his own wit, and suffering his lust to have the full reins," he was invoking the standard critical view, not only of actors and playwrights in the commercial theaters, but of their mass audience, too. "You are no sooner enter'd" in the theater, writes the theater-hating Stephen Gosson in his *Schoole of Abuse*, "but liberty looseth the reins."[36] The sonnet-speaker agrees: "public means" breed "public manners," not as the imaginative range of the poet but rather as the scandalous behavior of the profligate.

This same self-accusatory view of theatrical liberty or licentiousness figures prominently in a rival sonnet sequence written by Shakespeare's nearly exact contemporary Michael Drayton. In 1594, Drayton had published a conventionally Petrarchan sequence of sonnets entitled *Ideas Mirrour: Amours in Quatorzains*. But then in 1599, and again in 1600, 1602, 1603, and 1605, Drayton issued a radically different version of these sonnets, called simply *Idea*. Drayton set the tone for his new sequence in two opening sonnets addressed to the reader, which present him as a "Libertine" who writes "wanton verse," "wild, madding, jocund, & irregular."[37] What accounts for the change? Starting in December 1597, as the diary of the theatrical entrepreneur Philip Henslowe informs us, Drayton began to write plays for the commercial stage; by the time he published his revised sonnets a year or two later, he had already collaborated on seventeen or eighteen plays for Henslowe's company.[38] Scholars have long noted that the 1599 *Idea* shows Drayton importing a newly dramatic style of writing into his sonnets.[39] But the opening sonnets to the reader also express a new mass-entertainment conception of the poet, who now maintains that his verse inclines to "the choice of all variety": "And in all humors sportively I range."[40] For Keats, that range would count as the hallmark of the sublimely protean poetical character, but for Drayton it is the brand of the wantonly commercial playwright.[41]

And yet there is nothing particularly libertine, licentious, or vulgar about the sonnets Drayton proceeds to write in *Idea:* wantonness turns out to be less a practical than a theoretical feature of the dramatist's poetry.[42] The difference between Shakespeare's and Drayton's sequences in this regard is nicely captured by a sonnet of Drayton's, first published in the 1605 edition of *Idea*, on the subject of Drayton's playwrighting:

> In pride of wit, when high desire of fame
> Gave life and courage to my laboring pen,
> And first the sound and virtue of my name,
> Won grace and credit in the ears of men:
> With those the thronged Theaters that press,
> I in the circuit for the Laurel strove,
> Where the full praise I freely must confess,
> In heat of blood and modest mind might move:
> With shouts and claps at every little pause,
> When the proud round on every side hath rung.
> Sadly I sit unmov'd with the applause,
> As though to me it nothing did belong:
>   No public glory vainly I pursue.
>   The praise I strive, is to eternize you.[43]

Like Greene's Shakespeare, who longs to be the only "Shake-scene" in a country, Drayton hears "the sound and virtue" of his "name" ringing throughout the theater as he strives for the sovereignty of a laurel crown. But the throng and press of the mass audience dismay him: he feels that whatever triumph the audience applauds must belong not to him personally, but to the theater at large, "the proud round." So he abandons the theatrical pursuit of "public glory" for the more exclusive literary praise he can win by eternizing his beloved. This is the pose that Shakespeare adopts, and then drops, in his own sonnets. The difference, it seems, is that after 1601, when Drayton stopped writing for Henslowe, he became increasingly disenchanted with the stage and its "thick-brain'd Audience," while Shakespeare had so entirely committed himself to the stage as to buy a share in the new Globe theater.[44] This is not to say that Shakespeare renounced the elitism proclaimed on title page after title page of *Venus and Adonis;* if he had, then why would his sonnets represent his theater work as disgraceful? Instead, reversing the trajectory of Drayton's sonnet, Shakespeare in his own sonnet sequence decided both to acknowledge and to enact the shame of publicity that Drayton could (as he says) "freely . . . confess" only hypothetically: the "shouts and claps" of the theater audience "*might* move," Drayton allows, but "I sit unmov'd."[45] Yet how could Shakespeare turn "public glory" into a sovereign sufficiency that belonged to him and him alone? Only by presenting himself as the embodiment of the audience's commonness, the one of their many: "Think all but one, and me in that one *Will*."[46]

A surprisingly empowering debasement of sovereignty is, after all, a central theme of Shakespeare's history plays. In the Henriad, Hal redefines kingship as something common and vulgar yet still regal. Although Hal's father King Henry believes that Hal has "lost thy princely privilege/With vile participation," Hal proves that by consorting with lowlifes and transforming himself into "all humors" he can attain a miraculously supreme authority. Even the familiar name "Hal," like the familiar name "Will," helps the prince secure this privilege: while the more respectful "Henry" and "Harry" are names that Hal shares with his father and his chief rival, among others, the more common "Hal" is a title uniquely applied to the prince, belonging to him exclusively.[47]

But Shakespeare was no prince, nor do the sonnets show him turning away his disgraceful self as Hal does. The last two of the sonnets are among the most tawdry of the sequence, representing the speaker as a man sexually "diseas'd" and unhelped by any "sovereign cure." Startled critics have often cautioned readers that, since the speaker is "grossly and notoriously profligate," as James Boswell the younger put it in his 1821 edition of sonnets, we should never mistake the speaker for Shakespeare himself.[48] Other scholars, such as W. H. Auden, have accepted the sonnets as autobiographical but at the same time insisted that Shakespeare never intended to publish them: according to Auden, Shakespeare wrote the sonnets "as one writes a diary, for himself alone, with no thought of a public," and therefore he "must have been horrified" when they appeared in print.[49] Yet the speaker of the sonnets repeatedly insists that he has *made* himself a motley to the view: "I am shamed by that which I bring forth," he declares, elsewhere lamenting "the injuries that to myself I do" and assuring the young man that "thou canst not, love, disgrace me half so ill,/ . . . / As I'll myself disgrace, *knowing thy will.*"[50]

It is this peculiar readiness to shame himself that makes the speaker seem distinctive in his own eyes. He repeatedly admits that he shares too many "frailties" with other "wills" to claim the *sui generis* individuality he praises in the young man: "that you alone are you." When the speaker declares "I am that I am," he means that he can at least acknowledge his faults, unlike those who "level / At my abuses" and in the process unwittingly "reckon up their own." But the terms of his self-acceptance change once the dark lady enters the picture: "my bad angel" who "makes me sin." The speaker finds that he is so addicted to harming himself by his profligacy, "longing still / For that which longer nurseth the disease," that he cannot help but pursue the further self-injury of parading his faults. This double perversity—his irrational lust and his even more irrational publicizing of it—turns his failings into a paradoxically singular commonness: "I love what others do abhor."[51]

The best the speaker can make of this worst is that it amounts to a confession: "With mine own weakness being best acquainted,/ Upon thy part I can set down a story / Of faults concealed wherein I am attainted."[52] A will to confess suits the preacherly tone that the speaker often adopts in the sonnets, as in the poems that begin, "Sin of self-love possesseth all mine eye," or "Poor soul, the center of my sinful earth," or "Love is my sin." In my book *Shakespeare's Tribe*, I argued that one of the ways theater people habitually defended their low profession was to present themselves as accommodationists who deliberately posed as libertines in order to capture the attention of the profane theatergoer and then convert him or her to a better life. In his preacher's manual *The Faithfull Shepheard*, published two years before Shakespeare's *Sonnets*, the clergyman Richard

Bernard advised his fellow clerics that a minister who hopes "to make applications to his hearers" and "do it profitably" must similarly "preach to them from knowledge out of himself, feeling the corruption of nature."[53] The archetype of such preachers was the apostle Paul, who called himself the chief of sinners and confessed that, to save other sinners, he had made himself all things to all men. If the speaker of the sonnets believes that the young man can count as "beauty's pattern to succeeding men," perhaps he also believes that his own "defects" can serve as a kind of pattern, too, just as Paul in his first letter to Timothy claims that Jesus endured and then forgave Paul's sins so that Paul might become "a pattern to them which should hereafter believe on [Christ] to life everlasting." Indeed, the speaker admits to *more* sin than the chief of sinners does. Although Paul in his letter to Timothy confesses that he was "a blasphemer, and a persecutor" before his conversion, he never accuses himself of adultery or lust.[54] In sonnet 129, conversely, "lust" becomes the all-in-one vice, "perjur'd, murd'rous, bloody, full of blame,/ Savage, extreme, rude, cruel, not to trust"—and the Will sonnets go on to personify lust as the speaker, "Will."

In some respects, the young man himself lights the way toward a remedial view of the speaker's confessions. Possessed like Prince Hal with "both grace and faults" that "are lov'd of more and less," he shows the speaker how frailties might be excused even as they are expressed: "How sweet and lovely dost thou make the shame/Which ... /Doth spot the beauty of thy budding name." But the dark lady provides no such model for the amelioration of "sins." On the contrary, her presence in the sonnets weakens any penitential claim by the speaker, who admits to loving her, not in spite of her faults, but because of them: "all my best doth worship thy defect." The surviving evidence of the sonnets' contemporary reception indicates that readers were consequently puzzled, at best, by the extremity of Shakespeare's self-disgracing in these poems. In the three decades after the initial publication of the sonnets, when Shakespeare's complete plays were twice printed and his earlier long poems *Venus and Adonis* and *Lucrece* appeared in ten further editions, the sonnets themselves were never reissued. "What a heap of wretched Infidel Stuff," one contemporary reader of the 1609 edition jotted down in the margins after the final sonnet. Of the mere twenty-eight transcriptions of individual Shakespeare sonnets that are scattered across twenty-five different manuscripts surviving from the seventeenth century, only two derive from the dark-lady sequence—and one of these is copied from an earlier poetical miscellany, *The Passionate Pilgrim*, not from the 1609 *Sonnets*.[55] For contemporary readers, Shakespeare's self-representation as "Will" seems to have been a failure. But that failure was, in its way, a logical consequence of Shakespeare's conceptualizing himself in the sonnets as something other than a poet only. To popularize his more capacious, or more motley, role as an actor-author, he would have to transfer it once again to the stage.

Coda

According to Greene, the only way that Shakespeare could impress as a dramatist was through "bombast"—that is, through rhetorical padding and stuffing. But the sonnets self-critically link the speaker's psychological amplitude with the stranger and even more discreditable "defect" of his perversity: being "against myself" is what opens the speaker to more than a single or particular identity. In chapter 2, I will show how "myriad-minded" Shakespeare used the stage to highlight the spectrum of characterological possibilities for the self-various person who finds a kind of distinctiveness and even sovereignty in disgrace.

In *Measure for Measure*, for instance, Duke Vincentio begins the play already vested in the "power" of his office, but he temporarily removes himself from office for reasons that he never makes entirely clear to his subjects. Instead, he perversely strives to shake their confidence in him: "the Duke is very strangely gone from hence," comments one subject; "every letter he hath writ hath disvouch'd the other," adds another; "in most uneven and distracted manner," says a third. But the fate of this third character, Angelo, the man whom the duke had named as his substitute, demonstrates how the role of duke can itself prove distracting. Taking the place of the duke who himself stands for his subjects, internalizing their multiplicity in his royal "we," Angelo finds himself becoming divided by conflicting desires. "When I would pray and think," he confesses in soliloquy, "I think and pray/To several subjects." Specifically, Angelo longs to uphold a law against premarital sex and yet also to engage in such sex himself—with a novice nun. While his "tongue" may speak of "heaven," his "blood" registers a sexual arousal that floods his "heart," "dispossessing all my other parts/Of necessary fitness." Trying to grasp how his magisterial refusal to be "partial" in office could ever have given way to his pathetic disintegration into "parts," Angelo compares his internal chaos to two different scenes of "one" who is overcome by many: "So play the foolish throngs with one that swounds," he reasons, "and even so/The general subject to a well-wish'd king/Quit their own part, and in obsequious fondness/Crowd to his presence."[56] As duke, Angelo finds that the particularity of his old identity has been overwhelmed by the generality of "subjects" both outside and also within him: the throngs crowd *into* his presence, making him self-various.

When the poet Sir John Davies (c. 1594) imagined a person who suffered from a similar excess, he chose a theatrical analogy to express it.

IN COSMUM

Cosmus hath more discoursing in his head,
Than Jove, when Pallas issued from his brain,
And still he strives to be delivered
Of all his thoughts at once, but all in vain.
For as we see at all the play-house doors,
When ended is the play, the dance, and song:
A thousand townsmen, gentlemen, and whores,
Porters and serving-men together throng,
So thoughts of drinking, thriving, wenching, war,

And borrowing money, raging in his mind,
To issue all at once so forward are,
As none at all can perfect passage find.[57]

For Davies, the masses gathered in a playhouse suggest not the loss of particularity, as one might expect, but rather the concentration of generality within a single character. Like Cosmus (whose name already makes him stand for the world), Angelo feels himself distracted by such concentration. But Duke Vincentio finds "passage" for the internal multiplicity of his desires by acting on the theatrical analogy and devising new parts for himself and his subjects to play.

To emphasize this difference, Shakespeare has Vincentio first voice his opposition to theatricality. "I love the people," the duke confides to Angelo and Escalus in his opening scene, "But do not like to stage me to their eyes." "I have ever lov'd the life removed," he confesses to another confidant, a friar, in his next scene. After delegating his power to Angelo, however, Vincentio chooses to conduct himself more like Greene's johnny-do-all than an unapproachable ruler. Disguising himself as a friar, Vincentio takes himself to prison, where he immediately begins directing various of his subjects in his "plot"; by the end of *Measure for Measure* he has grown so invested in play-acting that he stage-manages not one but two spectacular public entrances for himself when he decides to reclaim his dukeship. The effect is extraordinary on Angelo in particular, who is so mystified by the shows the duke has arranged that he now compares his "dread lord" to "pow'r divine." Yet as Davies's democratizing vision of the playhouse suggests, with its indiscriminate mingling of gentlemen, servingmen, and whores, the duke's newfound love for staging himself necessitates his demeaning himself in pursuit of theatrical glory. Public means breed public manners: worse than the debasement of pretending to be a "poor" friar is the fraud of it, an offense the duke compounds by using his false identity first to encourage the premarital sex he supposedly wants stopped and then to condemn himself publicly for his own laxness. Once again,

Angelo clarifies the duke's perversity by contrast. When his own crimes are finally revealed, Angelo proves incapable of bearing the "shame" and hopes that his "confession" of "guiltiness" will bring instant "death." Yet the duke's experimentations with theatricality have taught him how to live with shame, and thrive by it, too. After pardoning certain "slanders" against himself, Vincentio ends *Measure for Measure* with a characterization of his "palace" as no longer a sanctuary for the life removed but now an open stage for his own confessions, "where we'll show/What's yet behind, that's meet you all should know."[58]

The Author Staged

But, observe his Comic vein,
Laugh, and proceed next to a Tragic strain,
Then weep; So when thou find'st two contraries,
Two different passions from thy rapt soul rise,
Say, (who alone effect such wonders could)
Rare *Shake-speare* to the life thou dost behold.
« A commendatory poem in *Mr. William Shakespeares Comedies, Histories, and Tragedies* (1632) »

Long before Shakespeare began his theatrical career, it was commonplace to think of plays as the expressions of two different agencies: "the *Poets* which pen the plays" and "the Actors that present them upon the Stage," as the theater-hater Stephen Gosson put it in his 1582 *Playes Confuted,* while heaping scorn on both parties.[1] Ideally, these separate agencies were understood to be working as one, jointly pursuing their common goal of pleasing the audience. "We that are th'actors have ourselves dedicate/With some Christmas device your spirits to recreate," declares the prologue to the 1553 *Respublica,* "And our poet trusteth the thing we shall recite/May without offence the hearers' minds delight." The prologue to the 1567 *Triall of Treasure* makes the same distinction while insisting on the same uniformity of purpose: "our Author desireth your gentle acceptation,/ And we the players likewise, with all humiliation."[2]

If author and actor thus generally conspired to present a united front to their audience, the potential for rivalry between the two was strong on the side of authors especially, who often complained that actors gained more from their working partnership than they deserved. "With mouthing words that better wits have framed," the scholar Studioso complains of actors in the Cambridge play *The Return from Parnassus* (acted c. 1601–2), "They purchase lands, and now Esquires are named," while the authors, those better wits, live in poverty: "Vile world, that lifts them up to high degree,/ And treads us down in groveling misery." Studioso tries to shift the blame for authorial misery from the world to the actors: echoing the bitter denunciation of players by his fellow university dramatist Robert Greene in *Greenes Groats-worth of Wit*, Studioso depicts actors as deplorable ingrates who "prize" authors at no better than "a hireling rate." But Studioso's protest acknowledges a deeper, more structural imbalance in the relation between authors and actors than the contingent matter of profit-sharing. For all the language of collaboration in the prologues and epilogues of plays, authors were generally not the partners of actors: they were rather their employees. What a "pity," Greene lamented in his *Groats-worth*, that "such rare wits" as his fellow dramatists "should be subject to the pleasure of such rude grooms."[3]

And this inequality on the business side of theater life was only part of the basic asymmetry between authors and actors. No matter how indispensable the dramatist's pen may have been to the creation of plays, the actors were the ones who presented the plays before audiences of thousands. "Sit in a full Theater," writes the playwright John Webster (1615) in his "character" of "An Excellent Actor," "and you will think you see so many lines drawn from the circumference of so many ears, whiles the *Actor* is the *Center*." In performance, as dramatists like Webster well knew, players could command the attention of their audience without mouthing a single authorial word. The traveler Fynes

Moryson (c. 1617–20) recalled how a company of English play-ers on tour in Germany, "having neither a Complete number of Actors, nor any good Apparell, nor any ornament of the Stage, yet the Germans, not understanding a word they said, both men and women, flocked wonderfully to see their gesture and Ac-tion." No more bothered than the Germans by the lack of any comprehensible script, "many young virgins" in the Netherlands, too, according to Moryson, "fell in love with some of the play-ers, and followed them from City to City, till the magistrates were forced to forbid them to play any more"—and in both cases these were "cast[-off] despised Stage players," "straggling broken Companies" who failed to make it in London, yet "the people not understanding what they said, only for their Action followed them with wonderful Concourse."[4]

Whether from a lofty indifference to the actor's charisma or an envious hatred of it, authors repeatedly celebrated their own theatrical agency by reversing the dynamics of performance and erasing the actors from the experience of plays. Elsewhere in his *Playes Confuted*, the former dramatist Gosson referred sim-ply to "the *Poet* on stages" and to playwrights who "fill" the the-aters. In the prologue to *If This Be Not a Good Play, The Devil Is In It* (1612), Thomas Dekker more elaborately redrew the lines that Webster traced from audience to actor by claiming that a playwright's eloquence "can call the *Banish'd* Auditor home, And tie / His Ear (with golden chains) to his Melody: / Can draw with *Adamantine Pen*, (even creatures / Forg'd out of *th'Hammer*,) on tiptoe, to *Reach*-up, / And (from *Rare silence*) clap their *Brawny hands*, / T'*Applaud*, what their *charm'd* soul scarce understands."[5] No professional dramatist labored more doggedly to assert his central importance to the theatrical experience than Ben Jonson, and in the eyes of contemporary observers no event better epito-mized the violent ambitions of Jonson as an author than the duel in which he actually killed an actor, Gabriel Spencer.

Taking their cue from Jonson, recent historians of the theater have magnified such local hostilities into an all-out war that pit-ted authors against actors and the audiences who applauded them.

According to Richard Helgerson in *Forms of Nationhood* (1992), Jonson was joined on the battlefield by Shakespeare. Helgerson claims that Shakespeare's playwriting career coincided with a momentous "shift" in Renaissance dramatic culture from a communitarian "players' theater" to a hierarchical "authors' theater." The players' theater, Helgerson argues, was "essentially artisanal," its primary spokesperson "the clown," its primary audience "the common people." At the start of Shakespeare's career, his "position" in the theater resembled that of the clowns Richard Tarlton and Robert Wilson: he was merely "a player who collaborated in generating the plays his company put on." Yet "others" at the time—"the 'university wits' most prominent among them—were being engaged and being recognized solely as writers." Tempted by the wits, Shakespeare soon repudiated his populist, artisanal, and above all collaborative roots for the lordly eminence of an author "defined by his social superiority to the institution for which he wrote." During the 1590s, Helgerson maintains, Shakespeare as author began to receive "a sharply increasing share" of the "public attention" that had previously belonged to his company collectively, and the more famous he grew, the more his drama moved "in the direction of greater exclusion, which is also the direction of an authors' theater as Marlowe, Nashe, Greene, Marston, and the other university wits were defining it."[6]

At first glance, this tale of collaboration lost seems backed by compelling evidence. After 1590 playwrights did receive more press than they had before, the university wits did style themselves as gentlemen, and several of them did mock players. But this series of developments falls well short of the theater's supposed conversion into an authors' world so anticollaborative and elitist that its aim was to "exclude all those below the rank of gentleman" from theaters and plays. "Gentlemanly" is not a label one could easily apply to such plays by the university wits as Marlowe's *Jew of Malta* or Nashe's *Isle of Dogs.* Greene's attacks on players pale by comparison to the full-scale antitheatrical diatribes of the dramatists Gosson and Anthony Munday a decade earlier, when Helgerson claims a players' theater reigned. As for

Nashe, foolish and bombastic players were the objects of his scorn in his 1589 preface to Greene's *Menaphon,* not actors with "deserved reputation." Three years later, in *Pierce Penilesse,* Nashe mounted one of the strongest defenses of the commercial theaters to that date, going so far as to promise that he would spread the fame of the clown Tarlton and other talented English players throughout Europe, "if I ever write anything in Latin." In his 1616 *Workes,* Jonson himself praised the actor Edward Alleyn for having "out-stript" the "glories" of the classical stage, and offered his encomium as a kind of restitution for his murder of Spencer: "'Tis just, that who did give / So many *Poets* life, by one should live."[7]

Such complexities in the relations between authors and actors have nevertheless seemed beside the point to historicists who share Helgerson's views on the rise of an author's theater and yet attribute that development to relatively objective market forces: in particular, to the growing interest of publishers in advertising plays as literature rather than popular entertainment. For these historicists, as I noted in my Introduction, there simply were no dramatic authors before publishers invented them; but this is only half the story they tell. At the start of Shakespeare's professional career, they argue, "play texts . . . did not yet demand an author, and in some sense they did not deserve one, the text being so fully a record of the collaborative activities of a theatrical company." To transform plays "from the ephemera of an emerging entertainment industry to the artifacts of high culture," publishers therefore had to do more (in the historicist account) than promote the fiction of dramatic authorship: they also had to suppress the fact of theatrical teamwork. Consequently, the process of "legitimating plays" meant not only "associating" plays "with a single source of origin and authority," but also "dissociating them from the disreputable commercial playhouses where players, shareholders, theatrical entrepreneurs, and playwrights collaborated." Plays "had to be cut off from the milieu of their production in order to be lifted into the timeless, transcendent place inhabited by the Author himself."[8]

Historicists have cited the title pages of plays published during the Renaissance to prove not only that dramatic authorship came into being around 1600, but also that authors soon came to matter more than actors. For instance, James Saeger and Christopher Fassler have identified a "downward trend" throughout the period in title pages that mention acting companies but not authors: such "company-only attributions," as Saeger and Fassler call them, account for "very roughly half of all editions" of plays before 1600 but less than "10% even a decade before the 1642 closing." At the same time as company-only attributions fell, "author-only" attributions rose, from below 20 percent of all published commercial plays in 1591 to nearly 50 percent of the total in 1621. Here, it seems, is the quantitative proof that authors replaced acting companies as the presumptive "originating producers of plays." But the statistics of Saeger and Fassler turn out to sketch as partial a picture of Renaissance theater culture as Helgerson's more discursive analysis does. The title pages of Renaissance plays that single out an acting company typically offer the play "as it was presented" or "acted" or "played" or "performed" by that company: none of these title pages, to my knowledge, ever claims that a company *wrote* a play. What's more, if authors did indeed replace actors in the public mind, we would expect to see a decline not just in company-only attributions but also in the *total number* of company attributions during the Renaissance. Yet Saeger and Fassler concede "that throughout the period of the active theater, and even in the decade following," the total number of company attributions on the title pages of published plays "remained relatively constant (at or above 60%)."[9] How could an authors' theater have superseded an actors' theater if acting companies continued to be cited on the majority of dramatic title pages?

A later analysis of title pages by Alan Farmer and Zachary Lesser confirms the steady state of company attributions throughout the period while also identifying a different but equally striking trend: a growing number of attributions to *theaters* after 1600, "reaching over 65% of all commercial title pages by the mid-1640s."[10] The 1609 title page of *Pericles*, for instance, links the play to a specific building as well as to a specific company and author: "As it hath been diverse and sundry times acted by his Majesty's Servants, at the Globe on the Bank-side. By William Shakespeare." As Farmer and Lesser rightly conclude, the concomitant development of theatrical and authorial attributions seriously weakens the notion that "the rise of the author served to distance plays from their theatrical origins."[11] Although they do not say so directly, the findings of Farmer and Lesser also suggest that publishers began to see a promotional value in *broadening* the advertised provenance of plays, beyond acting companies to authors and playhouses and audiences as well. According to Farmer and Lesser, the first published commercial play in England to cite a theater on its title page was *Cynthia's Revels* (1601), a play attributed on the same page to the supposedly anticollaborative author *par excellence,* Jonson. Jonson's 1616 *Workes* proved to be even more innovative in marketing plays as the products of diverse collaborative forces. As G. E. Bentley notes, "each of the nine tragedies and comedies in the volume was accompanied by a list of the names of the players who had created the principal roles. . . . Such formal recognition for the lowly players had never been shown in an English book before."[12] In Jonson's folio, greater prestige for the playwright meant greater prestige for the players also. Farmer and Lesser's statistics point to a similar trend on a larger scale: as the status of professional dramatists rose during this period, so did the status of the professional theater generally.

But ultimately the title pages of plays constitute no more than a subsidiary issue in deciding whether an authors' theater ever supplanted an actors' theater during the English Renaissance. Authors could never "dominate" the "theatrical scene" after 1590 as Helgerson maintains, because the memory of the clowns Tarlton and Wilson faded in the light of new *players* also—men such as Alleyn, Richard Burbage, and Nathan Field, whose contemporary fame belies Helgerson's notion of a theater predicated on authors. To a considerable extent, the modern scholarly vision of authors triumphing over actors amounts to an anachronistic retrojection of the current state of affairs, in which the scripts of Renaissance playwrights have survived the bodies of Renaissance players. A similar anachronism helps explain the strangely prosecutorial stance of recent theater scholars toward authors. Their disapproval seems driven by a vaguely marxist or at least populist preference for groups of laborers over single workers— even though the players in Shakespeare's company were the capitalists, and the authors their part-time wage slaves.[13] But perhaps the decisive factor in sustaining the scholarly fantasy of an authors' theater is the tendency among theater historians to homogenize the heterogeneous means by which commercial Renaissance plays were produced: in Helgerson's vision of the theater, for instance, it was either actors or dramatists who created plays, but never both at once.

This imagined dichotomy has led Helgerson and others to gloss over one of the most extraordinary features of the commercial theater in Shakespeare's time: the remarkable prominence of *actor-authors* on the Renaissance stage. As it happens, the two actors whom Helgerson associates with the artisanal, collaborative, and popular players' theater—Tarlton and Wilson—were also celebrated playwrights. In defending the commercial stage against Gosson's attacks, Thomas Lodge (c. 1579) cited Wilson's comedy *Short and Sweet* as "the practice of a good scholar," while both Gabriel Harvey and Thomas Nashe (1592) praised Tarlton in print for "his famous play of the seven Deadly sins."[14] Conversely, the two main figures whom Helgerson associates with an authors' theater—Jonson and Shakespeare—were both actors, and were long remembered as such. In his 1643 *Chronicle of the Kings of England*, Sir Richard Baker ends his catalogue of Elizabethan "Men of NOTE" with the players Burbage, Alleyn, and Tarlton, and then the playwrights Jonson and Shakespeare, who "had been Players themselves"; no other dramatists are mentioned.[15]

The uncommon celebrity and success of the actor-authors Jonson and Shakespeare in their own day demands a more balanced conception of the relation between actors and authors in the Renaissance theater than a narrative of intransigent struggle allows. Clearly, acting helped Shakespeare and Jonson grasp what would and would not work on stage. But their experience as players also encouraged a theater-conscious and thus multifarious conception of their authorship as well as their dramaturgy. Underscoring what he calls the "bifold authority" that dramatists and players shared on the Renaissance stage, Robert Weimann (2000) has powerfully demonstrated how Shakespeare and his playwriting contemporaries were capable of viewing the inevitable "contrariety" or "tension" between actors and authors as a "source of strength," a means of broadening the resonance of plays in characterization especially, where the "gap" between word and deed could be "deliberately inscribed in the represented image of character" and thus help generate "a new, almost unfathomable dimension in characterization." I want to supplement Weimann's bracing account by highlighting the new dimensions in *authorship* that could also result from an author's joining forces with "the basest trade," as *The Return from Parnassus* calls actors. I will trace the *dramatization* of authorship in Jonsonian comedy and Shakespearean tragedy, by which I mean not only the use of authorship as a dramatic subject, but also the conceptualization of authorship in specifically dramatic terms. Contrary to the view in current scholarship, staging the author as Jonson and Shakespeare did was no unambiguous assertion of power. As late as 1640, a commentator urged the actor-author Thomas Heywood to confine himself henceforward to print, which "will become thy age,/ And better please than groveling on the stage."[16] For both Jonson and Shakespeare, the author who engaged in mass entertainment might dream of riches, but it was "humiliation," as the prologue to the *Triall of Treasure* says, that he knew he would share with actors for a certainty.

Jonson on Stage

Near the end of the Elizabethan theater controversy that Thomas Dekker termed the "Poetomachia," or Poets' War, Ben Jonson took the extraordinary step of writing an "apologetical

Dialogue" in which a child actor (or, more likely, Jonson him-self) appeared on stage as the "Author" in order to defend both his character and his writings. This Apology must have added fuel to the controversy's fire, because Jonson was forbidden to publish it as an epilogue to his comedy *Poetaster* in 1601 and, according to Jonson, it was enacted "only once." In the text of the Apology as it was eventually printed in Jonson's *Workes,* we meet two London wits who are anxious to "see" how the Author "looks" after the most recent theatrical assaults on him. Rather than seek him out at the playhouse, however, they "steal upon him" in his study. There, the wits endure two hundred lines of the Author's fulminations against nearly every other participant in the London theater world besides himself: actors, playwrights, audiences. The scene ends with the Author turning his back on his visitors and the theater generally. "Leave me," he commands; "there's something come into my thought,/That must, and shall be sung, high, and aloof,/Safe from the wolf's black jaw, and the dull ass's hoof." "I reverence these raptures," replies one of the wits, "and obey 'em."[17]

This scene, so characteristic a mixture of Jonsonian arrogance and self-exposure, seems the perfect evidence for the claim of Peter Stallybrass and Allon White in their *Politics and Poetics of Transgression* (1986) that Jonson "constituted his identity" as a self-styled "master-poet" "in opposition to the theater." Jonson's Apology even dramatizes the "separation of the scholar's study and library from the theatrical marketplace" that Stallybrass and White regard as fundamental to Jonson's sense of his literary identity. And, since the Apology actually places a figure called the Author on the stage, the scene would appear to mark a wa-tershed moment in what Stallybrass and White identify as "the construction of the domain of 'authorship' in the period," when the very idea of an author first "emerged" in Renaissance Eng-land and began transforming the drama from a collaboratively produced mass entertainment to an elite literary art.[18]

One problem with Stallybrass and White's account of the au-thor's emergence is that, by the time Jonson wrote his Apology, authors had long been given speaking parts in English plays. A character called "the poet" appears in two early sixteenth-century religious plays, where he speaks the prologue and epilogue, and, for one of the plays, serves as chorus, too.[19] "The poet" also delivers the prologue and epilogue in a 1520 English version of Terence's *Andria,* and another speaks the prologue to Nicholas Udall's 1553 *Respublica.* None of these author-figures, it is true, pits the dramatist against the players as the Apology does: in each case, the poet refers to the actors as "we." Yet a notional distance between author and stage existed long before Jonson gave such exaggerated voice to it. In all the plays I mention, the poet is a commentator separated from the action; in the Terence adaptation, he ends the prologue, conventionally, by explaining, "But I must go[,] I may no longer tarry[,]/The players be come[,] now I do them see." The stage direction that begins the epilogue in the 1568 edition of *Jacob and Esau* makes sure to wall off the author from the actors even as it places them all together on the stage: "Then ent'reth the Poet, and the rest stand still, till he have done."[20]

For the first audience of the Apology, who also happened to be its last audience, the real innovation in the playlet they witnessed would have been Jonson's *staging* of the imagined gap between author and performance. The author as dramatized in the Apology is no longer merely conceptually distanced from the play as the actors present it: we see him in his study and hear him denouncing players there. The difference comes clearer when we set Jonson's self-dramatization beside a similar account of the poet in the prologue to John Day's *Isle of Gulls* (1606). Day's prologue takes care to insist that the poet disdains theatrical performance: he is not present to see his play, nor can he be found "on the stage amongst gallants, preparing a bespoke Plaudite." Instead, like Jonson in his Apology, the poet in *The Isle of Gulls* is said to be "close in his study writing hard."[21] The difference is that Jonson's Apology imports the author's study *into* the theater.

To maintain with Stallybrass and White that Jonson generally affirms his authorship by rejecting the loathéd stage is, then, to capture only half the story of the Apology. We have grown so accustomed to the thought of Jonson's antitheatricality that the paradox has lost much of its force *as* a paradox. When Stallybrass and White argue that "the notion of 'authorship' to which Jonson dedicated his poetic career was in every way in contradiction to . . . the theater," they necessarily gloss over the fact that Jonson authored *plays*.[22] After lambasting the London theatrical world in his Apology, Jonson authored plays, indeed, for thirty years more; the Apology itself informs us that Jonson is about to try his hand at tragedy. If it is plausible to say with Stallybrass and White that Jonson's self-portrayal in the Apology puts a kind of literary pressure on the theater, it is just as plausible to counter that the Apology puts theatrical pressure on the essentially literary paradigm of authorship that Jonson inherited from English drama as well as literature. Rather than oppose authorship to the theater, Jonson attempted to give authorship dramatic life and in the process submit the dramatist, more fully than earlier plays had, to the theatrical experience.

However distinctive a figure Jonson cut in the world of the Elizabethan stage, he was not the only playwright who encouraged this process of theatricalization. Dramatizations of the author appear in every play of the Poets' War; they are, indeed, a defining feature of it. While recent criticism has tended to characterize any representations of authorship in the Renaissance theater as inherently idealizing and elitist, the references to authors in the Poets' War were just as often coarsely satirical. Jonson told the poet Drummond that the war began when Marston "represented him in [*sic*] the stage," as if the sheer act of staging the author were injurious to him. There is no more richly detailed portrait of a contemporary author in all of Elizabethan literature than Dekker's dramatization of Jonson as "Horace" in his comedy *Satiro-Mastix* (1601), and yet the characterization is a brutal send-up. For those theatergoers who were as interested as the wits in Jonson's Apology to "see" how Jonson "look"ed, *Satiro-Mastix* presented him "in his true attire," as a "lean" and "hollow-cheekt Scrag" with a face "parboil'd," "like a rotten russet

Apple, when 'tis bruised," and acne-scarred, or as Dekker puts it, "puncht full of Oylet-holes, like the cover of a warming-pan." The play also reported on and jeered at various characteristics of Jonson as a literary figure: for instance, that he found it "sore labor" to lay his poetical "eggs"; that he made "faces, when he reads his Songs and Sonnets"; and that, if he failed to earn money as a poet, he could always return to his original occupation of laying bricks.[23]

Satiro-Mastix is especially concerned to record details about Jonson's life in the theater. The most shocking is that Jonson killed an actor, and was saved from hanging only because another actor intervened to help him. From no other source than Dekker's play do we learn that Jonson was once "a poor Journeyman Player" who walked beside the "play-wagon" as it rolled from town to town, or that he played the parts of "Zulziman" and "Hieronimo," or that he borrowed a gown from a fellow actor and returned it full of lice. *Satiro-Mastix* even reports on Jonson's customary behavior when one of his plays was performed. According to Dekker, Jonson watched the action from the gallery and made "faces at every line, to make [G]entlemen have an eye to you, and to make Players afraid to take your part." Then, after the play was done, Jonson, like the author Day despises, would "venture on the stage" and "exchange courtesies, and compliments with Gallants in the Lords' rooms, to make all the house rise up in Arms, and to cry that's *Horace*, that's he, that's he, that's he, that pens and purges Humors and diseases." By thus locating the author on the stage, Dekker clearly hoped to dismantle Jonson's self-portrayal as a poet "high and aloof" from the business of playing. *Satiro-Mastix* does not even allow Jonson to separate himself from the stage in the act of writing. In Horace's first scene, we find him "sitting in a study behind a Curtain, a candle by him burning, books lying confusedly," struggling to find the words for a nominally rapturous poem he is composing:

> For I to thee and thine immortal name,
> In—in—in golden tunes,

For I to thee and thine immortal name—
In—sacred raptures flowing, flowing, swimming, swimming:
In sacred raptures swimming,
Immortal name, game, dame, tame, lame, lame, lame. . . .[24]

The surprise is that Dekker takes his cue in this scene from Jonson's own dramaturgy. Perhaps in response to *Satiro-Mastix*, the Apology to *Poetaster* places the author in a study outside the theater and outside the action of the play; but *Poetaster* itself opens with a scene of an author in his study, and in this case the enraptured poet, Ovid, is part of the fiction.[25] Ovid may hardly seem a figure for the *dramatic* author, yet Ovid's father will shortly accuse him of writing "for the common players," and while Ovid may scorn the charge—"I am not known unto the open stage,/Nor do I traffic in their *theaters*," he declares—he does admit to having "begun a *poem* of that nature."[26] This taint of the theater links Ovid with the poetasters Crispinus and Demetrius, the only two avowed dramatists in the play, and distances him from Jonson's primary surrogate Horace, who is shown to have no other relation to the stage than to be threatened with Demetrius's abusive representation of him "in a play." According, then, to the hierarchy of authorship in *Poetaster*, the further a poet is from the stage, the more admirable he becomes. By the end of the play, Ovid has been banished from Rome, and the master-poet who replaces him, Virgil, expresses a more unequivocal antitheatricality than Ovid ever had, lumping "players" with the other "*buffon*, barking wits" who "tickle base vulgar ears" with "their beggarly, and barren trash."[27]

Yet Virgil is just as much "in the play" of *Poetaster* as Ovid is. And he is not a strictly literary figure there: Caesar commands him to read aloud a passage that the emperor has chosen at random from Virgil's "book." The portion of *The Aeneid* that Virgil is thus enjoined to recite is the famous scene of royal Dido and Aeneas in "a cave," which gives way to the image of "Fame" or Rumor as a monster with "many tongues," "mouths," and "ears" who is "stalking" the world as *Poetaster* says players "stalk" the stage (the word *stalk* appears six other times in *Poetaster*, always in association with the stage). Virgil never finishes his performance, however: he is interrupted by a kind of dramatization of the passage he is declaiming, as two malicious informers burst into the court to declare that they have found a "seditious libel" among the papers in Horace's "study." There is no space in *Poetaster* that can be set apart from the degrading "traffic" in "tongues"—not the imagined cave, not the study, not even the high and mighty sanctuary of Caesar's court. Like Ovid, Jonson may deplore the vulgarity of the "open stage," and like Virgil he may strive to be "most severe / In fashion, and collection of himself," but the playwright Demetrius calls Jonson's closest surrogate Horace "the most open fellow living": the most vulnerable to attack, Demetrius seems to mean, but also in Jonson's view the least deterred by libelous tongues, as Jonson tries to prove in *Poetaster* by boldly recording the charges that Marston and Dekker lodged against him. Although we later hear about Horace's study, we first encounter him composing his poetry, not in rapturous isolation but in the open street.[28]

No matter how the author is represented in *Poetaster*, one might argue, the effect of his being represented at all remains essentially antitheatrical: by turning authorship into such an absorbing center of attention, the play inevitably elevates the author over other collaborative forces in the theater. Near the end of the Apology, the Author claims that if the tragedy he is now writing "prove the pleasure but of one, / So he judicious be; He shall b' alone / A *Theater* unto me": in fantasy, Jonson compresses even the select audience of the private theater into a mirror image of, and thus another surrogate for, himself. This same imagined reduction of the theater to the author helps explain Jonson's decision to write *Poetaster* for a company of child actors. In *Satiro-Mastix*, Dekker has Horace contemptuously refer to the adult players as the "workmasters" of the dramatists Crispinus and Demetrius. Jonson had already claimed to upend this demeaning subservience of author to actors in an adult-player comedy two years earlier, *Every Man Out of His Humor*, where, reversing the conventional designation of the author in prologues and epilogues as "our" man, Jonson had become the first English dramatist, to my knowledge, who called the actors "his."[29]

If the Apology shows Jonson's literary bias driving him toward an even more isolating emphasis on his own masterful creativity, *Poetaster* itself tempers this drive by dramatizing a heterogeneous group of authors and by identifying Horace as less than the best of the group. While this diffusion of authority might be said to increase the prominence of authorship in the play, it also problematizes the relationship between Jonson and a whole series of possible authorial surrogates who cannot readily be conflated with him. Conversely, simply to take the part of Horace is for Jonson to sacrifice the critical detachment enjoyed by the poet in the prologues and epilogues of older English plays and to surrender the author instead to a theatrical fiction.

If we think of *Poetaster* as Stallybrass and White encourage us to do, as an early step in the emergence of the author, we would expect Jonson's subsequent work to show him becoming still more self-assertive and isolated, still more committed to a select audience who approximate the authorial theater of one. Yet, many years after the Poets' War had ended, Jonson returned to dramatize the author for adult actors and mass audiences. The Induction to *Bartholomew Fair*—first performed at the arena theater, the Hope, in 1614—begins with a Stagekeeper who makes fun of Jonson's inability to capture the essence of the fair in his play. As if in response to this criticism, the Bookkeeper appears, accompanied by a Scrivener, who reads a contract "drawn out in haste between our author" and the audience, "Articles of Agreement" about how each party should behave toward the other. In one respect, Jonson could hardly have hit upon a more telling enactment of his aim to impose his single authorial will on the theatrical experience. But in other equally striking respects, the Induction extends Jonson's attempts in *Poetaster* and the Apology to devise a theatrical as well as literary account of the author, to open his study to the stage. According to the conceit of the contract, the Induction dramatizes authorship as (1) a negotiation; (2) a negotiation involving intermediaries; (3) a negotiation not with a readership but with an audience; and (4) a negotiation with an audience that is not elite but mixed. A pressing issue in the Induction is whether Jonson has or has not succeeded in addressing his *entire* audience, "as well the curious and envious as the favoring and judicious, as also the grounded Judgments and understandings." In his proffered contract, Jonson's stated goal is not to seek out the one true theatergoer who mirrors the author himself but rather "to delight all, and to offend none."[30]

What's more, while Jonson may refer to himself in the Induction as a "Master-*Poet*" (the phrase is in fact the Stagekeeper's, and he means it to be sarcastic), the Induction also dramatizes Jonson as a backstage figure who is helping to put on the play. The Stagekeeper complains that the belligerent author has "kick'd me three, or four times about the Tiring-house, I thank him, for but offering to put in, with my experience."[31] In the Induction to Jonson's next commercial play, *The Staple of News*, performed in 1626, Jonson once again shifts the scene of his labors from the study to the theater.[32] The main speaker in the Induction, the character Mirth, tells us that Jonson is back exerting himself in the tiring-house, "rolling himself up and down . . . i' the midst" of the actors like a barrel of wine. But "never did vessel of wort, or wine work so!" Mirth adds; "his sweating put me in mind of a good Shroving dish." This characterization of Jonson as by turns an overheated laborer, a drunkard, and a festive meal—"a stew'd *Poet*," Mirth exclaims in summary—seems radically different from the picture offered by Stallybrass and White of an essentially literary author who aimed to transcend the saturnalian commonplace of popular drama.[33] If anything, Jonson's self-portrayal in *The Staple of News* recalls the caricatures that Dekker and Marston had drawn of him in the Poets' War. Rather than isolate him high and aloof from the degrading traffic in tongues, the Induction to the *Staple* appears to give theatrical libels the power not merely to touch but also to *shape* the author.

The Induction ends with Mirth's informing us that Jonson has grown so frustrated with the preparation for his comedy that he has "torn the book in a *Poetical* fury, and put himself to silence in dead *Sack.*" The fiction proper is thus ushered in by an image of failed collaboration: Jonson's raging against "his" actors, whom Mirth predicts "will abuse him enough" in return. But while the Induction histrionically exaggerates the traditional differentiation of poet from performance, it also transforms the poet's very antitheatricality into a performative and indeed theatrically generative role. Tearing his book, Jonson opens his play. [34]

Shakespeare on Stage

Shakespeare inherited a tragic as well as comic tradition of representing playwrights in plays. One of the parts that Dekker roasts Jonson for having acted was Hieronimo, an author-figure from a play that is often characterized as among the first to realize the full potentiality of mass entertainment on the popular stage: *The Spanish Tragedy.*[35] In that drama, Hieronimo originally appears as the author of a masque that he hopes will entertain his master the Spanish king and the Portuguese ambassador. The masque is silent, a dumb-show, and Hieronimo assumes the conventional stance of the stage-poet as a supervening commentator on the action. But he is considerably more active in the performance of the play than previous stage-poets had been. Entering with a drummer and three knights, he also "fetches three kings," and his first line of commentary is followed by a stage direction that tells us how he "takes" a "scutcheon" from one of these actors "and gives it to the king."[36] This breach of the notional wall between poet and player is no minor feature of *The Spanish Tragedy:* by the end of the play, Hieronimo has composed a far more elaborate entertainment in which he himself participates as an actor. How has tragedy empowered an author-figure to take so direct a role in a play?

In part, the change seems related to the higher class of personages represented in tragedy than in comedy. Hieronimo himself insists that "comedies are fit for common wits"; "Give me a stately written tragedy," he declares, "*Tragedia cothernata,* fitting kings,/ Containing matter, and not common things." If *The Spanish Tragedy* exposes an author to the stage, it also elevates that author into a thoroughly respectable character, the Lord Marshal of Spain. And over the course of the play, Hieronimo becomes an even more important figure to his country than its chief judicial officer. Believing that his son Horatio has been murdered by the king's nephew Lorenzo and that he therefore cannot receive justice through normal channels, Hieronimo takes the law upon himself by convincing Lorenzo to act in his play and then killing him both in fiction and in fact. Although Hieronimo stages this play for the king, he no longer thinks of himself as the king's servant. Instead, he wants the court to witness the birth of a new authority: "princes, now behold Hieronimo,/ Author and actor in this tragedy."[37] Like Greene's Shakespeare, who thinks himself the only "Shake-scene" in a country, Hieronimo appears to believe that his newly comprehensive role as both playwright and player has given him a kind of sovereign power; in stabbing Lorenzo, a fellow actor as well as a political adversary, he seems to make clear that he will brook no rivals on stage or off it.

Yet, like the counter-king in Shakespeare's sonnets, Hieronimo cannot rise without sinking, too. Over the course of the play we see him go mad, and when he proceeds to kill the father of Lorenzo for no good reason, his extralegal pursuit of justice turns out to be inseparable from this madness. What's more, his insanity subjects him to other forms of disgrace besides crime. In an earlier scene, four citizens present various legal documents to Hieronimo in his capacity as lord marshal, but Hieronimo tears up the papers and then taunts the citizens to "catch me if you can" as he races from the stage. (*Satiro-mastix* recalls this notorious scene when it mocks Jonson for the time "thou ranst mad for the death of Horatio.") Immediately before his final play, Hieronimo once again descends to coarse physical exertions, as we watch him hammer up the curtain for his stage. "How now, Hieronimo," his future victim the Duke of Castile wryly asks him, "where's your fellows,/ That you take all this pain?" In the duke's eyes, Hieronimo now exhibits what Greene would regard as the true professional identity of the actor-author who fancies himself a monarchical Shake-scene: the *Johannes fac totum* or johnny-do-all who makes a fool of himself by taking "all" the parts. Hieronimo's response to the duke anticipates Jonson's jocular assurances to the audiences of *Bartholomew Fair* and *The Staple of News* that his backstage labors are fully compatible with his authorial dignity: "Oh, sir, it is for the author's credit/To look that all things may go well." Yet as Hieronimo's play-within-the-play unfolds, it soon becomes clear that his hands-on involvement with the performance has substantially altered his conception of himself as an author. Even after the death of all his "fellows" leaves him alone on the stage and free to assert his authorial sovereignty over the performance, Hieronimo chooses to remain true to his new role as actor, proclaiming that he "will as resolute conclude his part/As any of the actors gone before."[38] His final pieces of acting are grisly reminders of his mad paper-tearing. First he bites off his tongue, reducing himself to the sort of dumb-show from which he stood apart as authorial commentator in his opening scene, and then he stabs both the duke and himself with his own pen-knife, fusing his writing and his playing in an act not of kingly self-aggrandizement but of suicide.

After Hieronimo's death, the complexly ambitious and disgraceful dynamics of actor-authorship in *The Spanish Tragedy* famously reappeared in another highly popular Elizabethan revenge play. Shakespeare seems to have based *Hamlet* on an earlier version of the story by Thomas Kyd, the author of *The Spanish Tragedy,* but the affiliations between *Hamlet* and *The Spanish Tragedy* are obvious nonetheless. Hamlet's father was murdered by a member of the royal family—indeed, by the king himself. In his extralegal quest for justice, Hamlet comes to rival the king as a center of the court's attention. And Hamlet stages a play-within-the-play as a form of counter-justice. A crucial difference between Shakespeare's and Kyd's revenge plays, however, is that Hamlet himself belongs to the royal family. This new princely status for the Hieronimo figure is part of the reason that Helgerson links Shakespeare's tragedy to a growing elitism on the Renaissance stage.

Even more damning evidence of this elitism, for Helgerson, is Hamlet's speaking ill of clowns. In the process of schooling the actors who will stage his play (it is for the author's credit to look that all things may go well), Hamlet commands them:

> Let those that play your clowns speak no more than is set down for them, for there be of them that will themselves laugh to set on some quantity of barren spectators to laugh too, though in the mean time some necessary question of the play be then to be consider'd. That's villainous, and shows a most pitiful ambition in the fool that uses it.

Helgerson insists on the inevitable "tension" between the improvisatory "clown, the central figure of the old players' theater, and the playwright, the *sine qua non* of the emerging authors' theater"; "the author's perspective," he maintains, is "the perspective Hamlet adopts in his instructions to the players." But why should we believe that Hamlet speaks for Shakespeare in this scene? As evidence, Helgerson cites a suspicious development in Shakespeare's acting company shortly before *Hamlet* was first performed: the "disappearance" of the company's chief clown, Will Kemp, in 1599. "Was the author's theater and the hegemony of the script clamping down on him?" Helgerson asks, and then answers his own question: "A few months after Kemp's departure from the Chamberlain's Men, Hamlet pointed to its primary cause." James Shapiro is even more definite on the connection between Hamlet's speech and Kemp's resignation: "The parting of ways between Shakespeare and Kemp . . . was a rejection not only of a certain kind of comedy but also a declaration that from here on in, it was going to be a playwright's and not an actor's theater, no matter how popular the actor."[39]

In reality, we have no idea why Kemp left the Chamberlain's Men.[40] But an entirely different picture of the relationship between clown and author appears in the last of the Cambridge *Parnassus* plays. During that comedy, written around the same time as *Hamlet,* Kemp takes the stage in his own person to defend Shakespeare against elitist critics such as Greene: "Few of the university pen plays well," Kemp declares; "they smell too much of that writer *Ovid,* and that writer *Metamorphoses,* and talk too much of *Proserpina & Jupiter.* Why here's our fellow *Shakespeare* puts them all down." "*Our* fellow": Kemp praises Shakespeare as his colleague, his fellow professional, and when he applauds Shakespeare in this way he is addressing a third colleague on stage, the actor Richard Burbage. Ironically, Helgerson's and Shapiro's account of a titanic struggle for supremacy between Kemp and Shakespeare effectively erases all the other Chamberlain's Men from the picture, reducing the company to single agents in just the way that Helgerson and Shapiro suppose an authors' theater did. (For Helgerson, in fact, the clown was already lord of the stage before the author asserted his elite status: in the "players' theater," he maintains, "the clown dominated the theatrical scene.")[41]

By conflating Hamlet with Shakespeare, what's more, Helgerson and Shapiro gloss over the fact that Hamlet's strictures on clowning are clearly in character for him, manifesting various personal obsessions, such as his own anxiety about attending to a "necessary question" and his antipathy toward any expressions of "ambition." As authors, Hamlet and Shakespeare seem quite different from one another in several crucial respects. Hamlet is a university man, an amateur participant in the play he is helping to stage, and when that play goes well (by his lights), he only jokes with Horatio that it could win him "a fellowship in a cry of players." Shakespeare, by contrast, never attended university; he was a professional actor and playwright, with an actual share in a theatrical company. Finally, Hamlet does directly echo a contemporary dramatist in his instructions to the players, but that dramatist is not Shakespeare. In Jonson's Apology to *Poetaster,* again, the Author says of his forthcoming tragedy that "if I prove the pleasure but of one,/ So he judicious be; He shall b' alone/ A *Theater* unto me"; Hamlet likewise tells the actors that clowning will make "the judicious grieve; the censure of which one must in your allowance o'erweigh a whole theater of others."[42]

So intent was Shakespeare on underscoring *contrasts* between styles or conceptions of drama in *Hamlet* that he built an unusual topical digression into his play on the subject of the Poets' War. Two scenes before Hamlet's advice to the players, the prince wonders why the "tragedians of the city" who will eventually stage *The Murther of Gonzago* are touring Denmark, when "their residence, both in reputation and profit, was better both ways." Rosencrantz explains that adult players are no longer "the fashion" in the city; they have lost ground to child actors, who "so berattle the common stages—so they call them—that many wearing rapiers are afraid of goose-quills and dare scarce come thither." As the reference to "goose-quills" makes clear, it is not the children who have intimidated playgoers so much as "their writers." ("Common stages" is another Jonsonian phrase, from his 1600 children's theater comedy, *Cynthia's Revels*.)[43] What's more, according to the information Rosencrantz provides, the boys' companies have managed to "carry . . . away" the reputation and profit of the adult companies by exaggerating the distinction between writers and actors: "for a while," says Rosencrantz, the boys' companies even succeeded in creating a market where "no money" was "bid for argument, unless the poet and the player went to cuffs in the question." Hamlet observes that, by making the children disparage the adult players, the authors of the boys' theater should rightly be considered the adversaries of all actors, including the children: "will [the boys] not say afterwards, if they should grow themselves to common players (as it is most like, if their means are no better), their writers do them wrong, to make them exclaim against their own succession?"[44] Shakespeare's play may indeed bear witness to the "fashion" for a theater where authors clash with players, but that is pointedly *not* the stage for which Shakespeare writes. Against the divisive elitism he associates with the boys' companies, Shakespeare attempts to dramatize a different kind of theater in *Hamlet*, exemplified by a different kind of author—the *Johannes fac totum* Greene had scoffed at, the player-author.

Hamlet on Stage

Hamlet himself personifies the composite figure of an actor-author, in his amateurish way. To identify a speech he has asked the visiting players to recite, Hamlet delivers its opening lines, and Polonius applauds his fine performance: "'Fore God, my lord, well spoken, with good accent and good discretion." Next, Hamlet tells the players he will "set down" another speech "of some dozen or sixteen lines" that he wants inserted in *The Murther of Gonzago,* a speech he later mentions he has "pronounc'd" to the players. Briefly, then, Hamlet becomes a player-poet. To treat him as a vehicle for "the unitary voice of the author," Helgerson must disregard more than Hamlet's acting in the company of the players, however; he must also overlook Hamlet's self-appointed role as a *co*author, a reviser of the *Murther.*[45] In his final scene, Hamlet appears as a reviser once again, when he recounts to Horatio how he undertook the "play" of rewriting a royal commission and then passing off this new "writ" as if it were the original. By breaking the king's seal and commandment, this second act of coauthorial revision clearly places Hamlet on the side of the "unauthorized speech and action" that Helgerson believes the "author" proscribes. Yet even Hamlet's initial revision to *The Murther of Gonzago* causes the players to "speak . . . more" than the original "author" had "set down for them" and in so doing assimilates Hamlet to the extemporizing clown. When the *Murther* is performed, Hamlet becomes a clown in earnest—"your only jig-maker"—before twice interrupting the play as he worried the clowns would and then breaking off the *Murther* altogether.[46] Hamlet's instructions to the players thus fail to match his own dramatic practices, not to mention Shakespeare's.

Shakespeare's conceptualization of Hamlet as not merely author and player but also coauthor and clown is most powerfully realized after Hamlet vows to the ghost of his father that he will be nothing more than what the ghost has just "set down" within him:

> Remember thee!
> Yea, from the table of my memory
> I'll wipe away all trivial fond records,
> All saws of books, all forms, all pressures past
> That youth and observation copied there,
> And thy commandment all alone shall live
> Within the book and volume of my brain,
> Unmix'd with baser matter.

In the larger context of the play, Hamlet's advice to the players turns out to be a relatively casual instance of the injunction, imposed here by Hamlet acting for his ghostly father, that one strictly adhere to "prescripts." When Claudius dispatches Cornelius and Voltemand to Norway, for instance, he gives them "no further personal power / To business with the King, more than the scope / Of these delated articles allow"; God, having "fix'd / His canon 'gainst self-slaughter," sets similar limits on Hamlet, just as the ghost is "forbid / To tell the secrets" of his "prison-house." And yet immediately after Hamlet vows to confine himself to his father's script, he exceeds the scope of that "writ" by turning his attention to other people and in the process becoming a rival author himself:

> O most pernicious woman!
> O villain, villain, smiling, damned villain!
> My tables—meet it is I set it down
> That one may smile, and smile, and be a villain!
> At least I am sure it may be so in Denmark.
>   [*He writes.*]
> So, uncle, there you are.

This bizarre note-taking is effectively coauthorial, insofar as Hamlet learned of his uncle's villainy only from the ghost and now paraphrases the ghost from the "table" of his memory. What

distracts Hamlet enough from the ghost's writ to make him ex-
temporaneously supplement and thereby revise it in writing is
the image of Claudius smiling, like the clown who laughs to set
others laughing when some necessary question must be considered. And Claudius's good humor does indeed prove contagious.
"Hillo, ho, ho, boy! Come, bird, come," Hamlet soon cries out
in high spirits to his friends, who then hear his plan "to put an
antic disposition on"—a course of action, needless to say, that the
ghost had not prescribed.[47]

Young Hamlet's life thus turns out to be a part that Claudius
is helping old Hamlet to write, along with Gertrude, the thought
of whom first diverts Hamlet from his father's script. Even Polonius assists in guiding the revisions begun on Hamlet's tables:
who else could have inspired Hamlet to record the fatuous "saw"
that a man may smile and smile and yet be a villain? Near the end
of the play, Hamlet invokes a further parental influence, more
lineally the progenitor of his clowning than either Claudius or
Polonius: the jester Yorick, whose "gibes" and "gambols" were
"wont to set the table" (an echo of Hamlet's memory-book and
writing-tablet) "on a roar." Hamlet remembers riding on Yorick's
back "a thousand times" and kissing his lips "I know not how
oft," occasions of a physical intimacy that figures in none of the
prince's other relationships. But Hamlet does not act like a fool
because he was raised by a jester: his own gibes and gambols
allow the hands of rival authors to appear in his father's script
because such clowning marks Hamlet as unconsumed by grief
for his father. What would the tragedian do, Hamlet asks himself, "had he the motive and the cue for passion/That I have?"
Hamlet answers, "He would drown the stage with tears." "O that
this too too solid flesh would melt": and yet Hamlet cannot reduce himself to the tragic part his father has set down for him;
unaccountably—or is it madly?—he indulges in "flashes of mer-
riment" from his very first lines.[48]

By taking Hamlet's instructions to the players out of dramatic
context, Helgerson thus encourages three related misreadings of
authorship in the play: first, that the play champions the unitary

voice of the author; second, that the play distances authorship from clowning; and third, that the author must suppress clowning in order to pursue his "necessary questions." This last misreading seems the most significant one. Contemporary playgoers were capable of admiring *Hamlet* for its distinctive *infusion* of comedy into tragedy: in the preface to his 1604 *Daiphantus,* Anthony Scoloker thinks of "*Shakespeare's tragedies*" as "where the *Comedian* rides, when the *Tragedian* stands on Tip-toe."[49] Subsequent commentators have pointed out how such generic heterogeneity enabled Shakespeare not only to complicate Hamlet's professed disdain for clowning, but also to present himself as an author in the popular mold. Holding the stage to presumptively classical standards of unity, Sidney's *Defence of Poesie* had famously condemned "all" English plays as "neither right Tragedies, nor right Comedies," and had urged English playwrights no longer to "thrust in Clowns by head and shoulders, to play a part in majestical matters." In *Hamlet,* Shakespeare follows Sidney's advice with characteristic perverseness: rather than "mingle Kings and Clowns," he merges the two. So radical a defense of a "mongrel" native tradition against classical "rules" hardly fits the picture of the refined university wit in whose image Shakespeare was supposedly remaking himself.[50] But then Scoloker understands "friendly" Shakespeare to be working in "the vulgar's *Element*," and he wishes his own *Daiphantus* could "please all, like Prince *Hamlet*."[51]

Ignoring such direct testimony to Shakespeare's broad appeal as a dramatist, Helgerson pursues the vision of the author he sees in Hamlet's request for a speech that, like Jonson's Apology, "was never acted, or if it was, not above once; for the play, I remember, pleas'd not the million, 'twas caviary to the general, but it was—as I receiv'd it, and others, whose judgments in such matters cried in the top of mine—an excellent play."[52] Summoning this elitism once again in his instructions to the players, Hamlet asks the players to believe that whatever makes "the unskillful laugh" will cause "the judicious" to "grieve," and yet he cannot separate his own noble sorrow from vulgar merrymaking.

Nor can he cleanly distinguish his royalty from "the million." As Claudius complains, "he's lov'd of the distracted multitude," "the general gender"; the prince habitually addresses his social inferiors, including the players, as his "friends."[53] When Scoloker states that Prince Hamlet pleases all, he can just as easily mean the character as the play.

This is not to say, in simple opposition to Helgerson, that Hamlet's—or, for that matter, Shakespeare's—true allegiance lies with the distracted multitude: the prince's companionability no more displaces his hauteur than his clowning erases his grief. To please all is to delight both high and low, the judicious as well as the unskillful: around the time that Scoloker published his praise for *Hamlet*'s popular mixture of comedy and tragedy, the university man Gabriel Harvey privately noted in the margin of a book that Shakespeare's "Lucrece, & his tragedy of Hamlet, Prince of Denmark, have it in them, to please the wiser sort."[54] The idea that a play should be as heterogeneous as its audience was itself a traditional English view of theater. As the dramatist Ulpian Fulwell puts it in the prologue to his 1568 *Like Will to Like*,

> diverse men of diverse minds be,
> Some do matters of mirth and pastime require:
> Other some are delighted with matters of gravity,
> To please all men is our author's chief desire.
> Wherefore mirth with measure to sadness is annexed,
> Desiring that none here at our matter will be perplexed.[55]

Along with such generic mixtures, a mass audience was thought to require another kind of variety, too. In a dedicatory letter to his *Posies* and *Woorkes* addressed "To the Readers generally," the playwright George Gascoigne defended his decision to publish writings that are sometimes "moral," sometimes "sauced with wantonness," by observing that the apostle Paul "glorieth that he could (as it were) transform himself into all professions, thereby to win all kind of men to God: saying that with the Jews he became a Jew: with them that were under the law, he seemed also under the law: with the feeble, he showed himself feeble.

And to conclude, he became all things to all men, to the end that he might thereby win some to salvation."[56] I have elsewhere noted the centrality of Pauline accommodationism to protheatrical discourse during the English Renaissance; my point here is to emphasize how Gascoigne believed that a diverse audience should be mirrored not only in a mongrel play but also in a multiform author, who makes himself "all things to all men." Before it became a staple of Romantic criticism, the notion of a "myriad-minded" playwright was a Renaissance ideal.[57]

Within the play of *Hamlet*, Shakespeare mediates the various registers of diversity in his audience, his play, and his authorship through the internal heterogeneity of the clown-prince. Prince Hamlet has it in him to please all sorts of playgoers because Shakespeare makes him self-various. This embodiment of "diverse minds" in one character suggests a more complex theory of the audience, however, than the taxonomical view of Fulwell and Gascoigne, where the mirth in a play corresponds to one set of playgoers, the gravity to another. Hamlet himself repeatedly categorizes playgoers in this reductive fashion: against the connoisseurs he sets the "barren" spectators who laugh at clowns, Polonius who wants "a jig or a tale of bawdry, or he sleeps," and, of course, "the groundlings, who for the most part are capable of nothing but inexplicable dumb shows and noise." But the representation of character in the play militates against such reductiveness, just as the play's heterogeneous dramatic form resists the Polonian classification of drama into "tragedy, comedy, history, pastoral, pastoral-comical, historical-pastoral, tragical-historical, tragicial-comical-historical-pastoral." Hearing Osric praise Laertes as a gentleman "full of most excellent differences," Hamlet drolly refuses "to divide" Laertes "inventorially," as if he were a collection of discrete parts. When Ophelia, her father's daughter, nevertheless inventories Hamlet as "the courtier's, soldier's, scholar's, eye, tongue, sword," she fails to make his parts ("soldier's . . . tongue," "scholar's . . . sword") line up with one another. "Groundling" is an even cruder reification that helps to divide spectators inventorially, by class or station. Yet it proves inadequate to the wit of the gravedigger Hamlet meets, a "clown" not only on the "ground" but in it, whose wordplay leads Hamlet to remark that these days "the toe of the peasant comes so near the heel of the courtier, he galls his kibe." Although Hamlet defensively keeps his eyes on the ground here, it is minds, not feet, that he sees as too close to one another for comfort. How then can Shakespeare have intended *Hamlet*, or any part of *Hamlet*, for one sort of spectator exclusively, when the play regularly presents class as an imperfect determinant of minds, and minds as essentially mixed?[58]

Shakespeare expresses his own hybrid identity as player-author through more than the generic and characterological mixtures of *Hamlet*, however. He also scripts events in the play that emphasize how an author's writ becomes theater only through the willing collaboration of players. The digression on the boys' theater and Hamlet's instructions to the players are two notable occasions when the audience is urged to think of the actors on stage as actors. A third is *The Murther of Gonzago*, which begins with a prologue begging the audience's indulgence of the actors as a collaborative group, "for us, and for our tragedy." But the most extraordinary instance of the play's playerliness is once again the scene following Hamlet's first encounter with the ghost, when Hamlet's clowning appears to disrupt not only the ghost's script but Shakespeare's, too.

HAM. Never make known what you have seen tonight.
BOTH [*Hor., Mar.*]. My lord, we will not.
HAM. Nay, but swear't.
HOR. In faith,
    My lord, not I.
MAR. Nor I, my lord, in faith.
HAM. Upon my sword.
MAR. We have sworn, my lord, already.
HAM. Indeed, upon my sword, indeed.
    Ghost cries under the stage.
GHOST. Swear.
HAM. Ha, ha, boy, say'st thou so? Art thou there, truepenny?

Come on, you hear this fellow in the cellarage,
Consent to swear.
HOR. Propose the oath, my lord.
HAM. Never to speak of this that you have seen,
Swear by my sword.
GHOST. Swear.
HAM. *Hic et ubique?* Then we'll shift our ground.
Come hither, gentlemen,
And lay your hands again upon my sword.
Swear by my sword
Never to speak of this that you have heard.
GHOST. Swear by his sword.
HAM. Well said, old mole, canst work i' th' earth so fast?
A worthy pioneer! Once more remove, good friends.
HOR. O day and night, but this is wondrous strange!

This "recklessly comic throw-away of illusion," as William
Empson calls it, confuses the fictional and the theatrical action
of the play, allowing each to serve as commentary on the other.[59]
By insisting on the stage-mechanics of the ghost's descent,
Hamlet extends the foolery begun with his vision of a smiling
Claudius; makes that foolery explicitly disrespectful of the ghost,
whom Hamlet mocks as "boy," "truepenny," "fellow," "old mole";
and then caps this clownish rebellion from his father's writ by
gesturing to the ghost as an actor rather than author. Simulta-
neously, Shakespeare treats Hamlet's clowning as an opportu-
nity to highlight the performance of the play over its text and
thereby acknowledge his own complex identity not only as the
pre-scriptor of *Hamlet* but also as a "fellow" collaborating on its
enactment—especially if the old report is true that the ghost in
the cellarage was originally played by Shakespeare himself.[60]

To say that Shakespeare figures as both author and actor in
this ghost scene is by no means to claim that he alternates between these roles: on the contrary, the scene makes them as hard
to distinguish from one another as it does tragedy from comedy.
Hamlet's clowning with his ghostly father suggests instead that
Shakespeare wants to dramatize the playing in authorship and

the authorship in playing, an anti-"inventorial" goal he pursues by incorporating disruptive improvisation into his script.[61] Helgerson terms this surprising maneuver an "improvisation effect," and he is deeply suspicious of it: "Shakespeare wrote parts for Kemp—including the part of Falstaff—that conveyed an 'improvisation effect' even as they eliminated the real thing." But Helgerson provides no evidence that unscripted improvisation was ever actually "eliminated" from the Shakespearean stage; he bases this theater history on the fiction of Hamlet's instructions to the players. What's more, the improvisation effect in *Hamlet*'s ghost scene is scarcely as controlled as Helgerson implies. Reckless, Empson calls it; Horatio, wondrous strange—as it must surely have appeared to the scene's original audience, most of whom would probably have had no idea that the breaking of illusion was part of the script. Shakespeare's own self-variousness as player-author means that his sympathies in *Hamlet* are never wholly on one side or the other of the battle-line Hamlet draws between scripting and clowning. Like the theater company Polonius praises, Shakespeare the *Johannes fac totum* is adept at "the law of writ *and* the liberty": what marks him as a professional, he thinks, is his readiness to perform both.[62]

Shakespeare as Do-all

And yet the concern that Helgerson shares with Greene—the suspicion that Shakespeare aimed to preempt his colleagues by doing it all himself—cannot be allayed by recourse to Shakespeare's professionalism alone. Even if we set aside the imputation of bad faith, Shakespeare's very brilliance at mixing comedy and tragedy, kings and clowns, prescription and improvisation, authorship and acting, must have distinguished him from the rest of his company, no matter how responsive to them he may have intended to be. Contemporaries repeatedly singled out famous actors as a kind of equipoise or equivalent to their fellows. "Would any man think that *Burbage* should be content with a single share, who was the flower and the life of his company, the

Loadstone of the Auditory, and the *Roscius* of the Stage?" asked John Gee in 1624; according to Jonson, Edward Alleyn "dost so contract" the "worth in all" other actors that the others "speak, but only thou dost act." "Burbage his company," "*Ed. Alleyn* and his Company": these contemporary references recalled classical allusions to the legendary first actor and also first dramatist Thespis, who "led about *his* players," in Thomas Drant's 1567 translation of the *Ars poetica*.[63] So Jonson called actors "his," and Leonard Digges in 1640 claimed that the King's Men were Shakespeare's, able to "live" because of him alone.[64]

The notion that one person could contract the worth in all is a constant theme in Shakespeare. "That due of many now is thine alone," the sonnets' speaker declares of the young man, after admitting that he craves a similar comprehensiveness for himself, "wishing me like to one more rich in hope, / Featur'd like him, like him with friends possess'd, / Desiring this man's art, and that man's scope." Shakespeare translates this desire for all-inclusiveness to a theatrical setting in his most straightforward staging of dramatic authorship, *A Midsummer Night's Dream* (c. 1595), where he handles the issue comically. The dramatist we meet there, Peter Quince, belongs to an amateur playing company whose collaborative ethos is strong. Each of the first lines in the company's first two scenes expresses concern for their togetherness: "Is all our company here?"; "Are we all met?" We see the troupe conferring about the tragedy they plan to stage, and Quince promises to revise his script along the lines they suggest, downplaying his personal agency in the process: "Well; we will have such a prologue, and it shall be written in eight and six"; "Well, it shall be so." But Quince is the only member of the company who writes as well as acts, and this double role seems to make him (like Posthaste in *Histrio-Mastix*) the de facto leader of the troupe, prompting him to direct rehearsals and to exhort his fellows not to fail "me" personally.[65] None of Quince's fellows questions his authority, nor do they ever treat it as a breach of their collaborativeness.

Neither does the troupe seem bothered by the conspicuous overreaching of a second fellow, Nick Bottom, who asks to play the female as well as male protagonists of their drama, and the lion, too. Quince does insist that Bottom "play no part but Pyramus," but he later acknowledges that the troupe cannot go "forward" without Bottom, who is "the best" of their group.[66] In the meantime, supernatural forces have enabled Bottom to play a double role of human and animal after all, and when he returns to his company, his own authority has grown large enough that he acts as director, too, urging his fellows to "get your apparel together," "meet presently at the palace," and "every man look o'er his part." During the actual performance of the tragedy, Bottom even encroaches on Quince's authorial role, becoming a clownishly supervenient commentator on the action: "You shall see it will fall pat as I told you," he assures the audience. ("You shall see anon," Hamlet twice interjects during the performance of his own play-within-the-play.) No one, including Quince, complains.[67] In the play's comic imagination of an acting company, a collaborative ethos can do more than accommodate the desire to be distinguished from one's fellows, to be the writer, the leader, even to play all the parts; it can actually spur these ambitions, by encouraging each fellow to think of himself in collective terms, as exemplary of the group. Bottom's first words express this logic by way of a farcical confusion: he advises Quince to call the company "generally, man by man, according to the scrip." From the elite perspective of Duke Theseus, it may be the low-class anonymity of the company rather than their cohesiveness that makes the individual and the general seem so interchangeable, but the conceptual result is the same. Reflecting on the drama he has just witnessed, Theseus envisions the company—author and actors—as many in one: "Marry, if he that writ it had play'd Pyramus, and hang'd himself in Thisby's garter, it would have been a fine tragedy; and so it is, truly, and very notably discharg'd."[68]

With the higher class of characters in the actually tragic *Hamlet* comes a greater political charge to the notion of one person's playing all the parts. King Claudius repeatedly refers to himself as a multiplicity, as "Denmark," "we," "ourself." "Never alone / Did the King sigh, but with a general groan," his flatterer Rosencrantz later assures him, just as the First Player hyperbolically imagines that "senseless Ilium" felt a "blow" aimed at its king. In Claudius's view, the king provides the coherence to his country that the distracted multitude decidedly lack: his first words in the play portray his sorrow for his dead brother as pervading "our whole kingdom," which he claims has been "contracted in one brow of woe." This monarchical compression of the many into the one is conspicuously unstable in *Hamlet*, however. Along with the single brow of woe, Claudius also invokes "our hearts," a plurality he cannot incorporate within himself, and he goes on to acknowledge political limitations to his comprehensiveness: "nor have we herein barr'd/Your better wisdoms." More disquietingly, the contraction to one brow of woe results from grief for a different king than Claudius, for "*buried* Denmark," whose memory produces a division in Claudius's ostensible singleness: "we with wisest sorrow think on him/Together with remembrance of ourselves." Claudius would like to end this self-division and celebrate a new "contraction," his marriage to the realm and to the old king's wife: "So much for him./Now for ourself." But the pressure of having to incorporate the thought of both kingships in one leads Claudius to sketch grotesque images of his royal rule as well as brow: he states that he has married Gertrude "with an auspicious, and a dropping eye,/With mirth in funeral, and with dirge in marriage." Such rhetorical difficulties are, of course, nothing in comparison to the trouble Claudius faces from the old king rematerialized in his son, the prince whom Claudius himself characterizes as a rival embodiment of the king's comprehensive multiplicity: "be as ourself in Denmark."[69] This new version of the all-in-one monarch turns out to be a revenging counter-king.

Famously, however, Hamlet has a much harder time than Claudius does in managing the thought of his own royal comprehensiveness. He experiences his presumed indispensability to "the safety and health of this whole state" as a curb on his will, which must "be circumscrib'd/Unto the voice and yielding of that body/Whereof he is the head." Then all the other agencies

that he finds at work within him—of his father, Claudius, Gertrude, Polonius, Yorick, and more—make him feel so painfully
self-divided, so "distracted," that he longs to kill himself. Yet this
self-variousness is at the same time Hamlet's primary weapon in
his duel with Claudius. Where the idealizing king insists on the
unity he brings to his kingdom and therefore flatly rejects any
suspicion that "our state" is "disjoint and out of frame," Hamlet
repeatedly confesses to a "sore distraction" that better correlates
him with Claudius's own view of his people as distracted. Indeed,
Hamlet's calling *his* royal brow "this distracted globe" links him
not only with Denmark but with the world at large, even reaching outside the play to the audience of the Globe Theater. Such
overdeterminations seem to betray the sweeping ambition that
Greene and Helgerson detect in Shakespeare, as Rosencrantz
and Guildenstern detect it in Hamlet.[70] But for Hamlet no less
than Hieronimo, the price of his counter-kingly inclusiveness is
an "antic" and ultimately suicidal self-debasement. Hamlet sees
"ambition in the fool," too, and he calls it "pitiful."[71]

"O, what a noble mind is here o'erthrown!" Ophelia exclaims
after witnessing the spectacle of a distracted Hamlet; "Th'observ'd
of all observers, quite, quite down!" The disturbing proximity of
celebrity and humiliation in Ophelia's account of Hamlet recalls
contemporary judgments on the commercial player, whose "Profession," one commentator maintained in 1628, "has in it a kind
of contradiction, for none is more dislik'd, and yet none more applauded." If Shakespeare the actor-author had confined himself
to strictly literary work, he might perhaps have found a more
respectable way to achieve fame and even to emulate the player's
feat of "acting all men's parts."[72] Around the start of Shakespeare's
theatrical career, the jurist and literary critic Gentili (1593) noted
"that all the arts of peace and war are comprehended in Aeneas alone [uno in Aenea cognitur]," "and so Fulgentius once
compiled a book of moral precepts from Vergil alone [ex uno
Virgilio]."[73] But Hamlet exemplifies a range of identities that
exceeds the genteel limits Gentili takes for granted in belles-
lettres. As a prince, Hamlet extends this range beyond the limits
even of *The Spanish Tragedy,* by incorporating royalty into the

comprehensive self-variousness that distinguishes the distracted counter-king from the "high and mighty" reigning sovereign.[74] "They fool me to the top of my bent," Hamlet exclaims at the end of his play-within-the-play, confounding high and low like the actor whose "profession" another contemporary (1615) described as "compounded of all Natures, all humors, all professions"—as, in a word, "Motley."[75]

Coda

Several years before Jonson's self-mocking self-representation in *The Staple of News* as a man who has drowned himself in drink, he painted a similarly ignominious picture of himself for the Scottish poet William Drummond. In conversation with Drummond, Jonson recalled the time that he had served as tutor to Sir Walter Raleigh's son and accompanied him to France, where the pupil "caused" the master "to be Drunken & dead drunk, so that he knew not where he was, thereafter laid him on a Car which he made to be Drawn by Pioneers through the streets, at every corner showing his Governor stretched out & telling them that was a more Lively image of the Crucifix than any they had." Jonson could hardly have expected this story to reflect well upon him, except perhaps as a demonstration of his willingness to discredit himself. But then it was Jonson's degradation in the story that made the young Raleigh see him as so lively an image of Christ. In fact, Jonson's anecdote presents him as Christlike in no other respect than in his humiliating exposure to public view—an exposure that Jonson reprised in part by re-telling the story to Drummond.

By the time he wrote *The Staple of News*, Jonson had long ceased making a spectacle of himself as an actor, dedicating himself instead to the loftier role of poet: in the prologue to *The Staple* he styles himself one of the "few" who "can think,/Conceive, express, and steer the souls of men,/As with a rudder, round thus, with their pen." But in the induction to *The Staple* Jonson nonetheless went out of his way to vulgarize himself for the audience by having Mirth report on the sight of him dead drunk, just as Jonson had reported it to Drummond. And when Mirth, "the daughter of *Christmas,* and spirit of *Shrovetide,*" compared that sight of the stewed poet to a shroving dish, Jonson once again suggested, as he had to Drummond, that his personal humiliation be seen as a festive occasion for devotional, even sacramental remembrance. To write for the public theater was not merely a kind of elective disgrace, Jonson implied in *The Staple of News:* it was also a kind of sacrifice. "For your own sakes, not his" is how the poet begins his comedy.[76]

In *Julius Caesar,* Shakespeare makes playing to an audience seem as disabling as it is empowering. Early in the tragedy, Casca reports to Brutus on Caesar's thrice refusing the crown, a scene that for its cheap theatrics Casca dismisses as "mere foolery": "If the tag-rag people did not clap him and hiss him, according as he pleas'd and displeas'd them, as they use to do the players in the theater, I am no true man." Much to Casca's disgust, Caesar so relishes seeing how his displays of humility electrify his audience that he takes his self-sacrifice even further: "when he perceiv'd the common herd was glad he refus'd the crown, he pluck'd me ope his doublet, and offer'd them his throat to cut." But the offer proves too effective: in their wild acclamation, "the rabblement . . . utter'd such a deal of stinking breath" that it almost "chok'd Caesar, for he swounded, and fell down at it"—a humiliating show of weakness that would have made Casca "laugh" if he himself had not feared "opening my lips and receiving the bad air." The image that Casca conveys to Brutus of Caesar's "speechless" body before "the vulgar" does more than foreshadow the public display of Caesar's corpse after his assassination; it actually helps inspire that murder, which Brutus envisions in terms that Caesar's histrionics appear to have suggested to him: "Let's be sacrificers," Brutus urges his co-conspirators, "let's carve him as a dish fit for the gods." In my next chapter I'll show how Shakespeare imagined his own exposure to "vulgar company" in the theater as staking out his claim for a kingliness that was indistinguishable from sacrifice.[77]

3

The Author Sacrificed

Why then begin, great King! ascend Thy Throne,
And thence proceed, to act Thy Passion.
« ROBERT HERRICK, *"Good Friday:* Rex Tragicus, *or Christ going to his Cross"* (1647) »

By the time he completed *Henry V* in 1599, Shakespeare had
written or cowritten two four-part sequences of English history
plays. Taken together, these two tetralogies formed a coherent
historical narrative, a cycle. No other dramatist for the Elizabethan arena theaters had ever attempted such a cycle; none
had even written more than a two-part sequence of plays. The
only significant analogue to Shakespeare's achievement were the
miracle plays that in earlier times had been performed in towns
such as York and Chester during the festival of Corpus Christi.
These cycles, dozens of plays apiece, were religious drama, telling
the history of the world from the Creation to the Last Judgment. They were also Catholic drama, and the Protestant church
eventually shut them down. But the Corpus Christi cycles lasted
long enough for Shakespeare, his fellow actors, and members
of his audience to have been able to witness them.[1] Why did
Shakespeare take the unprecedented step of imitating or emulat-
ing these old religious plays with a commercial theatrical cycle
of his own?[2]

Over the past forty years, theater scholars have largely accepted the answer formulated, in different ways, by C. L. Barber, Alvin Kernan, Louis Montrose, and Stephen Greenblatt: that Shakespeare aimed to present a secular alternative to the miracle plays.[3] Intensely skeptical himself, and believing that the Reformation had seriously weakened the hold of Christianity on the rest of English society, Shakespeare (these critics argue) assumed that his audiences were just as anxious as he was to embrace a more realistic, desacralized vision of the world. But Shakespeare also realized that his theater could do more than confirm his audience's doubts about the old religion: it could help satisfy what Barber called a "famished, insatiable spiritual hunger" for Catholic "ritual" in Elizabethan England, by offering audiences the compensatory mystique of its own spectacles.[4] Writing in praise of a history play that may have been the first installment in Shakespeare's cycle—the first part of *Henry VI*—the Elizabethan playwright Thomas Nashe (1592) exclaimed, "How would it have joyed brave *Talbot* (the terror of the French) to think that after he had lien two hundred years in his Tomb, he should triumph again on the Stage, and have his bones new embalmed with the tears of ten thousand spectators at least (at several times), who, in the Tragedian that represents his person, imagine they behold him fresh bleeding." In Barber's view, Elizabethan theater scenes such as Talbot's bleeding both recalled and redefined the central element of the Corpus Christi plays: the sacrament of Christ's body and blood. "Can the need that tragedy meets in the [Elizabethan] theater," Barber asked, "be unrelated to the elimination, in the church, of the image of a supreme voluntary sacrifice, and the elimination of the Mass understood as an actual, present reenactment of that sacrifice?" From the perspective of Barber and his followers, Talbot bleeds, but not for God: Shakespeare's history cycle appropriated the spiritual "energy" of the miracle plays by fashioning a secular religion of the nation.[5]

In my book *Shakespeare's Tribe*, I tried to underscore several problems with this widely accepted account of secularization in the Elizabethan theater. First, I argued, neither Shakespeare's histories nor those of his playwriting contemporaries were ever so zealously devoted to a nationalist celebration of England as modern critics maintain. Second, Barber could characterize the Shakespearean theater as "post-Christian" only because he equated Christianity with Catholicism, dismissing the fact that the Reformation generated new popular forms of Christianity and that these new religions appropriated the spiritual energies of Catholic worship far more directly than the commercial theater ever could. Third, I maintained, Barber and his followers approach Renaissance theater history with a surprisingly antitheatrical as well as Catholic bias: just as they implicitly deny the status of a genuine religion to any Christianity besides Catholicism, so they implicitly deny the status of a genuine Christian to anyone who worked in the Elizabethan theater. Yet throughout the English Renaissance, as I showed in *Shakespeare's Tribe,* theater people and their audiences repeatedly asserted that "there might be as much good many times done by a man in hearing a play, as in hearing a sermon." Such contemporaneous defenses of the theater suggest the possibility that Shakespeare modeled his history cycle on the miracle cycles so as to underscore his *religious* purpose in dramatizing Lancastrian *realpolitik*.[6]

Claims of the spiritual value in plays were, it is true, severely discountenanced at the time, so much so that they were recorded only in antitheatrical diatribes or in court cases against those who voiced them. In the court case I've just quoted, the statement that plays might do people good is entered as evidence of a witness's unusually bad character. It is also alleged against the witness in question (one James Smith in 1633) that it is "usual" for him "to swear and Curse bitterly and fearfully"; that "for money and reward, [he] may be drawn to swear any thing whether true or false"; that "for these 4 years last past [he] hath been a poor and needy person living by Cozenage and Cheating"; that he is "much given to excessive drinking," and spends "whole night[s] and days abroad drinking and keeping of ill Company"; and finally that this Falstaffian "frequenter of alehouses[,] playhouses[,] and bowling alleys" has kept "Company" with "players."[7]

So dubious was the social status of theater people in Renaissance England, I noted in *Shakespeare's Tribe,* that attempts to praise them generally required some acknowledgment of their ill repute. Even the most aggressive defenses of the religious potentiality in plays admitted that theater people consorted with low-lifes, although protheatricalists insisted that this familiarity with roguish "good fellows" enabled theater people to encourage true Christian fellowship in the profane better than churchmen ever could. Smith's balancing of plays against sermons in particular suggests a further standard element in the praise of theatrical religiosity. Unlike puritans, it was said, who used their preaching to promote sectarian divisiveness, theater people avoided doctrinal controversies: on Nashe's imagined stage, the most divisive issue in Christianity—the contemplation of a bleeding body—becomes the occasion for unity among thousands of spectators at a time. Singling out puritanical exclusivism as the primary source of sectarian disunity in English society also enabled the theater's defenders to distinguish the theater's inclusivist approach to religion from an adversarial stance toward the church per se. The player-lover James Smith was no mere roisterer: a drunkard, a liar, and a cheat, if we take the word of the witnesses against him, he was also a clergyman—or an ex-clergyman: "within these twelve months," one of his opponents claimed, he had been "turned out of his Cure or lecture in St. Botolph's Billingsgate for keeping excessive Company with players." Smith's counter-witnesses saw nothing but apostasy in his ties to theater people: Smith and the players, they claimed, "styled themselves of the Order of the Fancy," a mock sodality whose "practice" was not to study scripture or perform charitable works but "to drink excessively, and to speak nonsense." Yet shortly after his court case Smith resumed his clerical career, and three decades later he ended his days as the rector of Alphington and Exminster and the precentor of Exeter Cathedral.[8] Even as the court records confirm the picture of Smith's libertinism, they highlight his commitment to a religious theory of plays that he had little practical reason to endorse: Smith had been heard to "extol the society of players and their faculties, and said that he loved the Company of players above all, and that he thought there might be as much good many times done by a man in hearing a play, as in hearing a sermon, and that he thought it a Credit to keep them Company."

Smith's example underscores the limitations of a scholarship that posits as strict a division between the sacred and the profane as Smith's detractors did. But a secularist bias is not the only feature of current criticism that makes it hard for scholars to think of Shakespeare's history cycle as a possible vehicle for religious inclusivism. While the old Corpus Christi plays—the communal endeavor of guilds and townships generally—were anonymous productions, the final two plays in Shakespeare's Lancastrian cycle both end with references to their "Author." These are the earliest surviving plays of Shakespeare to do so, seeming to capitalize on Shakespeare's unparalleled success at writing and completing his cycle. And the nature of these authorial references appears to support the recent scholarly view that such special attention to the author spelled doom for "the communal enterprise of the public stage."[9] The epilogue to the second part of *Henry IV* portrays the "author" as willing to "continue" a "story" whose plot is a secret he has yet to share with the players: in the next installment of the cycle, declares the actor of the epilogue, "Falstaff shall die of a sweat," "for anything I know." This next play, *Henry V,* ends with a still more striking depiction of the author. In the epilogue to that play—the climactic statement on Shakespeare's history cycle as a whole—the story is said to have been "pursu'd" not by the actors on the stage but rather by the author "bending" over his "pen."[10] The only other figures of comparable singularity in the epilogue are kings. How can Shakespeare have intended his cycle as the medium for an inclusive religious fellowship when he ends the cycle by distinguishing himself even from his professional colleagues?

In this chapter I will show how Shakespeare's emphasis on his authorship of the history cycle is not only compatible with the religious inclusivism habitually espoused by Renaissance theater people but also strongly suggestive of that inclusivism. As I have argued in my previous chapters, the notion of a single author did not suddenly thrust its way onto the stage in the seventeenth century but was instead generally accepted at the time as the standard, received model for understanding how scripts got written. This notion was essentially literary, however: it was not equipped to treat the playwright's engagement with other artistic forces in the theater as anything but a struggle for authority. Although Shakespeare did not invent authorship in his plays, he did help theatricalize the concept by acknowledging the formative power of actors and audience on his playwriting. Yet so dominant was the literary model of authorship that Shakespeare could not or would not entirely dispel its bias against collaborative mass entertainment. Instead, embracing the thought that an author writing plays for the commercial stage must suffer a loss of sovereign authority as well as respectability, Shakespeare idealized that loss. In the last plays of his history cycle, he conceptualized the author as both a king and a martyr—two seemingly disparate identities that Christ made one on the cross.

I begin my discussion by examining the Elizabethan poet John Weever's preoccupation with Shakespeare, which I take as evidence supporting three related claims about Shakespeare and authorship: first, that Shakespeare's contemporaries were fully capable of seeing him as an author; second, that Weever's literary conception of authorship differed from the theatrical conception Shakespeare dramatized in his plays; and third, that this difference hinged in part on Shakespeare's ability to treat authorship as sacrifice. I will then show how even the theater's detractors at the time acknowledged the power of the stage to evoke Christ's sacrifice, although they tried, like Barber and his followers, to dismiss this power as sacrilegious. Throughout his later histories, Shakespeare seems to concede these antitheatrical claims by repeatedly dramatizing the hypocrisy of characters who allude to the Passion, especially kings who play on their "anointed" role as "God's substitute" for their personal gain.[11] Yet for Shakespeare, these characters ultimately testify to the power of Christ's sacrifice in ways they do not intend; even the outright profanations of Falstaff the counter-king illuminate the potential spirituality of the stage. I will end my discussion by focusing on the sacrificial implications of the epilogue to *Henry V,* where, in one of the most extraordinary passages in English literary history, Shakespeare alludes to the entirety of the history cycle he has authored at the very moment that he overturns its triumphalist narrative of conquest and summons his audience instead to the contemplation of bleeding.

Authorship and Sacrifice

In the years immediately following the completion of Shakespeare's history cycle, the poet John Weever was fairly obsessed with him. As Ernst Honigmann notes, "four of Weever's five . . . publications" during this period allude to Shakespeare. A sonnet entitled "Ad Gulielmum Shakespear" in Weever's 1599 *Epigrammes* constitutes "the first extant poem addressed to the dramatist."[12] Weever's epyllion *Faunus and Melliflora,* published in 1600, recalls Shakespeare's *Venus and Adonis;* it even picks up and revises the story of Shakespeare's poem. The next year, Weever's *Whipping of the Satyre* invoked two characters from Shakespeare's second tetralogy, Falstaff and John of Gaunt.[13] The most notable of Weever's homages to Shakespeare, *The Mirror of Martyrs, or The Life and Death of . . . Sir John Old-castle Knight,* also published in 1601, implicitly attacked Shakespeare for portraying Falstaff as a libertine. In Shakespeare's history cycle, Falstaff was originally named Sir John Oldcastle, a historical contemporary of Henry V whom many Protestants, particularly his puritan Elizabethan descendant Lord Cobham, revered as an early martyr to the cause of religious reform. In part, the epilogue to the second *Henry IV* play mentions the author so that he can make his "humble" amends for any offence the Oldcastle references had caused: "Falstaff shall die of a sweat, unless already 'a be kill'd with your hard opinions; for Oldcastle died Martyr, and this is not the man." When Weever calls the subject of his *Mirror of Martyrs* the "first true Oldcastle," he means to exploit the vulnerability of Shakespeare to sectarian critique as a way not simply to imitate Shakespeare but to rival and outdo him.[14]

What Weever never attempted in his publications was any competition with Shakespeare as a dramatist. And yet, by the evidence of the *Mirror of Martyrs*, it was Shakespeare's theater work that Weever envied most. Early in the *Mirror*, Weever's Oldcastle marvels at the drawing power of plays and then claims that his own saintly story will, or at least should, command a far greater audience: "If thousands flock to hear a Poet's pen," he declares, "To hear a god, how many millions then." The rivalry with one poet-dramatist in particular becomes more explicit in Oldcastle's very next lines, which turn the thought of thousands flocking to the theater into a bitterly strife-torn scene from another Shakespeare play of 1599 besides *Henry V, Julius Caesar:*

> The many-headed multitude were drawn
> By *Brutus'* speech, that *Caesar* was ambitious;
> When eloquent *Mark Antony* had shown
> His virtues, who but *Brutus* then was vicious:
> Man's memory with new forgets the old,
> One tale is good until another's told.

As the passage suggests, Weever wants to tell a new literary tale about Oldcastle that will make his readers forget Shakespeare's theatrical version. Yet Shakespeare is such a commanding figure for Weever that Shakespeare's recent plays—not only the two parts of *Henry IV* but also *Julius Caesar*—define the terms of Weever's "ambitious" rivalry with him.[15] In fact, Weever sees *Julius Caesar* as so mightily expressive of his own competitiveness that the play appears to him to exemplify three different modes of rivalry at once—each, as it were, in rivalry with the others. The first is an imperial mode, where power resides successively in one lone figure after another: after Caesar comes Brutus, after Brutus comes Antony, just as Weever hopes to supplant Shakespeare as the popular "Poet." The second mode of rivalry

The Author Sacrificed 105

is less adaptable to Weever's purposes: in this republican mode, power resides in the "multitude" who support one figure after another and who prefigure the multiplicity of possible leaders by their own many-headedness. Weever's anxiety about his ability to sway a popular audience underscores a third mode of rivalry in the passage, between the "Pen" of the poet and the "speech" of the actor. Weever's metonymic formulation of the theatrical experience as the hearing of a poet's pen grants a singular imperial power to the poet by erasing actors from the scene of communication between playwright and audience. Yet the archetypal imperial figure in the *Julius Caesar* stanza is a dead man, whose ability to sway the multitude now belongs to the eloquence of others—though Weever softens this blow to authorship by presenting his speakers in the author's image, only one at a time. In short, Weever's literary imagination converts the mass entertainment of a Shakespearean play into three authorial plots that either compete for preeminence with one another or else are superimposed upon one another as if they were one indeed: single author against single author; single author against many-headed multitude; and single author against single actor. What these authorial plots do not allow the theatrical experience to mean for Weever is the enactment of any *fellowship*.

For all his reductive fixation on the poet's pen, Weever strangely omits the one element from the Shakespearean scene in *Julius Caesar* that concerns authorship most directly. He omits the will of Caesar, with its bequests to the common people, that Antony reads to the multitude. What's more, because Weever's fantasy of the stage as an authorial space limits its occupancy to only one person at a time, Weever omits Caesar himself. For in Shakespeare's scene Caesar is not simply dead and gone; Antony presents Caesar's corpse to the multitude, and he calls that corpse an author. "Let me show you him that made the will," Antony cries. Only after he has displayed the body, with bloody wounds he depicts as "dumb mouths," does Antony begin to read the will aloud. "Let but the commons hear this testament, " he had exclaimed when he first mentioned the will, "And they would go and kiss dead Caesar's wounds,/And dip their napkins in his sacred blood."[16] This rhetorical association of Caesar's will with bloody cloth helps Antony equate Caesar's bequests, even the very writing of those bequests, with Caesar's bleeding.

A testament in sacred blood: the scene as Shakespeare wrote it almost demands reference to another "J.C." But Weever ignores the christological resonance of Shakespeare's play because it fails to suit the literary notion of authorship he defines in competition with Shakespeare the playwright. After all, it must in part have been the pagan setting of *Julius Caesar* that recommended the play to Weever as emblematic of the profane theater in which Shakespeare would think to mock the martyr Oldcastle. The only Elizabethan work of Weever's that does not invoke Shakespeare is Weever's *Agnus Dei*, published the same year as the *Mirror for Martyrs*. The *Agnus Dei* is a miniature life of Christ in verse that figures Christ's "wounds" on the cross as possessing more drawing power than any stage scene ever could: "Who would not stand and view that dropping gore." Yet the *Agnus Dei* is no more interested in representing the Crucifixion as a mass spectacle than the *Mirror for Martyrs* was interested in representing the murdered Caesar as a sacrifice to the people. While "th'unconstant multitude" thirst for Christ's "sacred blood" in the *Agnus Dei* and jeer him on his way to the cross, they do not follow him there; only Mary, in Weever's account, "beholds her Son, and weeping stood,/Whilst nailéd to the Cross he streaméd blood."[17] Like Shakespeare, Weever links exposure to the multitude with bleeding, but his contempt for the multitude prevents him from conceiving of an author who bleeds for the sake of his audience.[18]

Staging the Passion

Nothing drew the ire of Renaissance theater haters so dependably as that chief spectacle in the Corpus Christi plays, the staging of the Passion. To prove that God could "endure nothing less than such profane and ridiculous handling of so serious and heavenly matters," Thomas Beard in his 1597 *Theatre of Gods Judgements* recounted how "in a certain place there was acted a tragedy of the death and passion of Christ in show, but indeed of [the actors] themselves, for he that played Christ's part hanging upon the cross was wounded to death by him that should have thrust his sword into a bladder full of blood tied to his side; who with his fall slew another that played one of the women's part that lamented under the cross; his brother that was first slain seeing this, slew the murderer, and was himself by order of justice hanged therefore." Beard mentions no other irreverence in the actors' "handling" of the Passion than the mere pretense of Christ's bleeding, "the death and passion of Christ *in show.*" But for Beard, faking the Passion counts as profanity enough to justify capital punishment, and the punishment has the added benefit of clarifying the crime: "this tragedy" of Christ, he writes, "was concluded with four true, not counterfeit deaths."[19]

A 1613 poem on *Christes Bloodie Sweat, or the Sonne of God in his Agonie* takes Beard's antitheatricalism one step further and opposes Christ's sacrifice to *any* play-acted tragedy. The author "I. F." says of Christ on the cross,

> He died indeed not as an actor dies
> To die today, and live again tomorrow,
> In show to please the audience, or disguise
> The idle habit of inforcéd sorrow:
> The Cross his stage was, and he play'd the part
> Of one that for his friend did pawn his heart.

Again the target of antitheatrical hostility is the notion of Christ's dying "in show," but I. F. is more explicit than Beard in supposing that the counterfeit deaths of actors undermine the reality not just of Christ's suffering but of his resurrection, too. There are those, I. F. declares, who have "esteem'd" Christ's sacrifice "a fancy or a fable," and the actor who dies today to live again tomorrow only confirms such doubters in their worldliness.[20]

But I. F. does not simply condemn the analogy between players and Christ. The cross, he writes, was Christ's stage; Christ played a part. According to *The Shakspere Allusion-Book,* the final couplet in I. F.'s stanza even has a specific part in mind—Antonio's in *The Merchant of Venice.* "Repent but you that you shall lose your friend," Antonio assures Bassanio, "And he repents not that he pays your debt;/For if the Jew do cut but deep enough,/I'll pay it instantly with all my heart."[21] If the theatrical analogue here seems too general to count as a direct link, the same cannot be said of another reference that *The Shakspere Allusion-Book* does not mention. The very lines in which I. F. insists on the difference between real and enacted death are themselves a reworking of a famous passage from *The Spanish Tragedy,* at the point in the tragedy when Hieronimo begins explaining to his royal audience that the corpses on his stage bleed "in earnest":

> Haply you think, but bootless are your thoughts,
> That this is fabulously counterfeit,
> And that we do as all tragedians do:
> To die today, for (fashioning our scene)
> The death of Ajax, or some Roman peer,
> And in a minute starting up again,
> Revive to please tomorrow's audience.[22]

Something about the theater shapes I. F.'s thinking about Christ's sacrifice even as he opposes the theater to that sacrifice. The explanation appears to lie in two elements that I. F. sees as common to both: not only life after death, but also a resurrection "for" the audience.

I. F.'s uncertainty about whether to treat play-acting as a sympathetic or antipathetic imitation of Christ's sacrifice may have been resolved to some degree in his later authorial career: modern scholars have identified him as the future dramatist John Ford. At the time Ford published *Christes Bloodie Sweat,* writes Brian Vickers, he "seemed to be setting out on the career of a Christian moralist and essayist," yet a few years later Ford "switched careers" and chose playwriting instead.[23] But Ford did not have to abandon his first aims to pursue his second, as Vickers implies he did. Consider the parallel though reverse career of Ford's contemporary Thomas Goffe. In the final act of Goffe's c.1618 tragicomedy *The Careless Shepherdess,* two women fake their deaths, but when they hear their lovers and fathers weeping for them at their graveside, they decide to "live again." "*They open the[ir] Coffins,*" the stage direction reads, "*and rise from them.*" What could have appeared more pagan, in Beard's eyes, than these counterfeit deaths and resurrections—presided over in the play, what is worse, by the heathen god Apollo. Yet shortly after writing *The Careless Shepherdess* Goffe took holy orders, and the first of his works to be published in English was a 1627 sermon entitled *Deliverance From the Grave.*[24]

The Passion in Shakespeare's Histories

Of the forty-four references to Christ's name in Shakespeare's plays, thirty-nine occur in the Lancastrian history cycle. So do two-thirds of Shakespeare's direct references to the mass, as well as eight of his nine references to the word *sacrament.* In the second tetralogy or Henriad, bleeding and sacrifice are linked from the opening scene: at the start of *Richard II,* the future Henry IV likens the "blood" of the murdered Gloucester to "sacrificing Abel's." Shakespeare's only direct reference to Christ on the cross appears in the first scene of the next play, the first part of *Henry IV,* when King Henry announces his crusading purpose "to chase these pagans in those holy fields, / Over whose acres walk'd those blessed feet / Which fourteen hundred years ago were nail'd / For our advantage on the bitter cross." The next most explicit reference to the Passion occurs a few scenes earlier in the Henriad, when the fallen Richard speaks of the "Pilates" who have "deliver'd me to my sour cross." Richard is a thief and a murderer, so his imitation of Christ cannot help but sound self-servingly appropriative, as modern scholars have claimed about Shakespeare and religion generally. Henry has his own tainted reasons for invoking Christ. In the second part of *Henry IV,* he confides to his son Hal that his intended Crusades were merely a diversionary tactic, "to lead out many to the Holy Land,/Lest rest and lying still might make them look/Too near unto my state." At the end of *Richard II,* Henry had been even more specific about his personal reasons for crusading: after Exton brought him Richard's corpse, Henry said that he planned to voyage "to the Holy Land" so that he could "wash" Richard's "blood off from my guilty hand."[25] The switch from Richard's bloody corpse to Christ's at the start of *1 Henry IV* obscures the "advantage" that Henry gained from Richard's murder by piously universalizing both the guilt and the profit.

As hypocrites who vest themselves in religious discourse, neither Richard nor Henry can compete, of course, with Falstaff. "Well, and the fire of grace be not quite out of thee, now shalt thou be mov'd," Falstaff declares to the company about to witness his acting the part of the king. Shakespeare associates Falstaff with a travesty of the Passion in Falstaff's very first scene: Poins jokes that Falstaff sold his soul to the devil "on Good Friday last, for a cup of Madeira and a cold capon leg." The play that begins with Henry's sanctimonious reference to the Crucifixion ends with Falstaff's spurious resurrection: after Hal sees him "dead,/Breathless and bleeding," "*Falstaff,*" the stage direction notes, "*riseth up.*" It is the player's resurrection that had so outraged Beard and troubled Ford, a resurrection made possible by a counterfeit death that Falstaff defends in the worldliest of terms: "To die is to be a counterfeit, for he is but the counterfeit of a man who hath not the life of a man; but to counterfeit dying, when a man thereby liveth, is to be not counterfeit, but the true and perfect image of life indeed."[26]

In short, Shakespeare makes the notion that a person might pretend to religion, and trade on the spiritual power of Christ's death and resurrection in particular, a conspicuous feature of his history cycle. If Shakespeare is a similar pretender, as Barber and his followers have claimed, why would he continually expose such appropriations in his cycle? To write off Henry or Falstaff as mere hypocrites is in any case a drastic simplification of both characters. Although Henry's reference to the advantage he gained from Christ's sacrifice may mystify the advantage he gained from Richard's murder, it also gives new life to Richard's christological characterization of himself, while at the same time acknowledging the guilt that Henry seems to feel in relation to Christ as well as Richard: "my soul is full of woe," he declares at the end of *Richard II*, "That blood should sprinkle me to make me grow." No religious pose comes more naturally to Falstaff than that of the penitent: "Monsieur Remorse," Poins calls the man who repeatedly tells whoever will listen to him that "I must give over this life, and I will give it over." Yet the last play of Shakespeare's history cycle suggests that Falstaff may well have died in real anguish over the state of his soul. Hostess Quickly reports that on his deathbed he "cried out, 'God, God, God!' three or four times." "To comfort him," Nell adds, "[I] bid him 'a should not think of God; I hop'd there was no need to trouble himself with any such thoughts yet."[27] For Shakespeare, by contrast, not even the blatant hypocrite can be cleanly separated from the ranks of the religious, no matter how comforting the thought of that separation might be.

Falstaff—originally Oldcastle, the Protestant and especially puritan hero—mocks the desire for such separation in himself as well as others. *Company* is a favorite word of his, and the claim that "company, villainous company, hath been the spoil of me" a favorite penitential refrain. Because they treat the Reformation and the consequent dispersion of Christianity into a multitude of sects as a process of secularization rather than of religious pluralization, secularizing critics such as Barber fail to see how Falstaff's role as a satirist of puritan cant *avant la lettre* opens a possible space of religious moderation, rather than atheism, for Shakespeare to occupy. By the same token, Barber and his followers cannot allow the possibility that Shakespeare's depiction of King Henry's spiritual hypocrisy amounts to a moderate Protestant critique of Henry's Catholicism. Yet Protestant polemicists often claimed that Catholics who linked penitence with pilgrimage had made the carnal mistake of believing that

Christ was to be found more in one place than in another. A similar carnality seems to be manifested in Henry's oddly literal emphasis on the "fields" where Christ walked and the "feet" he walked with. Considered in light of the history cycle as a whole, however, Henry's evocation of the Passion has a spiritual resonance that exceeds the boundaries a sectarian spectator might try to draw around it. The next time in the cycle that Shakespeare mentions "fields" and "feet" together is in Hostess Quickly's report of Falstaff's death: "'a babbl'd of green fields," she says; "'a bade me lay more clothes on his feet."[28] Neither Falstaff nor the Hostess can intend a connection to a speech about the Passion that neither of them heard. Only for the players and audience of Shakespeare's history cycle could the Hostess's words link a once-counterfeit and now (as it were) real dead man to an image of Christ on the cross.

Authorship and Sacrifice in Henry V

In the final installments of Shakespeare's history cycle, the character who plays the religious part most effectively is not Richard or Henry or even Falstaff, but rather Prince Hal, or King Henry V. "The King is full of grace and high regard," the Archbishop of Canterbury declares in the first scene of *Henry V;* "and a true lover of the holy Church," adds the Bishop of Ely. This godliness astonishes both men, since Hal had seemed no better than a libertine before his accession to the throne. But the audience who have witnessed Hal in rehearsal with his old teacher "Monsieur Remorse" know that Henry's ostensibly "sudden" "reformation" had been in the works for some time. Once Hal reforms himself, his dubious connection with Falstaff, it would seem, must fade from memory; Falstaff must die a martyr to the cause of Henry's succeeding in his part. Yet, for Canterbury, the "wonder" of Hal's reformation *depends* on the knowledge of the villainous company he used to keep.[29] What others might view as evidence of

Henry's inauthenticity the Archbishop takes as proof of a nearly miraculous change in him.

Since Hazlitt's time at least, commentators have seen Hal's career path from libertinism to godliness as a kind of autobiographical fantasy for his author. Shakespeare, too, critics have felt, wished that he could rise from "courses vain" and "companies unletter'd, rude, and shallow" to the high regard that Henry comes to enjoy. And the second tetralogy would appear not only to dramatize that ambition but also to effectuate it, insofar as the miraculous tale of Henry's reformation demonstrates powers in Shakespeare that he, like Prince Hal, had hidden "under the veil of wildness."[30] Although critics rarely say so, it also follows from this account of the authorial plot built into the Henriad's royal story that Shakespeare imagined the later plays of the cycle as vindicating his own claims to piety and religious purpose. Yet the second tetralogy exposes Hal's capacity for hypocrisy as much as piety: does Shakespeare identify with Hal's humble "penitence" before God in *Henry V* or with his pretense of such humility?[31]

The comparison between the king and the playwright becomes most explicit in the final speech of the play, of the tetralogy, and of the cycle as a whole.

> Thus far, with rough and all-unable pen,
> Our bending author hath pursu'd the story,
> In little room confining mighty men,
> Mangling by starts the full course of their glory.
> Small time: but in that small, most greatly lived
> This star of England. Fortune made his sword;
> By which, the world's best garden he achieved:
> And of it left his son imperial Lord.

In its opening lines, the epilogue analogizes Shakespeare and Henry by singling them out together, the author with his pen, the emperor with his sword. At first, indeed, the "author" might almost be taken for that "Star of England," having "greatly lived" in the "small time" of his play. When Weever depicted the author in such an imperial mode, he envisioned a play as a direct communication between pen and audience that obviated the need for actors; Shakespeare's epilogue similarly begins by focusing on the author to the exclusion of the rest of his theater company. The very sonnet form of the epilogue suggests Shakespeare's stake in imagining the primacy of the author's page over the actors' stage.[32]

This is not to say that the imperial conception of authorship goes unchallenged in the epilogue. Even Weever had acknowledged the rival forces of actors and mass audience, but so unwilling was he to think of these forces positively that, when he did visualize them, he saw nothing but the author's death and the specter of civil war. In *Henry V,* the epilogue similarly links any expansion of focus beyond a single imperial lord with disaster:

> Henry the Sixt, in infant bands crown'd King
> Of France and England, did this king succeed:
> Whose state so many had the managing,
> That they lost France, and made his England bleed.

"Which oft *our* stage hath shown": once the royal tragedy has been evoked, the author as well as the king surrenders his exclusive hold on power. Just as proxy managers "succeed" Henry V, so the author at his desk is supplanted by the actors on the stage—and, according to the epilogue, to replace the "one" with the "many" is to suffer loss and bleeding.[33]

Yet both the author and the king had already been threatened with usurpation in the opening lines of the epilogue, by an analogy between them that constituted a rivalry as much as an equation. The differences between Henry and Shakespeare are, after all, more salient than their similarities. For a start, the author is no "conqu'ring Caesar"; in the epilogue, he is "bending" submissively, as Henry had promised to "bend" France "to our awe," and his pen has none of the sword's actual power to "mangle."[34] Nor was Shakespeare born a prince as Hal was, nor can he leave a royal title to his son as Hal does. Finally, King Henry V lost his power only when he died, but the author in Shakespeare's epilogue, "all-unable" to begin with, is simply cast aside as the epilogue proceeds.

Falstaff might reply that the real loser is always the dead man, not the living one. Henry dies, but the mirroring eclipse of the author in the epilogue is a counterfeit death like all the other instances of "bleeding" the stage is said to have "shown" throughout Shakespeare's cycle. It is worth pausing for a moment over the final lines of the epilogue to consider how double- and triple-edged they render the relationship between historical and theatrical death.

> Henry the Sixt, in infant bands crown'd King
> Of France and England, did this king succeed:
> Whose state so many had the managing,
> That they lost France, and made his England bleed:
> Which oft our stage hath shown; and for their sake,
> In your fair minds let this acceptance take.

Only with the mention of England's bleeding—"his" England, as if it were Henry's body—does the epilogue allude to the cycle of plays it brings to a close. Or to be more precise, the epilogue makes the thought of England's bleeding the occasion to bring the cycle to life again in the imagination of the audience, just as the cycle appears to be ending: "which oft our stage hath shown." This emphasis on previous plays seems to mark a victory for the author over his kingly rival, insofar as Henry's "small time" is lengthened into a durative triumph for Shakespeare. The further implication of *repeat* performances marks a certain moral advantage for the author over the king, as well. No matter how hypocritically humble Shakespeare may be in touting his stage successes or hypocritically penitent in regretting the mighty men he mangles with his pen, the actors who die on his stage revive again to please tomorrow's audience. Shakespeare faces no such "heavy reckoning" for his sins as the common soldier Williams says King Henry must face "when all those legs, and arms, and heads, chopp'd off in a battle, shall join together at the latter day" and the dead shall rise to bear witness against him. "God fought for us," the pious Henry claims after Agincourt, and the epilogue does credit him with having "achieved" a kind of second Eden—by the sword, however, and with pagan "Fortune" standing in the place of God as Henry's patron. Throughout his history plays, Shakespeare regularly depicts "the purple testament of bleeding war" as a demonic inversion of Christianity.[35] The epilogue's surprising shift from bleeding to the repeated enactment of bleeding ("which oft our Stage hath shown") distances Shakespeare's theater from Henry's sanctifications of violence by suggesting, in the spirit of Falstaff, that those who pretend to die gain rather than lose. They have a life after death.

Yet Shakespeare is not content to offer the theater as merely a harmless counterfeit of war or a profane rather than devilish imitation of religion. Unlike the "bleeding sword" that the French king pits against "Christian-like accord" a few lines before the epilogue, the author's pen generates unbloody versions of sacrifice, and unbloody is how both Catholics and Protestants described the celebration of Christ's sacrifice in communion. Protestant polemicists claimed that Catholics were disingenuous on this score: if, in Barber's words, Catholics understood the mass "as an actual, present reenactment" of Christ's sacrifice, then (according to Protestants) Catholics would also have to believe that the officiating priest makes Christ bleed anew. For Protestants, the Eucharist was instead a remembrance of Christ's sacrifice, and Shakespeare's distinction between actual and theatrical bleeding better accords with this sacramental theory than with the Catholic view. Whatever form of sacrifice Shakespeare's theater dramatized, of course, it could never count as an authorized religious ceremony, but in Shakespeare's cycle the clergymen who *are* authorized to perform such ceremonies prove to be deeply corrupt. At the start of *Henry V*, for instance, the Bishop and Archbishop who marvel at Henry's godliness are engaged in a sordid conspiracy: they have decided that "the clergy" will "part" with an enormous "sum" to fund Henry's war efforts in exchange for his blocking a bill that would "strip" the church of all its "temporal lands"—"the better half of our possession,"

Canterbury observes. These venal and ultimately warmongering church officials are Catholics; at no point in Shakespeare's cycle do we see a Protestant cleric who conceives of the church in such nakedly antisacramental terms, as a "cup" he does not want "the commons" to drink. But then neither do we see any Protestant clergyman who sponsors Christian unity. In the historical time that Shakespeare depicts, no Protestants have yet arrived on the scene; the only possible alternatives to the Catholic priests and laity on stage are the admittedly "flat unraiséd spirits" who impersonate them.[36]

For Shakespeare, a theatrical version of ministry may not have been a sufficient alternative to a corrupt church, but at least it was a beginning. By taking the place of the Corpus Christi plays, which had themselves shifted the celebration of Christ's sacrifice from the altar to the open air, Shakespeare's Lancastrian cycle as he seems to have understood it helped liberate communion from the Catholic monopoly on it so that the impact of Christ's sacrifice could be seen to pervade everywhere, not only in the sincere religion of other Christian sects but in hypocritical pieties, too, even in open profanities, such as Falstaff's "cup of Madeira" and "cold capon leg" on Good Friday, or in unintentional allusions such as the Hostess's on Falstaff's death. "Any manner of way" Christ is "preached," "whether it be by pretence, or by truth," writes Paul in his letter to the Philippians, "I joy therein, and will joy."[37] So persistently does the mass entertainment of the theater suggest to Shakespeare the communal partaking of Christ's body and blood that he ends the epilogue of *Henry V* by asking the audience to think of itself christologically, as acting "for" the "sake" of others. But this happens only after he has first performed a sacrifice of his own. Having begun the epilogue like Weever's poet, diverting attention away from the stage to the study, where he can take sole credit for the cycle he has just completed, the author in *Henry V* proves to be a king and no king, who yields his sovereign power without struggle to the theater's "many" and to the image of a body bleeding that they have repeatedly enacted and beheld.

Coda

Then as now, plays that returned to the stage after long absences were said to be *revived*. Richard Burbage told a court official in 1604 that the King's Men had "no new play that the queen hath not seen, but they have Revived an old one, Called *Love's Labor lost*."[38] Jonson's induction to *Cynthia's Revels* (1601) put the metaphor more colorfully: "the *Umbrae*, or Ghosts of some three or four Plays, departed a dozen years since, have been seen walking on your Stage here," a satirical boy claims to one of the actors. Books, too, could seem to bring plays back to life: the title page of *The Tragedie of Tancred and Gismund* (1591), which was first performed in the late 1560s, describes the play as "newly revived and polished according to the decorum of these days." And publication was said to resurrect dramatists as well as plays: "Wonder! who's here? *Fletcher*, long buried / Reviv'd?" asks Robert Gardiner in his prefatory poem to the 1647 Beaumont and Fletcher folio. Through new plays, dramatists could also seem to be reborn in other dramatists, their purported heirs. "Jonson's alive!" proclaimed one commender of Richard Brome's *Antipodes* (1640) a few years after Jonson's death. All these conceits of new life were encouraged by the ubiquity of counterfeit death on the stage. "We thought thee dead," wrote James Mabbe of Shakespeare in 1623, but the printing of the First Folio had reminded Mabbe that "an Actor's Art, / Can die, and live, to act a second part."[39]

In Shakespeare's late plays, heirs revive their parents without the parents' even having to die. Awakened from despair by the rediscovery of a daughter he had thought long gone, Pericles calls that daughter "the heir of kingdoms, and another life / To Pericles thy father."[40] Shakespeare wrote *Pericles* with another dramatist, George Wilkins; in my next chapter, I will ask whether Shakespeare believed that one *co*author could revive another.

The Author Revived

Look how the father's face
Lives in his issue.
« JONSON, *"To the Memory of . . . Shakespeare"* »

Perhaps the most surprising turn in Shakespeare's professional career was his decision, at the height of his fame and power as a playwright, to begin sharing the authorship of his plays once again with other dramatists. The decision looks all the more surprising from the perspective of recent scholarship on the Renaissance English theater, which, as we've seen, treats collective playwriting as both the practical and the theoretical norm in English theaters until single authorship began to appear at the end of the sixteenth century. It makes sense, by the light of this scholarship, that evidence should suggest Shakespeare might have cowritten such early plays as *Titus Andronicus* and the first part of *Henry VI*. It also fits the current view, at least to some degree, that little evidence of substantial coauthorship has been uncovered in Shakespearean drama written around the turn of the century. But the surprise from the current perspective is that the strongest evidence of coauthorship in the Shakespearean corpus should crop up where the supposed historical trajectory from plural to single authorship would lead us to believe it shouldn't, toward the end of Shakespeare's career—in *Timon of Athens, Pericles, Henry VIII,* the lost *Cardenio,* and *Two Noble Kinsmen.* Why would Shakespeare have returned to coauthorship after its heyday was past and, even more bafflingly, after he had already achieved unprecedented success as a single author?

Some of the perplexity vanishes when the presumed shift from collaboration to authorship vanishes too. Collective play-writing was never the norm for Renaissance drama, practically or conceptually, and by arguing that it was, theater scholars have actually obscured the historically specific contours of cowriting they hope to retrace. To claim with Foucault, for instance, that *all* writing was seen as collective until the seventeenth century is to miss the real innovativeness of large-scale coauthorship in the Renaissance theater. As G. E. Bentley points out, collective playwriting had never been so "notable" a feature of English drama as it became after "the appearance of the regular commercial theaters in London." These permanent playhouses created something new in English drama: a regularly returning audience, and with them a far greater demand for new plays than touring players had ever experienced. Collective writing helped speed up the process of satisfying this demand, but once "large repertories of actable old plays" had been assembled, coauthorship became "less necessary," and consequently after the 1620s "there appears to have been a decline in the number of collaborated plays prepared for the London stage."[1]

Even those historicists who reject Foucault's totalizing account and more modestly argue that all *play*writing was seen as collective until the seventeenth century end up masking the distinctive features of their historical subject. By generalizing the collaborative nature of theatrical performance into the claim that every kind of theatrical labor in the Renaissance, including playwriting, was equally collaborative, scholars not only ignore the importance of single authorship to Renaissance drama but also gloss over the astonishingly low profile of collective playwriting in the theater as well as in the culture at large. References to coauthorship in the prologues and epilogues of plays, for instance, are extremely rare. I can find no clear case before 1600, and only one in a commercial play printed before 1642: the epilogue to the 1607 *Travailes of the Three English Brothers* mentions "the authors," while the prologue more conventionally invokes a singular "muse."[2] Title page attributions to multiple authors also turn out to have been much less common in the period than one might have guessed. Charting their numbers, Brian Vickers concludes that printed acknowledgments of coauthorship were "frequent" in the seventeenth century, but his figures tell a different story. Between 1580 and 1649, by Vickers's count, 416 plays were published with acknowledgment of single authorship, versus 26 plays with acknowledgment of multiple authorship—a ratio of 16 to 1.[3]

Within these narrow limits, however, Vickers does seem right to claim that *recognition* of collective playwriting grew, even as the practice decreased for the economic reasons Bentley cites. Only three printed attributions of dramatic coauthorship surfaced during the last three decades of the sixteenth century, versus fourteen in the next three decades. What Vickers calls "an increasing readiness to acknowledge joint creations" came slowly, however, and it never made serious headway against the dominant single-author paradigm. According to the figures Vickers compiles, the largest number of attributed coauthorships in a single decade was 8 in the 1630s, when 129 single authorships were also acknowledged; this ratio of 16 to 1 is roughly the same as the ratio in the 1590s (17 to 1) and the 1600s (16 to 1).[4] Not until the 1647 publication of *Comedies and Tragedies Written by Francis Beaumont and John Fletcher*, with its attribution of more than 30 plays to collaborative writing—a number greater than all the earlier coauthorial attributions in Vickers's chart combined—did an English printer acknowledge coauthorship as a major feature of the English dramatic landscape.

Recent theater scholarship has stood this picture on its head. Even though the Beaumont and Fletcher folio was the first collection of avowedly coauthored plays to be published in England, Jeffrey Masten sees the volume as evidence that coauthorship was growing "increasingly inexplicable."[5] But a telling sign of the folio's innovativeness is the crudeness of its attempt to articulate the coauthorial practices it memorializes: as Vickers notes, the Beaumont and Fletcher folio "did not reveal the massive contributions made to that canon by Massinger, Webster, Jonson, Chapman, Shakespeare, Field, Rowley, Ford, and Shirley, names equally absent in its expanded reissue." By Bentley's count, Fletcher and *Massinger* were "the most productive collaborating partnership of the time," and yet, as Bentley elsewhere observes, "no play was published in the seventeenth century as a collaboration of Fletcher and Massinger."[6] So commanding a paradigm was single authorship that it made the common practice of collective playwriting difficult to notice, let alone promote.[7]

Thanks to its own absorption in a single-author paradigm, older criticism tended to view Shakespeare's return to coauthorship at the end of his career as a sign of disability only: of a weakness, weariness, or alienation that forced him to rely on others. It does seem to be true that Shakespeare wrote fewer plays in his later years than he had before, but Leeds Barroll has given us reason to think that this slackening may have resulted from external circumstances: namely, from plague, which "between 1603 and 1611," by Barroll's estimates, closed playhouses "off and on for a period of at least sixty-eight months." "When the circumstances were favorable—when the playhouses were open and stages available," Barroll maintains, Shakespeare continued to write "very rapidly indeed."[8] Whether or not Barroll is right, the argument from disability must contend with the extraordinary burst of creativity that generated Shakespeare's late comedies— his so-called romances—*after* he had resumed coauthorship in *Timon* and *Pericles.* The spotlight that Vickers has placed on the growing interest in collective playwriting during the seventeenth century helps us envision how Shakespeare might have actively *pursued* collaborative writing rather than have been forced into it. Throughout this book, I have been arguing that Shakespeare's authorial self-consciousness was fundamentally shaped by his immersion in the theater business. He came to regard the reigning authorial paradigm as an essentially literary concept that failed to capture the complexity of his means, aims, and methods as a theatrical professional—above all, the decisive effect of his audience and fellow actors on his dramaturgy. In this chapter, I consider Shakespeare's return to coauthorship as his attempt to develop a theatrical identity for his authorship that would build responsiveness to fellow *dramatists* into his writing as well.

Shakespeare's difficulty in expanding his conception of authorship to include the active participation of another author is apparent even in a play as profoundly invested in a mixed or heterogeneous dramaturgy as *Hamlet*. Although Shakespeare repeatedly depicts writing in *Hamlet* as the work of more than one hand, he rarely presents this shared labor as collaborative: cowriting in *Hamlet* is generally agonistic, one author revising another without his agreement or foreknowledge. Why could Shakespeare envision author and player as fellows in *Hamlet*, as I argued in chapter 2, but not author and author? The answer, it seems, is that while writing *Hamlet* Shakespeare could think of himself as embodying one fellowship but not the other, and only through an imagined internalization of multiple roles could he improvise a new authorial ideal from within the reigning paradigm of single authorship. One subtle instance of collaborative coauthorship in the play is the exception that proves the rule. Hamlet tells Horatio that after reading the king's commission to England, he found himself working with himself to revise it: "ere I could make a prologue to my brains,/They had begun the play." Earlier, Hamlet had pictured his "brain" as the ghost's "book"; in the scene with Horatio, Hamlet introduces his tale of inspired writing by assuring Horatio, "There's a divinity that shapes our ends,/Rough-hew them how we will."[9] By implication, Hamlet detects something like the ghostly hand of his father or of providence at work in his improvisation of a new commission. But this brief glimpse of collaborative coauthorship is overshadowed in the scene by the more salient contest of authorial will between Prince Hamlet and King Claudius, and it is also seriously restricted by the seemingly inescapable condition that the collaboration take place in a single mind.

Partnership with another writer would necessarily have entailed some sacrifice of this one-for-many comprehensiveness, and critics have marveled that toward the end of his career Shakespeare would stoop so low as to share authorship with a man like George Wilkins, the "very minor" dramatist, woman-beater, and, in all probability, pimp who helped Shakespeare write *Pericles.* Having noted that *Pericles* "contains Shakespeare's only sustained scene located in a brothel, where the man destined to marry the virginal heroine appears to be a regular customer," Katherine Duncan-Jones deplores "the coarsening influence" of Wilkins on Shakespeare and declares that "the period of Shakespeare's association with Wilkins was a distressing deviation from his commanding role as the King's Men's leading playwright."[10] But what if Shakespeare *chose* this deviation? *Pericles* begins with the stigmatization of a "leading" figure, the incestuous tyrant Antiochus, who would rather kill Pericles than surrender his daughter and eventually his kingship to him: "by his fall my honor must keep high," Antiochus rivalrously decides. The hero in the play is no alternative pillar of strength: fleeing from the monarch he says "frighted" him, Pericles spends most of the rest of his scenes in a state of virtual abdication from his own kingship in Tyre, renouncing that title for good at the end of the play, when he transfers his crown to his daughter and her formerly brothel-loving husband. A commanding role, in other words, is a troubling prospect in *Pericles.* I want to argue that, by opting to cowrite *Pericles* with Wilkins, Shakespeare purposely sought to diminish his honor and his sovereignty as a playwright—in particular, to end a uniquely triumphant run of tragedies that he had come to view as a self-limiting success.[11] He knew his business, of course: *Pericles* proved to be an immensely popular hit.[12] And the play itself registers Shakespeare's awareness of the gains that can accompany losses. When Pericles cedes his title to his heirs, he does not renounce all power: one form of sovereignty gives way to another. After performing the "sacrifice" that the goddess

Diana requires of him, Pericles accepts another kingship, which he inherits through his partnership with his wife.[13]

But what kind of sovereignty exactly could Shakespeare have hoped to gain through coauthorship? I begin my discussion of this issue by surveying the Renaissance book market to see how Shakespeare might have drawn on other genres of collective writing as guides to help him develop a more productive notion of coauthorship than the one he outlines in *Hamlet*. I then look more closely at *Pericles*, which reflects on collective writing so intensively as to modify and even transform Shakespeare's dramaturgy in the process. For with *Pericles* Shakespeare returned to comedy as well as coauthorship, after his long absorption in tragedy. The self-mortification of sharing *Pericles* with Wilkins proved to be self-renewing also, reviving for Shakespeare the versatility and range that he regarded as indispensable to a commercial dramatist's success. At the same time, the play's tragicomic linkage of death and rebirth helped Shakespeare envision coauthorship itself as a kind of revival, an inheritance. I end the chapter with a discussion of the coauthored play that may have been the last one Shakespeare had a hand in writing, *Two Noble Kinsmen* (c. 1613). Commentators have often interpreted this play and two others that Shakespeare cowrote around the same time as his attempt to bequeath his commanding role in the King's Men to his final writing partner, John Fletcher. In the sonnets published a few years earlier, Shakespeare's speaker had urged the fair young man to regard the creation of an "heir" as an act not of surrendering power but of restoring it: "To give away yourself keeps yourself still"; "This were to be new made when thou art old."[14] And yet *Two Noble Kinsmen* suggests that in the end Shakespeare found the will only to share authorship, not to cede it altogether.

The Acknowledgment of Coauthorship in Print

No one can say how many of the Renaissance publications that were advertised as single authorships were actually the products of multiple writers, but we *can* identify the books that were advertised as coauthorships and that therefore must have seemed, to writers or publishers in any case, to make sense as coauthorships. The most salient fact about these acknowledged cowritings is that they were relatively scarce, and the scarcest of them were coauthorships by living contemporaries, or what I'll call contemporaneous coauthorships. The majority of the contemporaneous coauthorships acknowledged during the period were the work of only two pairs of writers: the preachers John Dod and Robert Cleaver, and the playwrights Beaumont and Fletcher. By 1640 Dod and Cleaver had been identified as the coauthors of fourteen different titles printed in more than fifty editions, while Beaumont and Fletcher had been named as the coauthors of seven different titles in twenty-two editions, seven years before the first folio collection of their plays. So exceptional were these two partnerships that they had no serious coauthorial rivals. After Beaumont and Fletcher, the next most publicized team of dramatists were Dekker and Webster, with three titles published in a total of four editions, while the only clergymen to generate even two editions of acknowledged coauthorships after Dod and Cleaver were the Protestants John Deacon and John Walker, and the Catholics Thomas Preston and Thomas Green.

Before Dod and Cleaver arrived on the scene, contemporaneous coauthorships had the status more of curiosities than of ordinary occurrences. Only once a decade from 1565 to 1591, for example, was any play published as an acknowledged coauthorship. The first two attributed coauthorships from the commercial theaters—Marlowe and Nashe's *Dido,* and Lodge and Greene's *Looking Glass for London and England*—were not published until 1594, and no new acknowledged coauthorship from the theaters surfaced for the rest of the century. Then in 1603 Dod and Cleaver's *Plaine and Familiar Exposition of the Ten Commandements* appeared in two anonymous unauthorized editions, and when Dod and Cleaver issued a corrected version the following year, a floodgate opened for them. Prior to this 1604 edition, no coauthors in England had ever published more than one title together, but

within six years of their first acknowledged coauthorship Dod
and Cleaver were credited with ten more titles, yielding a total of
twenty-four Dod and Cleaver editions in seven years.[15]

The year 1604 also saw the first acknowledged coauthorship
from the commercial theaters in a decade: *The Malcontent. Augmented by Marston. With the additions played by the Kings Majesties
Servants. Written by John Webster.* Like Dod and Cleaver's *Plaine
and Familiar Exposition, The Malcontent* was followed by an unprecedented surge in other acknowledged coauthorships from
the stage as well as the pulpit: *East-ward Hoe . . . Made by Geo:
Chapman. Ben:Jonson. Joh:Marston* in 1605; *North-ward Hoe . . . By
Thomas Decker, and John Webster* (1607); *West-ward Hoe . . . Written by Tho:Decker, and John Webster* (1607); *The Famous History of
Sir Thomas Wyatt . . . Written by Thomas Dickers, and John Webster*
(1607); *The Travailes of the Three English Brothers,* with a dedication
signed by "John Day. William Rowley. George Wilkins" (1607);
and in 1608 *The Dumbe Knight,* credited to Gervase Markham
on its title page, but with a dedication by Lewis Machin that
mentions his "partner" in writing.[16] Dod and Cleaver either began or else rode the wave that first made contemporaneous coauthorship *interesting* to English printers and readers, and Shakespeare's serious return to coauthorship with *Timon* (c. 1604–8)
and *Pericles* (c. 1608) fits perfectly into the timeline of this new
fashion.[17]

Over subsequent decades, devotional and dramatic literature
continued to dominate the field of acknowledged coauthorship,
with devotional literature providing the most popular titles, and
plays providing the greatest number of different titles as well
as the greatest number of different coauthorial partnerships.[18]
In part, this overrepresentation of dramatic and religious literature among the contemporaneous coauthorships of the day
would seem to reflect the professions of the writers involved: in
particular, the ethos of fellowship shared by clergymen and theater people alike. Actor-playwrights such as Shakespeare were
"fellows" or partners of an acting company, but even unattached
dramatists were likely to be influenced by the actors' sense of

playmaking as a communal endeavor. In their brief dedicatory letter to *The Travailes of the Three English Brothers*, the first such letter signed by a play's coauthors, the three English dramatists Day, Rowley, and Wilkins speak of friends and friendship seven times.[19] Conversely, no closet drama between 1576 and 1642 was printed as a collaborative effort. This is not to say, as some historicists do, that dramatic coauthorship depended on a specifically *artisanal* sense of collectivity. The earliest plays that were published as coauthorships during the Renaissance came from the Inns of Court and were advertised as "compiled by the Gentlemen" there. By the same token, the first acknowledged coauthorships from the commercial theater were the products of the university wits Marlowe, Nashe, Lodge, and Greene; in his *Groats-worth of Wit*, Greene mentions that he wrote a play "together" with one of the dramatists he is warning about Shakespeare.[20] Clergymen did not belong to a guild or company either, but like university and Inns of Court students, they considered themselves members of a brotherhood. In their prefatory letter to *A Summarie Answere to . . . Master Darel* (1601), the preachers Deacon and Walker dedicate their work to "the Reverend Fathers, the Learned Preachers and Godly Brethren in this our English Church"; they extend "the *hand of fellowship*" even to their polemical adversaries; and they sign themselves "Your loving brethren assuredly in the Lord."[21]

Just as solidarities in church and theater seem to have encouraged coauthorship, so did the genres in which dramatists and preachers wrote. Theatrical and devotional literature was often easily divisible into units that could be parceled out to various writers: plays by scenes or acts or speeches, religious commentaries by sermons or scriptures.[22] Many advertised coauthorships of the period give different writers credit for different portions of the books they jointly authored. The title page of Dod and Cleaver's highly popular *Ten Sermons* (1609), for instance, specifies that Dod wrote "the six first" and Cleaver "the four last" sermons, while the title page of the Inns of Court play *Gorboduc* (1565) likewise declares that "three Acts were written by Thomas

Norton, and the two last by Thomas Sackville."[23] History writing—the next most prominent genre of contemporaneous coauthorship after devotional and dramatic literature—was also readily divisible into separate units of reigns or years or countries, and, like coauthored plays and sermon collections, histories that were advertised as coauthorships often gave credit to different writers for different portions of the work at hand.[24]

This parceling out of authorial responsibilities in religious, theatrical, and historical literature made the coauthorships in these genres seem less like exceptions to the rule of single authorship than proofs of it, as several single authorships bundled together. In the first edition of *The Chronicles of England, Scotlande, and Irelande* (1577), Raphael Holinshed notes that his publishers had enlisted the "help" of "William Harrison, and Richard Stanyhurst" in writing the *Chronicle*'s "descriptions" of England, Scotland, and Ireland, but these contributions were framed as being distinct enough from Holinshed's own work that they required separate prefatory letters signed by their respective authors.[25] In William Baldwin's letter to the reader of *A Myrroure for Magistrates* (1559), a verse history that picked up John Lydgate's translation of Boccaccio's *De casibus illustrium virorum* where Lydgate left off, Baldwin makes clear that he had "refused utterly to undertake" the project without the "help" of other "learned men," seven of whom eventually "consented" to share "the travail" with Baldwin. All these contributors, Baldwin explained, decided to retain Boccaccio's conceit of having the fallen princes "make their moan" to the narrator, but since "both Bochas and Lydgate were dead," the contributors also "all agreed that I should usurp Bochas['s] room, and the wretched princes complain unto me: and took upon themselves every man for his part to be sundry personages, and in their behalfs to bewail unto me their grievous chances, heavy destinies, & woeful misfortunes." The contribution of each cowriter, in other words, was purportedly limited to the "part" of the person or persons he played. Starting with the third edition of the *Myrroure* in 1571, separate "signatures" were "affixed to certain tragedies," just as separate signatures appeared at the end of separate acts in George Gascoigne and Francis Kin-welmershe's Inns of Court play *Jocasta*, first published in 1573.[26]

So authoritative was the single-author paradigm during the Renaissance that even acknowledged coauthorships were often treated as the work of one author only. Facing the title page of the Beaumont and Fletcher collection in 1647 was an engraving of only one playwright, Fletcher.[27] Twenty-one of the thirty-five commendatory poems to the volume addressed themselves to Fletcher alone, while only five focused steadily on Beaumont and Fletcher as coauthors.[28] Similarly, although both writers were named in the dedicatory letter to the most popular acknowledged coauthorship in the Renaissance, Dod and Cleaver's *Ten Commandements,* contemporaries nearly always referred to the book as the work of Dod alone, who came to be known as "Decalogue Dod."[29] One exception, a 1613 epigram that told how "Dod with his Cleaver cleaves the stony rock / Of our hard hearts through their laborious pain," nevertheless ended by insisting that the "pair of friends" were one and the same: "Though two in Name, in Nature yet not twain."[30] This was the keynote to the commendatory verses in the Beaumont and Fletcher collection that managed to treat the two dramatists as coauthors: according to these poems, Beaumont and Fletcher were "knit" together into "one wit," "one fair mind," "one Poet."[31] In a prefatory letter to their *Dialogicall Discourses of Spirits and Divels* (1601), Deacon and Walker made the same singularizing claim about themselves, recounting how the news of John Darrel's supposed exorcism of William Sommers "did so diversely affect our *minds* with a diverse and contrary *judgment* (the one very constantly *avouching,* the other no less confidently *impugning* that falsely pretended *action)*" that their friendship was nearly ruined, till "the favorable assistance of *God's holy spirit*" led them to "the very *truth* it self," "whereupon also, we eftsoons began to *speak both of us but one and the selfsame thing:* and (which is more) being now knit together in one *mind* and one *judgment* concerning these several matters, we determined forthwith to put down in writing, whatsoever had deliberately passed between us."[32]

One might think that Deacon and Walker's vision of coauthorship as a mutually achieved singleness would prove difficult to sustain in the more common form of acknowledged coauthorship during the Renaissance (more common than cowriting by contemporaries). This was *posthumous* coauthorship, in which a living writer was typically said to have "corrected," "augmented," "revised," "enlarged," "continued," or "finished" the work of a dead writer or writers.[33] The most popular posthumous coauthorship of the day, *Hero and Leander: Begun by Christopher Marloe; and finished by George Chapman* (1598), was so unmistakably a bundle of single authorships that each poet's parcel began with a separate dedication never mentioning the other poet in the venture. But the conceptual pressure to read coauthorships as single authorships did nevertheless make it possible to treat even posthumous cowritings as the work of "one *mind* and one *judgment*." The simplest method, again, was to ignore all but one of the coauthors. In Arthur Golding's translation of the one major classical precedent for any form of coauthorship, *Iustini ex Trogi Pompeii Historia,* or as Golding titled it *Thabridgment of the Histories of Trogus Pompeius . . . by the Famous Historiographer Justine* (1564), Golding claimed that Justinus had "obtained the name of a famous Historiographer" less "by his own industry" than "by the decay and loss of his Author Trogus." As if to prove Golding's point, George Wilkins later translated Justinus' abridgment of Trogus as *The Historie of Iustine . . . That Famous Historiographer* in 1606.[34] Similarly, when *An Epitome of Cronicles . . . First, by Thomas Lanquet . . . and Now Finished and Continued . . . by Thomas Cooper* (1549) was reprinted eleven years later, its title had changed to *Coopers Chronicle . . . by Me Thomas Cooper* (1560).

Such compression—or, as Baldwin more regally termed it, "usurpation"—could also happen without suppression.[35] For a culture that prided itself on reviving the classics, it was conventional to assert that a dead author had been *resurrected* in a living one. "As the soul of *Euphorbus* was thought to live in *Pythagoras,*" wrote Francis Meres in 1598, "so the sweet witty soul of *Ovid* lives in mellifluous & honey-tongued *Shakespeare.*" "*Ovid's* soul *revives* in *Drayton* now," declared William Alexander in 1600. The Pythagorean conceit insisted that the dead and living writers were one and the same. So in 1629 Robert Harvey assured James Shirley that "by transmigration of his soul" the "divine" portion of Beaumont was now "thine"; the same year Thomas May countered criticisms that John Ford had drawn *The Lover's Melancholy* "from Shakespeare's mine" by asking "What need?—when Shakespeare still survives in you."[36] According to some panegyrists, there were no limits on the number of authors who could be revived and infused into a single playwright: "Were old *Pythagoras* alive again," claimed Aston Cockaigne in 1632, Massinger's *Emperour of the East* might convince him "that all Poetic souls yet known / Are met in thee, united, and made one."[37]

In some cases these transmigrations were rationalized as inheritances. Writing in 1630, William Habington somewhat morbidly hoped that whenever Jonson died, Shirley would "live to make us see / The glory of the stage reviv'd in thee," and in 1638 D. Cooper duly proclaimed, "*Shirley* stand forth, and put thy Laurel on, / *Phoebus'* next heir, now *Ben* is dead and gone."[38] On occasion, a posthumous coauthorship was even presented as a straightforward bequest from the dead author to the living one. In *The Survey of London . . . Begun First by the Pains and Industry of John Stow, in the year 1598. Afterwards enlarged by the care and diligence of A[nthony].M[unday]. in the year 1618. And now compleatly finished by the study & labor of A. M. H[enry].D[yson]. and others, this present year 1633*, the later author Munday declared that the first author Stow had hoped to enlarge his *Survey* himself, "but prevented by infirmity, and Sickness-bringing Death," Stow had "imparted not only his good Intentions, but best Collections also unto me."[39] Holinshed told a similar story about the first compiler of the *Chronicles*, the printer Reyner Wolfe, whose heirs "willed me to continue" Wolfe's work, thus inspiring Holinshed to finish the *Chronicles* so as "to answer that trust which the deceased reposed in me."[40] A commendatory poem in *Maison Rustique, or The Country Farme. Compiled in the French Tongue by Charles Stevens and John Liebault Doctors of Physicke. And Trans-*

lated into English by Richard Surflet Practitioner in Physicke (1600) explained that Liebault was the "son in law" to Stevens or Estienne, who had died before he could finish his textual "house," but Liebault had "fully ended" what Estienne had "begun" and so was "due the praise of second birth."[41] Without usurping or otherwise disrupting the authorship of his predecessor, a living cowriter could assert his own authorship by taking the place of the dead author as his *heir.*

Coauthorship in Pericles

Pericles begins with a dead author revived. In place of the living dramatist or dramatists whom the text never mentions, the prologue to *Pericles* offers us the medieval English poet John Gower, one of the sources for the play, who declares that he has returned "from ashes" to "sing a song" he claims as "*my* rhymes." Somewhat incongruously, Gower also casts himself in the role of the living partner in a posthumous coauthorship: "I tell you what mine authors say," he declares, without informing us who these older authors might be.[42] This unstable substitution of the single author Gower for unnamed writers living and dead looms larger when we consider the overwhelming evidence that Shakespeare coauthored *Pericles* with Wilkins.[43] By attributing their modern play to a writer who died two hundred years beforehand and who acknowledges his own debts to earlier authors, Shakespeare and Wilkins introduce *Pericles* as only *figuratively* a single authorship.[44]

But why would living writers use the figure of a dead writer to signify their present collaboration? The evidence we can glean of Shakespeare and Wilkins's coauthorial practice in *Pericles* suggests that they drew on the logic of posthumous coauthorship to help them suppose a unity in their contemporaneous coauthorship. As G. E. Bentley notes, the advertised practice of "separate composition" by "individual acts" in Inns of Court plays such as *Gorboduc* became a "common" although not requisite procedure in the commercial Renaissance theater as well.[45] Like their amateur predecessors Sackville and Norton, Wilkins and Shakespeare appear to have divided the composition of *Pericles* this way, with Wilkins writing most of the first two acts and Shakespeare most of the last three.[46] This parceling out of *Pericles* suggests that the play was conceived from the start as a bundle of single authorships. But the conflation of old and new in Gower's opening resurrection gives an interesting cast to the division of labor that made Shakespeare's portion of the play the later work in the order of performance and reading, if not also of composition. When the "ancient" poet Gower claims to sing for these "latter times," he not only combines in one person the earlier and later positions of a posthumous coauthorship: he also figures the later writer as the earlier one *revived*.[47]

The first scene of *Pericles* renews this stress on a continuity between past and present, while also revising the terms of that continuity along lines suggested by the prologue. In place of Gower's ghostly revival, the play now speaks of children and inheritance: Pericles hopes to become "son to great Antiochus" by marrying his daughter, whom the prologue had called his "heir." From this beginning, inheritance becomes a defining concern in the play and indeed in most of the rest of Shakespeare's drama. *Successful* inheritance, that is. During the three or four years before he collaborated on *Pericles*, Shakespeare turned again and again to tragedy—*Othello, King Lear, Macbeth, Antony and Cleopatra, Coriolanus,* and *Timon of Athens.* His inability, or refusal, to try something new during this phase of his career corresponds to a bleakness about the future in the tragedies themselves, where the deaths of the protagonists overwhelm the lives of their children, too.[48] In the last of these tragedies especially, the loss of generationality is tied to protagonists who overvalue their singleness. Thus Coriolanus ends his life boasting of the exceptional prowess that earned him his honorific, not inherited, name—"Alone I did it"—while Timon in his own final scene obsessively proclaims his desire to "be alone." With the revival of comedy in *Pericles*, however, Shakespeare managed to envision a future of "new joy" beyond the single life of his protagonist, which in turn created a future for himself beyond the single genre of tragedy—and the change seems tied to Shakespeare's sense of having inherited the tragicomedy of *Pericles* from Wilkins.[49] As most critics of the play agree, the point in the action of *Pericles* where Shakespeare makes his entrance as an author is a spectacular scene of childbirth.

A spectacularly tragic scene: the mother dies and the child is abandoned.[50] Inheritance—the transmission of resources from one generation to the next—is no simple process in *Pericles*. This is true from the first of Wilkins's scenes as well. Antiochus does not want a son-in-law, or even exactly a daughter, whom his incest makes his "mother" and "wife" as well as "child." The man who chooses to short-circuit generationality this way is not coincidentally a tyrant whose "chiefest" city, Antioch, bears his name and no one else's; he is a demonically powerful version of the imperial single author.[51] At the end of Wilkins's contribution to the play, Pericles finds a better father-in-law in a ruler who is less "absolute" and "peremptory"—words that this second king, Simonides, applies to his daughter Thaisa's love for Pericles. Rather than force Thaisa to "frame" her "will" to his own, Simonides gives his "consent" to a marriage "agreed" upon by husband and wife that also happens to "agree" with Simonides' own desires.[52] For Wilkins, a generational future is made possible by a father who adopts a consensual rather than a conquering or imperialist approach to parenting—like the inveterate coauthor Robert Cleaver, who even in his single-authored tract *The Patrimony of Christian Children* (1624) stresses that the book was written "with the joint consent of Mr. John Dod."[53]

When Shakespeare inherits the script of *Pericles*, however, he underscores a resistance to generationality on the part of the child as well as the father in Wilkins's portion of the play. If Antiochus does not want a son to take his place, Pericles does not want to take the place of his father: instead, he searches for a foster father from whom he can *choose* and *win* his inheritance. Shakespeare insists on the tragic consequences of Pericles' refusal to conceive of himself as determined in any substantial way by his father's authorship of him: after his own child Marina is born, Pericles leaves her with foster parents, once again denying that father and heir have any essential bond between them.[54] Further sustaining Pericles' faith that he alone has authored the "volume" of his "deeds" is the apparent death of his wife in childbirth, which echoes the fate of Antiochus' wife "who died and left a female heir." A servant of Thaisa presents Marina to Pericles as "all that is left living of your queen." By abandoning the baby, Pericles distances himself from more than the identity he shares with the child; he also shuns the parentage he shares with the mother.[55]

Shakespeare joins Wilkins in blaming such tragic threats to generationality on an extreme, Antiochan investment in authorial mastery. But Shakespeare views Wilkins's consensual alternative as too weak to resolve these threats on its own, and too weak, by implication, to legitimate coauthorship in the face of the dominant single-author paradigm. One might guess that Shakespeare attributed this weakness to the awkwardness of Wilkins's having patterned consensual unity on heterosexual marriage: Shakespeare's discomfort with imagining his coauthor as his husband or his wife might explain why the climax of his portion of the play should turn on Pericles' coming to terms with his heir, not his queen.[56] But Pericles' heir is female, like Antiochus'; the gender difference and, thanks to Antiochus' incest, even the sexual complications of the marriage model still pertain in Shakespeare's representation of inheritance. What's more, the renewed bond between father and child does not end up displacing marriage in the play: it leads instead to the mother's return.[57] Like other contemporaries, Wilkins and Shakespeare tried to explicate their coauthorship through fictions of generational and consensual oneness that could assimilate their collective writing to single authorship, but Shakespeare more than Wilkins dramatized heterosexual discordancies in these fictional unions and therefore emphasized the difficulties of conflating one author or one model of authorship with another. More than Wilkins, Shakespeare also stressed the sheer variety of authorial models that *Pericles* evokes. Yet throughout his portion of *Pericles*, collective writing draws strength as a conceptual project from the very tensions that make the different theories of authorship in the play impossible to subsume under the "supremacy" of one hegemonic paradigm.[58] Each model as *Pericles* dramatizes them—the imperialist paradigm, which suppresses all but one author; the consensual paradigm, which makes one mind and judgment of two authors; and the generational paradigm, which treats the new author as the resurrected image of the old—possesses a certain narrative and cultural plausibility that, in concert with the plausibility of the other models, denies "absolute" power to any one of them.

If Shakespeare in the first of his romances thus outlined the possible *disintegration* of single authorship as a way to conceive of playwriting, he also acknowledged that coauthorship lacked the power to "contend" successfully against single authorship as a conceptual model and therefore had to rely on the reigning paradigm for its own intelligibility. After all, the first and last words in the play belong to Gower and Gower alone. Shakespeare seems to have felt that the best face to put on this dependency was to present it as a compromise. When, for instance, in the final movement of Shakespeare's contribution to *Pericles* the self-isolated father embraces his daughter as "thou that beget'st him that did thee beget," the terms of their reunion suggest how the generational theory of coauthorship could be understood as striking a balance between singleness and multiplicity. Rather than displace one another or else become as one, Wilkins and Shakespeare could instead regard each other as both progenitor and heir: even if one coauthor originated the script, the other might seem in the end to have developed issues from the script that the first coauthor neither recognized nor anticipated there. The last scene of *Pericles* forecasts how a similar balance between single and multiple authorship could be negotiated along consensual lines as well. Not until this final scene, when Shakespeare completes Wilkins's script, do Pericles and Thaisa ever jointly see their daughter. Their joyful response to her seems to hold the promise that each cowriter of *Pericles* could in the end acknowledge the authorial role of the other, while still legitimately claiming the "issue" of their collective enterprise as "mine own."[59]

Coauthorship in Two Noble Kinsmen

Children saved from death and in the process saving at least one of their parents figure in all three of the romances to follow *Pericles.* "Is not this boy reviv'd from death?" Belarius marvels in *Cymbeline* when he sees Imogen-Fidele again, anticipating the Soothsayer's propitious reading of Jupiter's oracle: "The lofty cedar, royal Cymbeline, / Personates thee; and thy lopp'd branches point / Thy two sons forth; who, by Belarius stol'n, / For many years thought dead, are now reviv'd, / To the majestic cedar join'd, whose issue / Promises Britain peace and plenty."[60] So in *The Winter's Tale* are Leontes and Hermione restored to life when they learn that their "heir" and "issue" lives, and in *The Tempest* Alonso receives a gift of "second life" when he discovers that his son lives, too.[61] But Shakespeare wrote these romances of revival on his own. Characteristically, he internalized the dynamics of coauthorship as *Pericles* had outlined them and fashioned his last great plays as a kind of self-succession, where the tragedies are recapitulated only to give way to comic endings marked by a new accord between older and younger generations.

After the romances, however, Shakespeare returned to coauthorship once more, and this time he committed himself so thoroughly to the project that he wrote what appear to have been his last three plays—*Henry VIII,* the lost *Cardenio,* and *Two Noble Kinsmen*—with the same coauthor, John Fletcher. Traditionally, these final coauthorships have been treated as a passing of the torch from Shakespeare to the new premier dramatist for his acting company. It certainly would have been conventional for Shakespeare and Fletcher to understand their theatrical partnership in generational terms, as we have seen. Fletcher was one of many a promising author whom Jonson was "proud to call . . . *Son,*" and Jonson's various adopted children were equally delighted to present themselves as his heirs: in the playwright Thomas Randolph's "Eclogue to Master Jonson" (c. 1632), for instance, Randolph has the Jonson surrogate Tityrus declare to Randolph's proxy Damon, "I meant to thee/Of all the sons I have, by legacy/To have bequeath'd my pipe."[62] The collegial ethos of the acting companies encouraged a generational as well as fraternal sense of connection between playwrights. One telling case in point is the actor-playwright Nathan Field, who began his theatrical career as a child actor. Jonson (1617) referred to Field as his "scholar" or student; the playwright George Chapman (1612) called Field his "Loved Son"; and in two surviving letters to the theatrical impresario Philip Henslowe, written in the same years as Shakespeare and Fletcher's plays, Field addressed his employer as "Father Hinchlow" while styling himself Henslowe's "loving and obedient Son."[63]

Shakespeare, too, had followers who proudly proclaimed themselves his sons. John Aubrey (c. 1681) reports with some amazement how the playwright William Davenant liked to tell friends "over a glass of wine" that he not only "writ with the very same spirit that did Shakespeare" but was actually Shakespeare's illegitimate son. Shakespeare himself repeatedly expressed his ambition to "will" his literary talent to the world. His dedicatory epistle to Southampton calls *Venus and Adonis* "the first heir of my invention," and in the sonnets the speaker replaces his initial demand that the young man generate an heir with his assurance that the man will forever be preserved in the "eternal lines" of the speaker's poetry.[64] In *Pericles*, however, Shakespeare questions generational models that portray creative power as flowing in one direction only, from old to young, and the Shakespeare and Fletcher play *Two Noble Kinsmen* continues the search begun in *Pericles* for alternative conceptualizations of inheritance. The main plot concerns two characters, the Theban princes Arcite and Palamon, who in typical Shakespearean fashion are easily confusable with one another: indeed, the word *twin* occurs more often in this play than in any other by Shakespeare. Yet Arcite and Palamon speak of each other as more than mirror images. In act 2 of the play, believing themselves to be imprisoned for life in an Athenian jail, they first lament that they will never father any "issue" to carry on their legacy—"No figures of ourselves shall we ev'r see/To glad our age"—but then quickly decide to adopt a more positive outlook on the straits they are in. Echoing the recursive, coauthorial representation of inheritance in *Pericles,* Arcite declares that "here being thus together,/We are an endless mine to one another": "we are father, friends, acquaintance;/We are, in one another, families:/I am your heir, and you are mine." In *Pericles,* of course, the mutual heirs were parent and child, and the two friends of *Two Noble Kinsmen* also share a biological tie as cousins. But the inheritance these friends envision is not so readily naturalized as the generational relationship in *Pericles.* "Dearer in love than blood," Palamon and Arcite think of each other as spiritual brothers, as "twins of honor."[65] More than the father and daughter of *Pericles,* in other words, the mutual heirs of *Two Noble Kinsmen* resemble the coauthors who devised them.

Unfortunately, the utopian solidarity of Palamon and Arcite is so short-lived that it fails to survive the scene in which the two friends first conceive of each other as co-inheritors. The pretext for their falling out is the "matchless beauty" of Emilia, which incites Palamon and Arcite to compete for the title of "the worthiest" to marry her. Yet the desire to stand out as matchless, to "exceed in all," pervades the world of the play, making twinship itself an incitement to a violence that would differentiate one noble kinsman from the other. Merely as a kind of opening gambit can Palamon and Arcite, "a pair of absolute men," "the only doers," wed their mutuality to the demand for singularity in Athens—the "only" place, says Arcite, dreamily mingling Emilia and excellence, where "fair-ey'd honor" dwells.[66] Historicists treat single authorship in the theater as driving a wedge between otherwise loving collaborators, but Renaissance discourse on the unanimity of cowriters can just as easily be read as a mystification of the potentiality for rivalry and conflict within joint authorship. If Shakespeare and Fletcher imagined Palamon and Arcite as "figures of ourselves," then they must also have seen their partnership as, at least to some degree, a battle for artistic supremacy.[67]

And, indeed, an author's wish to appear "the only star to shine" constitutes the very first expression of competitiveness in the play. Acknowledging that Chaucer was the "noble breeder" of the "story" to be dramatized, the Prologue of *Two Noble Kinsmen* worries that the play will fall so far "below his art" that Chaucer will "cry from under ground, 'O, fan/From me the witless chaff of such a writer/That blasts my bays.'" The Prologue's modest disclaimer of any desire to emulate Chaucer—"we" are too "weak" "to aspire" so high—is undercut by similar protestations of unworthiness later on, as Palamon and Arcite prepare to vanquish each other.[68] Yet Chaucer counts as a less immediate rival for the coauthors of *Two Noble Kinsmen* than each coauthor represents in regard to the other. Various stylistic analyses of the play have convincingly demonstrated that Shakespeare and Fletcher practiced a more complex form of coauthorship in *Two Noble Kinsmen* than Shakespeare and Wilkins did in *Pericles:* instead of giving one writer the first half of the play and the other writer the second, Shakespeare and Fletcher appear to have traded the writing of *Two Noble Kinsmen* back and forth, generating a script in which "the work of the two playwrights is tightly interlaced."[69] This decision to interweave their writing might seem to suggest the confidence of both coauthors in a shared purpose and perhaps even a shared ability. But it can also suggest the desire of both continually to outdo each other, to show up the other by a humiliating contrast of talent. "Lord, the diff'rence of men!" exclaims one character at the end of what most critics presume is Shakespeare's first portion of writing, just before Shakespeare hands his pen to Fletcher.[70]

The play itself offers as nearly straightforward a commentary as it can on this coauthorial "match" when Duke Theseus, having just witnessed the climactic battle between Palamon and Arcite, recalls how he once heard

Two emulous Philomels beat the ear o'th'night
With their contentious throats, now one the higher,
Anon the other, then again the first,

> And by and by out-breasted, that the sense
> Could not be judge between 'em.[71]

The speech underscores a basic Girardian paradox in the competition between Palamon and Arcite: that their mutual desire to differentiate themselves from the other amounts to a further likeness "between 'em." But the Philomel analogy only goes so far. Theseus encountered the birds at night, when nothing but their singing was available to "sense"; Emilia can only long for a "darkness" that would likewise cover Palamon and Arcite and so shield them from harm.[72] More important, the birds may have seemed equally matched in the end, but not Palamon and Arcite: "So it far'd / Good space between these kinsmen," Theseus continues, "till heavens did / Make hardly one the winner." The play's opening figure of rival authors intermixed as wheat with chaff tacitly admits that distinguishing between two writers on the basis of their poetry is practically more difficult than distinguishing between two embodied fighters or lovers. Perhaps this difference is the point: that the diffusive medium of poetry allows authors to compete nonviolently, which makes them capable of working for the good of one another, elevating each other to a sublime level of excellence. But Theseus' comparison implies that so happy an ending to contention exacts a cost: if writers can blend in ways that fighters cannot, that is because the writers are more like nightingales than warriors, because they lack any phallic means for differentiation, because they have surrendered their masculine vigor.[73]

"If we let fall the nobleness of this": from the very start of the play, the coauthors worry about their virility in comparison to a proven breeder. Since the breeder in question, Chaucer, was himself a "poet," writing alone cannot be the source of the effeminacy that troubles them. The play's first scene, with its tale of three fallen kings, identifies a different cause for concern. Having heard from the wives of these kings how the Theban Creon has killed their husbands and then denied them burial, Theseus recoils from the image of rotting corpses and finds himself recalling instead the matchless beauty of one queen at her marriage—but then the rot returns, and he thinks of the queen's "wheaten wreath" as now "thresh'd" and "blasted": "O grief and time,/Fearful consumers," he exclaims, "you will all devour!"[74] Less than a hundred lines after the playwrights worried about ruining Chaucer's bays, the destroyer is no longer posthumous revision but grief and time, and the wheat is fanned not to winnow it from chaff but to ready it for the fire. The difference maker, from the Prologue to the first scene, is Theseus' association of falling with aging.

Commentators on *Two Noble Kinsmen* have long noted the play's obsession with, and revulsion from, "the loathsome misery of age." Another side of the optimism that Palamon and Arcite briefly float in prison is the fantasy that "the loving gods found this place for us" so that the two friends would not die as "the great ones" in Thebes do, as "ill old men, unwept," with their only "epitaphs, the people's curses."[75] Living vicariously through Palamon and Arcite would have counted as a similar fantasy of escape for at least one of their creators. Shakespeare was hardly Fletcher's twin in age: fifteen years older than his writing partner, Shakespeare was nearly a generation separated from him. If he viewed the friendship of Palamon and Arcite as a fiction for his coauthorship with Fletcher, then there would seem to have been something Antiochan or quasi-incestuous about his desire to revive himself by coopting the relative youth of his ostensible heir.

But was he revived? The usual attribution of the play's final scenes to Shakespeare makes the older of the two playwrights the last man standing at the end of the play, like Palamon, and by analogy to Palamon's inheritance of Emilia from the dying Arcite, the older playwright, oddly, not the younger, inherits the prize of matchless beauty for which the two have contended.[76] Yet the tone of these closing scenes is almost entirely tragic. In the final speech of the play, which may have been Shakespeare's final piece of playwriting, Theseus declares that "the victor has the loss." What could Shakespeare have thought he lost by surviving? Perhaps he decided that the competition between coauthors was simply not winnable. After all, Shakespeare did not have to prove himself: he was the chief dramatist of the King's Men, and thus any labor to "distinguish" his writing from his junior colleague's might have seemed to argue a "pitiful . . . ambition," as Shakespeare's eighteenth-century editor George Steevens (1780) maintained. Or if Shakespeare succeeded in proving that Fletcher was the lesser writer, then Fletcher's noticeably weaker contributions might drag down the play, and Shakespeare with it; the general consensus of critics is that *Two Noble Kinsmen* does indeed represent a considerable falling off from the standard that Shakespeare had set for himself in his previous late plays, *The Winter's Tale* and *The Tempest.* Or perhaps Shakespeare concluded that, by competing with Fletcher, he had only accentuated their difference in age rather than overcome it. This, too, is a familiar judgment on *Two Noble Kinsmen:* "The Fletcherian parts of the play," writes Theodore Spencer (1939), "are first-rate theater; their contrasts and conflicts make an immediate and successful impression. The Shakespearean parts, on the other hand, are static, and though with splendor, stiff. . . . Their style is the style of old age, and their imagery is an old man's imagery."[77]

Ideally, we are reminded at the start of *Two Noble Kinsmen,* great art carries the promise of everlasting youth: in some unspecified "there," the Prologue assures us, Chaucer's story "lives," "constant to eternity." Several characters in *Two Noble Kinsmen* hope to find a similarly rewarding eternity for themselves: they dream, like Palamon and Arcite in prison, "of another world and a better." But the afterlife of the author-figure Philomel was nothing more glorious than metamorphosis into a bird, and as soon as the Prologue speaks of reviving Chaucer's story, its vision of a literary eternity shrinks to the dead Chaucer's crying "from under ground," where he amounts to nothing more than "bones." In the next scene, these bones reappear above ground, as the "mortal loathsomeness" of the kings' unburied corpses. And toward the end of the play Shakespeare and Fletcher offer a grotesque image of a corpse resurrected into a kind of living death. When Gower returned from ashes in *Pericles,* it was to shed a genial glow over an ultimately joyful story of rebirth; but when

Venus in *Two Noble Kinsmen* uses her power "to put life into dust," she inspires a "man/Of eighty winters" to marry "a lass of fourteen," even though

> the aged cramp
> Had screw'd his square foot round,
> The gout had knit his fingers into knots,
> Torturing convulsions from his globy eyes
> Had almost drawn their spheres, that what was life
> In him seem'd torture.[78]

Palamon is the one who describes this twisted "anatomy" of a man to us. From his first words in the play, the "strange ruins" and "decays" of age have haunted him as a nightmare realization of an afterlife. So it is that when facing execution after his loss to Arcite, Palamon finds comfort in the thought that he will die young: "There's many a man alive that hath outliv'd/The love o'th'people, yea, i'th'self-same state/Stands many a father with his child." By the end of the same scene, however, Arcite is the one who has gone to seek "Elysium," while Palamon—"O miserable end of our alliance!"—outlives him.[79]

Survival without revival: that is how Spencer conceives of the lifelessness that disturbs him in Shakespeare's portions of *Two Noble Kinsmen*. "It is the writing of a man who has come out on the other side of human experience, and who, in looking back, can no longer be interested in what he has once seen so vividly and so passionately felt."[80] Notoriously, the play does indeed recapitulate one of Shakespeare's earlier triumphs in a distinctly minor mode. Fletcher and Shakespeare chose to resuscitate Ophelia in the figure of the Jailer's Daughter and then devise a new, comic ending to her tragedy: although the Jailer's Daughter goes mad from unrequited love for Palamon, she is saved from drowning by another man. But the daughter never recovers her senses in the play, and she never marries Palamon: instead, the man who rescued her from death, the bourgeois "Wooer" she rejected in favor of Palamon, ends up disguising himself as her beloved "prince," and she is fooled into accepting the substitute.[81]

If Shakespeare's single-authored romances suggest that he internalized the lessons of coauthorship in *Pericles,* generating a new style of playwriting from a career he came to see himself as inheriting rather than extending, *Two Noble Kinsmen* repeatedly raises the ghost of a thought that Shakespeare could inherit from himself only by outliving himself—having become "a mere dull shadow" of the man he was.[82]

Epilogue

Did Shakespeare see himself as one of a kind? Throughout this book I've tried to underscore the complexity of his response to such questions. His popularity, his prestige, his brilliance as a playwright: these were undeniable distinctions, but he seems to have believed that they all depended on his willingness to surrender any claim to lofty superiority. He does not appear to have been a particularly loose or licentious man, as Greene and Marlowe were. Legend has it that he shunned "debauched" company.[1] What records we possess suggest that he never spent time in prison, as Marlowe and so many other of his chief rivals did, among them Kyd, Chapman, Dekker, Middleton, and Jonson. And we know for a certainty that he both sought and attained the rank of a gentleman. Yet he never disowned mass entertainment for some more high-toned or exclusive pursuit. Even in the midst of his greatest triumphs, he returned again and again to a dramaturgy that could embrace not only the collaborativeness of theater work but its vulgar commonness as well.

His ambition required range. From his earliest days as a playwright he had envisioned an aristocratic hero who could best establish his "unrivall'd merit" in "wild" rather than courtly company, as a "king" of outlaws.[2] But this professionally encouraged obsession with range meant that Shakespeare could no more reject the high than the low. In his most famous staging of dramatic authorship, which also seems to have been his last single-authored play, Shakespeare characteristically distanced himself from an elitist perspective on his playwriting by first engaging that perspective as intensely as he could. The playwright in *The Tempest* (1611) is a fantasmatic version of the imperial literary author: a former "prince of power," Prospero has achieved even greater power as a sorcerer by isolating himself on a deserted island with his books. True, Prospero is not entirely alone: he has an obedient daughter, Miranda, and a slave, Caliban, as well as spirits that he has also enslaved. Through his magic, he also maroons a boatload of his enemies on the island and quickly forces them to join the island's other inhabitants in enacting various plays he has created for them. These astonishing shows lead one castaway to exclaim, "Now I will believe / That . . . in Arabia / There is one tree, the phoenix' throne, one phoenix / At this hour reigning." According to fable, as George Hakewill explained in 1627, there is only "one" phoenix "at a time in the world." Prospero, himself "so rare and wonder'd," is the phoenix of his island, and the only shake-scene reigning there, with a control over his actors as absolute as that of a writer over his characters.[3]

Yet Prospero is not exactly the self-portrait of Shakespeare that scholars have generally traced in him. For much of *The Tempest* he more closely resembles Ben Jonson, or at least the caricatures of Jonson in other plays of the time.[4] Like the elitist Jonsonian playwright Chrisoganus in *Histrio-Mastix*, for example, Prospero is "rapt in secret studies," and like Jonson himself he draws on his classical erudition to craft a learned masque for a royal audience (Shakespeare, so far as we know, never wrote a court masque). But Prospero's attitude toward his "art" changes over the course of *The Tempest*.[5] Early in the play he reveals to Miranda that he was once duke of Milan, and yet he was so "dedicated / To closeness, and the bettering of my mind" that he asked his brother Antonio to execute "th' outward face of royalty" while he confined himself to "volumes" that he continues to

"prize above my dukedom." The brother betrayed him: "to have
no screen between this part he play'd / And him he play'd it for,"
Antonio deposed Prospero, actualizing Prospero's virtual exile
from his dukedom by setting him adrift at sea with his daughter
and his books. Eventually Prospero landed in another dream-
like analogue to his study, the island where he has now learned
how to tyrannize over those who play the parts he assigns them.
Yet Prospero's daughter has since come of age, and Prospero has
decided that he must allow her to act for herself. The result is
a profound transformation in his dramaturgy. Instead of using
the "spirits" he controls to "enact" his "fancies," he incorporates
humans in his shows; he even joins the action; and he kenotically
sacrifices his godlike power over his actors in order to promote a
more worldly and consensual theater, premised on the spectacle
of his daughter's love for his enemy's son. No longer phoenix-
like, "one of a kind," as Hakewill says, Prospero now conceives of
himself as "one of *their* kind."[6]

Until the epilogue, it seems. There we find that the newly
acting author Prospero has left the fellowship he has gathered
together and freely joined and now stands alone, like the older
figure of the dramatist as a commentator carefully segregated
from the players. In breaking away from his island society, however, Prospero has turned to address the even larger fellowship of
his audience:

> Now my charms are all o'erthrown,
> And what strength I have's mine own,
> Which is most faint. Now 'tis true,
> I must here be confin'd by you,
> Or sent to Naples. Let me not,
> Since I have my dukedom got,
> And pardon'd the deceiver, dwell
> In this island by your spell,
> But release me from my bands
> With the help of your good hands.
> Gentle breath of yours my sails
> Must fill, or else my project fails,

> Which was to please. Now I want
> Spirits to enforce, art to enchant,
> And my ending is despair,
> Unless I be reliev'd by prayer,
> Which pierces so, that it assaults
> Mercy itself, and frees all faults.
> As you from crimes would pardon'd be,
> Let your indulgence set me free.

Now Prospero treats his solitariness as a measure of the power in his spectators, assuring them that his "strength" is "most faint" without their aid and approval. Other contemporary dramatists similarly humbled themselves before their audiences. In the epilogue to *Sophonisba* (1606), for example, John Marston makes a kingly character "change" his "person" so that he can "hither bear / Another's voice"—the author's—"with a phrase as weak / As his deserts," who "craves" rather than "commands /. . . the justice of your hands," and "with constant modesty . . . doth submit, / To all."[7] Prospero takes this pose of humility considerably further than Marston does. "Mercy," not "justice," is his theme: to win the applause of his audience, he decides that he must not merely "submit" to them but also publicly confess to "crimes."

There are limits to the sacrifices that Prospero is willing to make at the end of *The Tempest*, however. Although he gives away a daughter whom he describes as "a third of mine own life," he gains something by the loss: the singleness he has always coveted. Indeed, he makes clear to Miranda and her fiancé that, once they all return to Italy, he expects them to take up residence in a different city than his own. This continuing reclusiveness highlights a second, more abstract way in which Prospero retains his commitment to a world that he alone defines. Several other fathers in Shakespeare's romances send a child away to distance themselves from the evidence that the child is "like" them, that as "the whole matter / And copy of the father," she has inherited their identity. Prospero seems equally troubled by the thought of inheritance: though he speaks repeatedly of his impending death, he never mentions any legacy he intends to leave or bequest he intends to make. His resistance to imagining a future that has no Prospero in it comes clearest in his otherwise selfless sacrifice of his magical powers. While he may surrender his daughter to another, he never surrenders his *art* to another. Rather than bequeath it, he buries it: "I'll break my staff,/Bury it certain fadoms in the earth,/And deeper than did ever plummet sound/I'll drown my book."[8]

But how *could* Prospero leave his art to anyone if, as the epilogue to *The Tempest* suggests, he now views it as a crime? The problem was not peculiar to Prospero, or to Shakespeare. On his deathbed, the Shakespeare-hating Greene disowned all the "vain fantasies" that had "famoused" him as a writer, asking the readers of his *Groats-worth of Witte* to "gather my follies altogether; and as ye would deal with so many parricides, cast them into the fire." Yet Greene's envy-ridden attack on Shakespeare in the *Groats-worth* makes his call for fire sound considerably more bitter than penitent. In the letter about Shakespeare that Greene addresses to three fellow playwrights, he seems to betray his own resistance to imagining a future with no Greene in it when he urges his friends and rivals to look where his profligacy has left him and then to write no more: "O that I might entreat your rare wits to be employed in more profitable courses: and let those Apes [viz., Shakespeare and his fellow players] imitate your past excellence, and never more acquaint them with your admired inventions." What Greene refuses to envision in his letter is any future theatrical success for his rivals; to save them from his dismal fate is also to forestall the possibility that any of them might ever prove a better dramatist than Greene himself. As for "new-comers," Greene predicts with similar wishfulness that the actors "will drive the best minded to despise them" and "make a jest" of the rest.[9]

For all its seeming care to pass on the tragic lesson of his life, *Greene's Groats-worth* is a tale of legacies either hoarded, lost, stolen, or else revealed as worthless. At the start, Greene tells us that his father was a usurer who "had gathered from many to bestow upon one," but the "one" he chose was not Greene, his

"fool" of an "eldest son," to whom the father bequeathed nothing more than "an old groat, (being the stock I first began with)
wherewith I wish him to buy a groats-worth of wit." Greene may
have gone on to attain a success in the theater that his father
could never have imagined, but his debaucheries make him end
where he began, "having but one groat left (the just proportion
of his Father's Legacy)." In a letter to his wife that concludes the
Groats-worth, Greene surprisingly reveals that he has fathered a
son who "is yet Greene, and may grow straight, if he be carefully
tended," but the author immediately labors to undo this patrimony, first by apologizing that "after so long waste" he has added
to his wife's burdens, and then by begging his wife to consider
that the child is more hers than his, "the fruit of thy womb, in
whose face regard not the Father's fault so much, as thy own
perfections." In the opening letter to the *Groats-worth*, Greene
had already expressed the fear that he would not survive to father
his pamphlet, which would therefore "be thrust into the world"
"like an Embrion without shape." The letter to his rivals replaces
an anxious or penitent account of Greene's failure to pass on a
legacy with an aggressive shifting of the blame to Shakespeare
and the players for having plucked Greene's theatrical "feathers"
from him. In every case, Greene turns his prodigality into an
argument that the "arch-playmaking" author has left no recog-
nizable heir.[10]

Further attempting to persuade his rivals that they should
"spend their wits" in some "better exercise" than "making plays,"
Greene reminds them that they are no less wasteful than he: "I
know the best husband of you all will never prove an Usurer."
The exception, of course, is Shakespeare, a hoarder in more ways
than in his refusal to share his money with playwrights in dis-
tress. Having ruined Greene's Prospero-like fantasy that actors
are merely the "puppets" of the author and that theatrical agency
belongs to the dramatist alone, Shakespeare as actor-author had
also (in Greene's mind) claimed a more "absolute" purchase on
the "scene" than any mere dramatist could possess—like another
actor-author earlier in the *Groats-worth* who declares that he

was "absolute Interpreter to the puppets" for a time and has now grown so wealthy in the theater business that his "very share in playing apparel will not be sold for two hundred pounds."[11] Where the literary dramatist wastes his powers on a medium that is beneath him, the theatrical professional as Greene imagines him enhances his powers by putting all the properties of the theater to use.

Shakespeare did indeed prove thrifty enough—even, to some critics, usurious enough—to pass on a substantial estate to his own daughters.[12] But how willingly, Prospero's and Greene's examples prompt us to ask, did he let it go? The will that Shakespeare drew up shortly before his death, with all its interlineations and strikeouts—so unlike the author who supposedly "never blotted out line"—indicates at the very least a certain hastiness or ambivalence in making provisions for his heirs. And his continued theatrical activity after the apparent farewell of *The Tempest* suggests that he found it difficult to step aside artistically as well.[13] Late in Jonson's life, several of his adopted "sons" accused him of a similar reluctance to cede his theatrical laurels to another playwright: "For shame," Nicholas Oldisworth chided Jonson in 1629, "engross not Age,/But now, thy fifth Act's ended, leave the stage."[14] "For shame": no matter how celebrated the dramatist or how princely his ambitions, his motives for playwriting could never entirely cease to appear disgraceful, even to himself. Though he repeatedly criticized Jonson for lording it over his fellow entertainers, Shakespeare the company man seems to have worried that he was not above regarding himself as an irreplaceable member of the company. When the sonnets urge a beloved to abandon "singleness" and "breed another thee," they have an element of self-address in them, warning their author not to be, as it were, "self-Will'd" only, a "glutton," "niggard," or "usurer" of his "treasure." Old Hamlet may have bred a young Hamlet, but the son cannot take the place of the father, who will not even stay dead. So Lear gives "all" to his daughters while still clinging to a kind of posthumous kingship.[15]

After Shakespeare's death, some of his own disciples complained that he had not better provided for them. At times their grievances sound like little more than conventional exaggeration, as when Leonard Digges in the First Folio declares that Shakespeare has left the stage "bankrupt." But John Dryden, writing four decades later, offers a more deliberate as well as resentful assessment. While he praises "the incomparable *Shakespeare*" in his *Essay of Dramatick Poesie* (1668) as "the man who of all Modern, and perhaps Ancient Poets, had the largest and most comprehensive soul," Dryden also insists that this inclusiveness had a cost. He maintains that Shakespeare, in league with his lesser but still prodigious "Rivals" Jonson and Fletcher, *exhausted* the resources of the stage: "We acknowledge them our Fathers in wit, but they have ruin'd their Estates themselves before they came to their children's hands." "We shall never equal them," Dryden continues in the vein of *Lear*'s final lines—but then "they could never equal themselves, were they to rise and write again."[16]

Notes

1. Both Francis Barker in his *Tremulous Private Body* (1984) and Catherine Belsey in her *Subject of Tragedy* (1985) traced the beginnings of modern subjectivity to a very specific moment in one Shakespeare play: the speech in act 1, scene 2 of *Hamlet* where the title character declares, "I have that within which passes show." In this line, according to Barker, "Hamlet utters . . . a first demand for the modern subject" (*Tremulous*, 32), while Belsey likewise maintained that the line begins "to define an interiority as the origin of meaning and action, a human subject as agent" (*Subject*, 42). For decisive critiques of these claims, see Aers, "Whisper"; and Maus, *Inwardness*. In *Shakespeare's Perjured Eye* (1986), Joel Fineman more specifically argued that "in his sonnets Shakespeare invents a genuinely new *poetic* subjectivity," which became "the governing model for subjectivity *in literature* after Shakespeare" (1 and 299; my emphases). For a sensible but nonetheless reductive critique, see Adams, "New Bards for Old," and his later "Reply to Fineman." As I will discuss at greater length in chapter 2, some historians of authorship also came to view *Hamlet* as the start of something new, although they shifted the dividing line between premodern and modern conceptions of agency to act 3, scene 2, where the title character demands that actors "speak no more than is set down for them."

2. Fynes Moryson (1617), in Hughes, ed., *Shakespeare's Europe*, 476; Gurr, *Playgoing*, 2.

3. Hall, *Virgidemiarum,* 1.3.13–18.

4. Shakespeare, *Mr. William Shakespeares Comedies, Histories, & Tragedies* [henceforth *FF* (for First Folio)], A3r (my emphasis), in Shakespeare, *The Riverside Shakespeare,* 95. For a fascinating exploration of the relation between plays and jury trials in the English Renaissance, see Lorna Hutson's *Invention of Suspicion.*

5. Quoted in Beal, "Massinger," 199; Dekker, *If It Be Not Good,* prol. 1–3; Middleton, *No Wit,* prol.1–2 (I retain the capitalization from the 1657 first edition); Day, *Isle of Guls,* prol. 140–42.

6. Day, *Isle of Guls,* prol. 138–39; Sir Edward Hoby to Sir Thomas Edmondes, 7 March 1606, quoted in *ES,* 3:286. For the satire in Day's play, see Burns, ed., *Isle of Guls,* 8–37.

7. Hall, *Virgidemiarum,* 1.3.11; *Henslowe Papers,* 69; Rowlands, *Letting,* A3r; Donne, Satire 2.13–14.

8. Carson, *Companion,* 64.

9. Hall, *Virgidemiarum,* 1.3.42–43, 1.1.7–8, 1.3.57–58.

10. *1 Henry IV* 2.4.5–6 and 18; *1 Henry IV* 3.2.41, 59, 150, and 88.

INTRODUCTION

1. Bloom, *Western,* 24 and 3.

2. Marcus, *Puzzling Shakespeare,* 28; Marcus does cite Shakespeare's "complicity" in this dream of transcendence (40–42) . See Dobson, *Making;* de Grazia, *Shakespeare;* Kastan, *Shakespeare;* Orgel, *Authentic* and *Imagining;* Stallybrass and White, *Politics;* Helgerson, *Forms;* Masten, *Textual;* and Erne, *Shakespeare.*

3. Masten, *Textual,* 10. Douglas Brooks similarly characterizes Shakespeare as a ghost who "continues to haunt our understanding of dramatic authorship" (*From Playhouse,* 4).

4. Cf. Stephen Greenblatt in his general introduction to *The Norton Shakespeare:* "It is not necessary to choose between an account of Shakespeare as the scion of a particular culture and an account of him as a universal genius who created works that continually renew themselves across national and generational divides" (2).

5. Bloom, *Western,* 38. Bloom argues that "the power to originate is an individual gift, present in all eras but evidently greatly encouraged by particular contexts" (44). If it makes sense to study the "rival playwrights" from whom "Shakespeare undoubtedly received provocation" (26), then why not widen the picture and study more of the context too?

6. Bloom, *Western,* 24.

7. Orgel, "What," 1; Orgel, *Imagining*, 1.

8. Orgel, "What," 1; Wall, "Dramatic Authorship," 2. Cf. Brooks: "the early modern London playhouse was a rather busy place that had no space for the 'coming into being' of the notion of 'author'" (*From Playhouse*, 17).

9. In *Dramatists and Their Manuscripts in the Age of Shakespeare, Jonson, Middleton and Heywood* (2006), Grace Ioppolo makes the case that a script "could return to the author at any or all stages of transmission: after the scribe had copied it; after a censor had licensed it; after the book-keeper had prepared the company book; after its rehearsal and performance; before one or more later revivals; and after it was printed" (99).

10. Nashe, *Works*, 5.29–33. After the performance of Chapman's two *Byron* tragedies in 1608, the French ambassador claimed that three "comédiens" were jailed at his request, "mais le principal qui est le compositeur eschapa" (*ES*, 3.257). Similarly, after the performance of Middleton's *A Game at Chess* in 1624, King James ordered the Privy Council to "call before you as well the Poet, that made the comedy, as the Comedians that acted it" (*JCS*, 4.872) and "to find out the original root of this offence, whether it sprang from the Poet, Players, or both" (875–76).

11. Cox and Kastan, "Introduction," 5, 2, 5.

12. Greenblatt, "Foreword," xiii-xiv; Cox and Kastan, "Introduction," 4.

13. Cox and Kastan, "Introduction," 5 (my emphasis), 4; Kastan, "Shakespeare," 5.

14. Michael Bristol offers a similar critique in *Big-time Shakespeare:* "The argument that works are the manifestations of discursive formations correctly insists that the institutional background against which artistic activity takes place must be specified in any historically cogent account of human creativity. However, if taken literally this idea is misleading. The flat statement that works are actually *produced* by discursive formations substitutes the vague operations of a ghostly metaphysical entity for more literal-minded notions of singular agency and purposive verbal activity" (53).

15. Cox and Kastan, "Introduction," 4, 2; Blayney, "Publication of Playbooks," 388.

16. Cox and Kastan, "Introduction," 5, 2. Cox and Kastan use the term *collaboration* in revealingly different ways. Usually, they mean it

to designate a general property of all work in "the collaborative econo-mies" (5) of the theater. But in the sentence I just quoted, where they turn their attention to playwriting in particular, they identify "collabo-rators" as a special set, only one among the many groups that "have a hand in shaping the text" (2). This special sense of collaboration as "co-authorship" is buried in the general sense of collaboration as "dramatic activity." Masten acknowledges that his own usages of "'collaboration' may risk an excessive broadening of the term" (*Textual*, 15), but he in-variably downplays the risk. Stallybrass more straightforwardly claims that "collaboration . . . in the broad and the narrow sense, was the norm" in the creation of playscripts ("Shakespeare," 597).

Production is another term that helps historicists conflate writing and performance, as when Gregory Chaplin claims that "collabora-tion was the dominant mode of play *production* in late sixteenth- and early seventeenth-century England" ("'Divided,'" 58; my emphasis), or Wendy Wall that "Renaissance plays were *produced* collaboratively un-der the auspices of theater companies rather than individual writers" ("Authorship," 65; my emphasis).

17. Cox and Kastan, "Introduction," 2.

18. Barthes, "Death," 1466–68; Cox and Kastan, "Introduction," 4.

19. Foucault, "What," 148–49.

20. As Brooks notes, "it would be difficult to overestimate the impact these essays by Barthes and Foucault, as well as the critical controversy they sparked, have had on a range of disciplines" (*From Playhouse*, 3). For superb Foucaldian accounts of authorship, see Mark Rose, *Authors and Owners* (1993); as well as Joseph Loewenstein, *Author's Due* (2002) and *Ben Jonson* (2002).

21. Burckhardt, *Civilization*, 1.143; Barthes, "Death," 1466.

22. Meres, *Palladis*, 280r. Incidentally, it is not often noted that Meres was a clergyman and that all his other publications besides the *Palladis* were devotional.

23. Masten, "Playwrighting," 368 (my emphasis); *Textual*,14, 13, 4, 102, 113; "Playwrighting," 370; *Textual*, 10.

24. McMillin, "Professional," 232; McGuire, "Collaboration," 541–42. See also Wendy Wall's anthology contributions, "Authorship and the Material Conditions of Writing," in *The Cambridge Companion to Eng-lish Literature 1500–1600* (2000); and "Dramatic Authorship and Print," in *Early Modern English Drama: A Critical Companion* (2006).

25. Stallybrass, "Shakespeare," 601, 611 (my emphasis); cf. de Grazia, *Shakespeare,* 7ff.

26. Masten, *Textual,* 13; Bentley, *PD,* 199. Cf. Masten, *Textual,* 14; and Masten, "Playwrighting," 357.

27. Nicholas Radel makes the same point in his 2001 review of *Textual Intercourse.* To question whether single or collective writing ever dominated theatrical practice is not to deny, however, that one mode of writing might have dominated dramatic *theory.*

28. *PD,* 199; Gurr, *Shakespearian,* 93 and 102; Carson, *Companion,* 57–58.

29. Kastan, *Shakespeare,* 33; Erne, *Shakespeare,* 45 and 47; Loewenstein, *Author's Due,* 86 and 24. Loewenstein's account of growing authorial prestige should not be confused with the more common historical claim of "an intensifying preoccupation with *individualized* authorial agency" in the period (Brooks, *From Playhouse,* xiv; my emphasis)—a claim that posits a pre-1600 stake in *collective* authorial agency.

30. Erne, *Shakespeare,* 40, 35, 33, 44. Cf. Alan Farmer in his "Shakespeare and the Book": "Dramatic authorship . . . was in fact produced in the book trade during the seventeenth century, as publishers went from marketing plays as unauthored collaborative pieces to selling them as the work of single individuals" ("Introduction"). See also Masten: "dramatic authorship emerges from the publishing house and only indirectly from the theater" ("Playwriting," 371); and Brooks: "the emergent notion of the individual author [was] principally generated in the printing house and ultimately ratified in the bookshop" (*From Playhouse,* 181).

31. Masten, *Textual,* 13; Meres, *Palladis,* 282r. Meres may be listing thirteen plays, if *"Henry the 4"* means both parts. The three plays that had been published with attribution were *Richard II* (1597), *Richard III* (1597), and *Love's Labors Lost* (1598). Sylvan Barnet notes that "many playwrights are mentioned" in Meres's work, "but Shakespeare's name occurs more often than any other, and Shakespeare is the only playwright whose plays are listed" ("Shakespeare," x-xi).

32. For the argument that Henry Chettle and not Greene authored the *Groats-worth,* see D. Allen Carroll's introduction to his edition (1–31). I think it is more likely that Chettle expanded on drafts by Greene, and I will later offer a parallel between Greene's *James IV* and the *Groats-worth's* attack on Shakespeare that supports the attribution of the attack to Greene, but the question of coauthorship is irrelevant to

my point here, which is that the title *Greenes Groats-worth* demonstrates a contemporary interest in authorship. According to the *Groats-worth*, what's more, Greene was "famoused for an Arch-playmaking-poet" (71) in his lifetime, even though no play of his was ever published in his lifetime—which again suggests that there is no necessary correlation between publication and public interest in authorship.

33. Greene, *Groats-worth*, 80, 83–85; *3H6* 1.4.137.

34. See, among many possible examples, the list of major Greek and Roman "authors" of plays in Thomas Langley's *Abridgement of . . . Polidore Vergile* (1546), (C2v–C3v).

35. Terence's plays were also featured—with attribution to Terence—in various compilations of translated excerpts, such as the playwright Nicholas Udall's *Floures for Latine Spekynge Selected and Gathered Oute of Terence*, which appeared in 1534, 1538, 1544, 1560, 1568, 1572, and, with further excerpts, in 1575 and 1581.

36. It is worth dwelling on the case of Edwards, because he was acknowledged as a playwright not only on the title pages of *Damon and Pithias* but in several other extant media as well. For instance, Miles Windsor in his manuscript narrative of the Queen's visit to Oxford in 1566 repeatedly mentions the play *Palamon and Arcite* and "Mr. Edwards the maker thereof" (Elliott and Nelson, eds., *Oxford*, 1.131–33); Stow in his 1570 *Chronicles* similarly records that *Palamon and Arcite* was "made by master *Edwards* of the Queen's Chapel" (408v; quoted in Elliott and Nelson, eds., *Oxford*, 1.141); and Barnabe Googe in 1563 and George Turberville in 1567 both eulogized Edwards as a playwright in printed poems that I will shortly discuss.

37. I am counting only those plays that were printed before 1600. In order of first publication date, they are *Fulgens and Lucres* (c. 1512), *The Nature of the .iiii. Elementes* (1520), *Of Gentylnes and Nobylyte* (1525), *Acolastus* (1540), *King Darius* (1565), *Pacient and Meeke Grissill* (1566?), *Triall of Treasure* (1567), *Like Will to Like* (1568), *Cambises* (1569), *Damon and Pithias* (1571 and 1582), *New Custom* (1573), *Apius and Virginia* (1575), *The Tyde Taryeth No Man* (1576), *Common Conditions* (c. 1577), *All for Money* (1578), *Susanna* (1578), *The Conflict of Conscience* (1581), *Fedele and Fortunio* (1585), *II Tamburlaine* (1590), *Midas* (1592), *The Pedlers Prophecie* (1595), *Woman in the Moone* (1597), *Octavia* (1598), and *Clyomon and Clamydes* (1599). The author is also invoked in at least three pre-1600 manuscripts that were never printed during the Renaissance: *Respublica* (performed 1553), *Misogonus* (performed 1570), and *Club Law* (1599). "The writer" and

"Poet" are mentioned in the printer's letter to the reader in *Menaecmi* (1595), A3r. And Hieronimo twice refers to himself as the "author" of his revenge play in act 4 of *The Spanish Tragedie* (c. 1592; 4.3.3 and 4.4.147). Finally, the Latin play *Christus Triumphans*, published in Basel in 1556, places "Autore Ioanne Foxo Anglo" immediately before the prologue, which twice mentions the "poeta" (pp. 228–31).

38. "Baleus Prolocutor" had earlier appeared in the Wesel editions of the *Chiefe Promises* (1547), of *The Temptacyon of our Lorde* (1547), and of *Three Laws* (1548).

39. *H5* epil.1–2; see Masten, *Textual*, 75.

40. Erne, *Shakespeare*, 63 (my emphasis). Cf. de Grazia and Stallybrass: "the relative insignificance of the author is particularly striking in the case of Shakespeare. Of his plays published before 1600, seven of the eight were first printed anonymously" ("Materiality," 274–75).

41. Masten, *Textual*, 119 (my emphasis); Berger and Lander, "Shakespeare," 400. Alan Sinfield similarly exemplifies this wavering in his response to Brian Vickers's contention "that writers in ancient Rome demanded and were credited with author-type attributes." "That doesn't mean we should expect not to discover distinct developments in early modern England," Sinfield reasonably counters, yet he immediately abandons this qualification, with its suggestion that models of authorship may be historically specific, for the blanket claim that "*Poetaster* is not documenting the author function, it is helping to constitute it." One might think that Sinfield means *Poetaster* helped constitute the *Renaissance* version of the author function, but his next sentence is absolute in its reference to "the emergence of the author" ("*Poetaster*," 82).

42. Erne, *Shakespeare*, 45. Our knowledge about the venues of many morality plays is too spotty to support any conclusions about their amateur or commercial provenance. But plays such as *Fedele and Fortunio* (c. 1583–84) were almost certainly staged commercially: see Richard Hosley's discussion of this in his edition of the play (93–95).

43. Erne, *Shakespeare*, 41 and 43. Katharine Maus and David Bevington also make the analogy to screenwriters in the general introduction to their anthology *English Renaissance Drama* (2002): "Most early modern playgoers were much more aware of the actors onstage than they were of the dramatists behind the scenes, just as modern moviegoers are far more aware of star performers than they are of screenwriters" (xxi).

44. *ES*, 4.286; Munday, *Blast*, 104; Gosson, *Playes*, in *Markets*, D𝟣v, D2r, D5v (cf. E6v, F𝟣v, F8r, and G𝟣r), and B𝟣r.

45. By Vickers's count, Shakespeare's name appeared "on a total of forty-nine quarto and octavo editions of plays and poems published between 1598 and 1622, far more frequently than any other poet or dramatist, indeed, more often than most professional writers" (*Shakespeare*, 6). Kastan, too, observes that, "in our various measures of Shakespeare's greatness, we have usually ignored the fact that in his own age more editions of his plays circulated than of any other contemporary playwright" (*Shakespeare*, 21).

46. "For more than half of his career in London Shakespeare shared in the enterprise of the Lord Chamberlain-King's company as actor, patented member, dramatist, and housekeeper, first of the Globe and then of both the Globe and Blackfriars. No other man of the time is known to have been tied to the theater in so many different ways" (Bentley, *Shakespeare*, 117). Bentley is right only if he means during Shakespeare's lifetime: the actor-dramatist Nathan Field was a housekeeper of the Globe from 1617 to 1619 (*JCS*, 2.435), and Richard Gunnell was an actor-dramatist-sharer-housekeeper on and off from 1618 (*JCS*, 4.516–20). Peter Thomson stresses that Shakespeare "was uniquely secure among late Elizabethan playwrights in his status as a member of the 'board of directors' of London's most successful theater company" (*Shakespeare's*, 80).

47. "From the formation of the Lord Chamberlain's company in 1594 to Shakespeare's death in 1616, there is no evidence that [Shakespeare] ever wrote any play for any other company—a longer period of fidelity than that known for any other dramatist, and one which was never interrupted, as Massinger's, Shirley's, and Brome's appear to have been" (*PD*, 279). Neil Carson points out that some dramatists wrote for one company even while contracted to another ("Collaborative Playwriting," 16, 18–19).

48. Erne calls the first tetralogy of histories "the most ambitious project the professional stage had yet seen": while "Marlowe had written a two-part play and so, it seems, had Thomas Kyd," "Shakespeare was not content to follow their precedent but seems to have been eager to outdo them" (*Shakespeare*, 2–5).

49. Weimann, *Author's Pen*, 124; Finkelpearl, *John Marston*, 124; Marston[?], *Histrio-Mastix*, in *Plays*, 3.250–51 and 299.

50. Finkelpearl, *John Marston*, 121; Marston[?], *Histrio-Mastix*

3.289, 247, 253 (my emphasis), 273–74. Posthaste's company punctures Chrisoganus's pretensions by emphasizing how histrionic his elitism sounds: Belch comments, "The fellow doth talk like one that can talk," and Gut adds, "Is this the well-learn'd man *Chrisoganus,*/He beats the Air the best that ere I heard"(274). Dekker's *Satiro-Mastix* offers a similar critique of Jonson's elitism, as I will show in chapter 2.

51. Bednarz, *Shakespeare,* 97; Marston[?], *Histrio-Mastix* 3.265, 264, 250–51.

52. Marston[?], *Histrio-Mastix* 3.281. Marston offers a similar triad of perspectives, with a mediator between two extremes, in the induction to *What You Will* (written 1601, published 1607).

53. Marston[?], *Histrio-Mastix* 3.295, 283, 251.

54. Marston[?], *Histrio-Mastix* 3.286, 291, 298.

55. Marston, *Parasitaster,* in *Plays,* 2.145; *Dutch Courtesan* 2.69; *What You Will* 2.235; *Parasitaster* 2.144.

56. Marston, "To my equal Reader," *Parasitaster* 2.143, and again in the final lines of the epilogue: "he protests he ever hath aspir'd,/To be belov'd, rather than admir'd"(2.225).

57. Jonson, *Poetaster,* "Ad Lectorem," 4; induct.1.s.d; 3.1.252–53, 5.3.624–25, 5.3.632. Jonson presents the urge to "satirize" as the opposite of envy (3.5.103ff.).

58. *HS,* 8.390 and 44.

59. Rowe, quoted in Craig, ed., *Ben Jonson,* 362. In reporting on a supper with Jonson in 1636, even Jonson's disciple James Howell expressed his dismay at Jonson's competitiveness: "One thing interven'd, which almost spoil'd the relish of the rest, that *B[en].* began to engross all the discourse, to vapor extremely of himself, and, by vilifying others, to magnify his own *Muse*" (quoted in Bradley and Adams, *Jonson,* 194).

60. Marston[?], *Histrio-Mastix* 3.281, quoting Ovid, *Remedio amoris* 369.

61. Marston[?], *Histrio-Mastix* 3.277.

62. Sir Vaughan in Dekker's *Satiro-Mastix* says that Horace/Jonson "*is* ambition" (4.3.253–54; my emphasis). In an early seventeenth-century revision to *Mucedorus,* Envy threatens to "make a poet"who sounds like Jonson; see *Mucedorus,* ed. Jupin, 4–9 and 160–62.

63. Meres, *Palladis,* 282r; Turberville, *Epitaphes,* 142v–143r. Barnabe Googe anticipated Turberville's praise of Edwardes in his *Eglogs[,] Epytaphes, and Sonettes* (1563): "O *Plautus* if/Thou wert alive again,/That Comedies/So finely didst endite./Or *Terence* thou/That

with thy pleasant brain,/The hearer's mind/On stage didst much delight./What would you say/Sirs if you should behold,/As I have done/The doings of this man?/No word at all,/To swear I durst be bold,/But burn with tears,/That which with mirth began,/I mean your books,/By which you gate your name,/To be forgot,/You would commit to flame" (F1r–v). The classical comparison was applied even to a shadowy amateur dramatist such as Samuel Brandon, with only one surviving play to his name: Brandon's "muse," claimed one commender (1598), "far surmounts the might of antique age," while a second writer added that "barking envy" had hunted Brandon from his "birth" (*Vertuous Octavia,* A2v–A3r).

64. "Cedite Romani scriptores, cedite Grai!" Propertius, *Elegies* 2.34.65–66. More generally, Renaissance readers knew from Plutarch that the ancient Greek theater was competitive: the Greek "poets" strove "one against another for victory" (*Lives,* 104).

65. Nashe, *Works,* 3.323 and 1.215. John Weever (1599) and Ben Jonson (1616) both wrote epigrams that compare Alleyn to his classical predecessors (Weever, *Epigrammes,* E6b; *HS,* 8.56–57).

66. Cf. Nashe, *Works,* 3.323.

67. *New Inn* epil.24. In his epigram to Sidney's daughter Elizabeth, Jonson maintained "that *Poets* are far rarer births than kings" (*HS,* 8.53). Bednarz underscores the "coupling of poet and sovereign" in three of Jonson's early comedies: "Asper and Queen Elizabeth in *Every Man Out,* Criticus and Cynthia in *Cynthia's Revels,* and Horace and Augustus Caesar in *Poetaster*" (*Shakespeare,* 62).

68. Puttenham, *Art,* 148–50.

69. *ES,* 1.279; Bentley, *Shakespeare,* 99. In *Histrio-Mastix,* the supposed and possibly fictitious patron of Posthaste's lowly company is merely a knight, "Sir Oliver Owlet."

70. Cf. Shapiro, *Rival:* "the writing of plays remained a commercial and therefore inescapably competitive enterprise" (14).

71. Puttenham, *Art,* 150; *ES,* 4.300; Hall, *Virgidemiarum,* 1.4.1–2.

72. Cf. Butler, *Theatre:* "The heterogeneity of the Elizabethan audiences . . . necessitated the drama's quite extraordinary range of social and cultural reference" (306).

73. *Hamlet* 2.2.328, 396–402; I quote the 1604 quarto for emphasis.

74. In his essay "Thomas Middleton: Lives and Afterlives" for *The Collected Works of Thomas Middleton,* Gary Taylor makes a strong case for viewing Middleton as Shakespeare's equal or superior in versatility:

"Thomas Middleton and William Shakespeare were the only writers of the English Renaissance who created plays still considered masterpieces in four major dramatic genres: comedy, history, tragedy, and tragicomedy.... [Middleton] wrote successful scripts for more theatrical venues than any of his contempories. The only seventeenth-century printed anthology of memorable passages from English drama [by John Cotgrave in 1655] quoted the Middleton canon more often than the works of any other playwright.... On and off the commercial stage, Middleton mastered more genres than any English writer of his time" (25). But this is a decidedly modern judgment of Middleton. "During his lifetime [Middleton] was never the subject of commendatory verses, and he was never singled out for particular praise in accounts of contemporary authors" (Barker, *Thomas Middleton*, 24).

75. E.g., Francis Beaumont writes to Jonson c. 1615, "here I would let slip / (If I had any in me) scholarship, / And from all Learning keep these lines as clear / As Shakespeare's best are" (quoted in *Riverside Shakespeare*, ed. Evans et al., 1971), while John Heminges and Henry Condell declare in a prefatory letter to the 1623 First Folio that "what [Shakespeare] thought, he uttered with that easiness, that we have scarce received from him a blot in his papers" (*FF*, A3r, in *Riverside Shakespeare*, 95). For more on contemporaneous interest in opposing Jonson to Shakespeare, see Bentley, *Shakespeare & Jonson;* Bednarz, *Shakespeare;* and Donaldson, "Looking Sideways."

76. "Alterutra veteres contenti laude: *Cothurnum* hic, / Atque, pari *soccum* tractat *Sol scenicus* arte"; in Jonson, *Volpone,* ¶4v, D.H. Craig's translation (*Ben Jonson,* 109). Cf. Michael Drayton in his disquisition "Of Poets and Poesie" in the 1627 *Battaile of Agincourt:* Jonson "long was Lord here of the Theater, / Who in opinion made our learn'st to stick, / Whether in Poems rightly dramatic, / Strong *Seneca* or *Plautus,* he or they, / Should bear the Buskin, or the Sock away" (quoted in *HS,* 11.389). See also William Bew's Latin epitaph in *Jonsonus Virbius* (*HS,* 11.479) and Herrick's "Upon M. Ben Jonson" (*HS,* 11.488).

77. Quoted in *HS,* 11.448. In the 1647 *Comedies and Tragedies* of Beaumont and Fletcher, G. Hills likewise calls Fletcher "*Proteus* of wit! who reads him doth not see / The manners of each sex of each degree! / His full-stor'd fancy doth all humors fill / From th' *Queen* of *Corinth* to the maid o' th' mill" (*BF,* F1v).

78. In his recent *Shakespeare, National Poet-Playwright* (2004), Patrick Cheney has provided a valuable corrective to studies that focus

on Shakespeare's plays to the exclusion of his poetry. But he overcorrects, I think, when he disputes the claim by the editors of *The Norton Shakespeare* that "the drama" was "Shakespeare's principal medium" (Cheney, *Shakespeare*, 71, on Greenblatt et al., "Preface," xi). I agree with the *Norton* editors, and I would add that Shakespeare's theatrical career dominated his sense of his authorship. This is not to say that Shakespeare was uninterested in literary publication: on the contrary, I am persuaded by Andrew Gurr ("Maximal"), Richard Dutton ("Shakespeare"), and Lukas Erne (*Shakespeare*) that Shakespeare expected his plays to be read as well as performed.

79. Stallybrass and White, *Politics*, 61.

80. Shakespeare, *2 Henry IV*, epil.27; *Sonnets*, 55, 137, 135–36, 129, 148.

81. Masten, *Textual Intercourse*, 108 and 111; Mullaney, *Place*, 149.

82. For a critique of this dichotomizing tendency in analyses of modern secularization, too, see my "'Sacred Songs Popular Prices': Secularization in *The Jazz Singer*."

CHAPTER ONE

1. Ackerman, "On the Bard's Brain," 2; Bentley, *Shakespeare and Jonson*, 63.

2. *HS*, 8.390–92.

3. Later in the century, Dryden claimed of Shakespeare that "however others are now generally preferr'd before him, yet the Age wherein he liv'd, which had contemporaries with him *Fletcher* and *Jonson*, never equall'd them to him in their esteem: And in the last King's Court, where *Ben*'s reputation was at highest, Sir *John Suckling*, and with him the greater part of the Courtiers, set our *Shakespeare* far above him" (*Essay*, 56).

4. Kastan, "Shakespeare," 5; *Shakespeare*, 78. Cf. Berger and Lander on the First Folio: "Here, Shakespeare, who never showed the least bit of interest in being a dramatic author while he lived, is identified as the privileged and singular source of literary meaning—an assertion that quite obviously flies in the face of the collaborative fluidity that typified playhouse practices" ("Shakespeare in Print," 409).

5. Greene, *Groats-worth*, 85.

6. Greene, *Groats-worth*, 71, 83; Bentley, *Shakespeare*, 121; Greene, *Groats-worth*, 84. After Shakespeare's time, Richard Gunnell (d. 1634) arguably became a more "complete" theater man than Shakespeare: not only was he an actor, dramatist, sharer, and housekeeper, as I noted ear-

lier, but he was also a manager and a builder (of Salisbury Court). John Heywood, too, over the course of his long theatrical career, was a sharer in several different acting companies.

7. Gentili, *Commentatio*, 256/235, 264/243, 271/248 (the dual numbers refer to the Latin original and the English translation). Gentili elsewhere concedes that it is not fair to blame the actors entirely: "I do not doubt that nearly all . . . [Roman] plays . . . were defiled and bespattered with many shameless and disgraceful words and deeds [*aspersas, et conspersas fuisse verbis, factisque inhonestis, et improbis*]; and others have noted the same. On account of which you may disapprove of the actors and the authors at the same time" (268/246).

8. *FF*, A5r, in *Riverside Shakespeare*, 99; Spenser, *Tears of the Muses*, 577; Drayton, *Idea* (1600), Q7r. Cf. *HS*, 8.28.

9. See, e.g., Smith, *Sir Thomas Smithes Voiage* (1605), K1v; Barnfield, *Encomion* (1598), E2v; Petowe, *Second Part* (1598), B2r and B2v; Weever, *Epigrammes* (1599), G1r; Lavater, *Of Ghosts* (1572), 44; and Davison, *Poetical* (1611), 95–96.

10. Jonson, *Cynthia's Revels* prol.17–18; quoted in *HS*, 11, 463, 468, 443, 382.

11. This manuscript poem of Alexander's was first published in 1711; see his *Poetical Works*, 2.541.

12. Spenser, *Tears*, 571 and 567; Jonson, *Cynthia's Revels* prol.7–8 and 13–14. Jonson's epigraph is from Horace, *Satires* 1.10.73–74: "neque te ut miretur turba laboros,/Contentus paucis lectoribus"; Jonson changes Horace's *te* to *me*.

13. Quoted in *HS*, 11.317, 325, 336, and 333; Digges in Shakespeare, *Poems*, *3r–*4r; *HS*, 5.19 (Herford and Simpson fail to capitalize "Multitude"). As James Bednarz points out, Jonson in his prologue to the 1616 version of *Every Man Out of His Humor* "summarizes Shakespeare's success as a series of ludicrous concessions to popular taste" (*Shakespeare*, 73).

14. Shakespeare, *Venus and Adonis*, p. 1799; Ovid, *Amores* 1.15.35–36 and 33; Ovid's poem is the *locus classicus* for the defense of poetry against the charge of trifling. The *Dictionary* (1538) of Sir Thomas Elyot glosses "Vulgus" as "the common people" (FF1r). The cast list on the title page of *Patient Grissel* (acted c. 1558–61, publ. 1566?) calls the allegorical character Vulgus "Common people," while other characters in the play refer to Vulgus as the "the common sort" (E1r) or "the commons" (G3v). Shakespeare's *vulgus* and Jonson's *turba* appear together in Cicero's let-

ter to Marius on the opening of Pompey's theater in 55 B.C.E., where Cicero writes of "admiratio magna vulgi atque turbae" ("great admiration among the vulgar and the crowd"; *Letters* 7.1.3).

In an unpublished essay, Adam G. Hooks argues that the epigraph to *Venus and Adonis* may have been supplied by the printer John Harrison: "Almost without exception, Harrison's title pages—of works in both Latin and English—include a Latin motto" ("'At the Signe'," 10). Whoever suggested the epigraph, it remained prominently displayed on the title page of every edition of the poem published during Shakespeare's life.

15. Shakespeare, *Rape of Lucrece,* p. 1816; Davies, *Scourge,* 76–77.

16. Davies, *Microcosmos,* 215; Crosse, *Vertues Common-wealth,* P4v; Northbrooke, *Treatise,* 63 and 65; Lodge, *Scillaes,* C4v; Davies, *Scourge,* 77; Honigmann, *John Weever,* 90; Weever, *Epigrammes,* E6r; Manningham in *WS,* 2.212.

17. My account of the sonnets is particularly indebted to Joel Fineman's incomparable *Shakespeare's Perjured Eye,* as well as to Booth's edition; Greene, "'Pitiful Thrivers'"; Kernan, *Playwright;* de Grazia, "Scandal"; and Greenblatt, *Will.*

18. Shakespeare, *Sonnets,* 63, 20, 53. Sidney in sonnet 107 of *Astrophil and Stella* (publ. 1591) refers to his beloved as his "princess," "sovereign," "queen," as Spenser in sonnet 74 of his *Amoretti* (1595) calls his own beloved "my sovereign Queen."

19. Shakespeare, *Sonnets,* 57, 26, 91, 29, 78, 55, and 18.

20. Shakespeare, *Sonnets,* 91, 23, 17, 36, 49, 103, 37, 62, and 91.

21. Shakespeare, *Sonnets,* 150, 147, 110. In his edition of the sonnets, Colin Burrow maintains that the "allusion to Shakespeare's activities as a player" in sonnet 110 "is at best a distant reference, since the role of fool was a specialized one which Shakespeare did not play" (*Complete Sonnets,* 600). But Burrow is too literal-minded about the actor as "a motley." Contemporaries often categorized all actors as fools: see e.g. the marprelatean attack (1589) on players for being "so base-minded, as at the pleasure of the veriest rogue in England, for one poor penny, they will be glad on open stage to play the ignominious fools for an hour or two together" (Pierce, *Marprelate Tracts,* 330), and Nashe's reference in his preface to *Menaphon* (1589) to "a company of taffaty fools with their feathers" (*Works,* 3.324). Burrow has no trouble glossing "public means which public manners breeds" in sonnet 111 as a reference to "the meth-

ods which the poet/playwright has to use to earn a living" (*Complete Sonnets*, 602).

22. Shakespeare, *Sonnets*, 111 and 112.

23. "Thy gift, thy tables, are *within my brain*/ Full charactered," says the speaker in sonnet 122 (my emphasis). Whereas the speaker had earlier conceived of his "lines" as overcoming "Time's injurious hand" (63), in sonnet 123 the "registers" and "records" belong to Time, not to the speaker, who is similarly alienated from writing in sonnet 134: "he learned but surety-like to write for me." Before the theater sonnets, the speaker refers to himself as a poet in sonnets 15–19, 21, 23, 32, 38, 39, 54, 55, 59, 60, 63, 65, 71, 74, 76, 78–86, 100–103, 105, 107, and 108, and the words *pen* and *verse* appear more often in the earlier sonnets than in any of Shakespeare's plays: *pen* in sonnets 16, 19, 32, 78, 79, 81, 84, 85, 100, and 106; *verse* in sonnets 17, 19, 21, 38, 54, 60, 71, 76, 78, 79, 81, 86, 103, and 105 (along with *verses* in 103). After the theater sonnets, however, neither of these words reappears in the sequence. Finally, in ten sonnets before the theater sonnets the speaker refers to his muse, but no sonnets mention her afterward.

Two of the sonnets' most influential readers, Alvin Kernan and Joel Fineman, overlook this shift in the sequence. Kernan argues that, "unlike the ideal courtly poet who concealed his personality and art beneath a surface of modesty and effortless ease," the "poet" of the sonnets "constantly betrays his professionalism by his interest in and discussion of poetic matters"; indeed, the poet grows increasingly more interested in the subjects of "poets and poetry" as the sonnets unfold (*Playwright*, 40–41). Fineman similarly maintains that the dark-lady sonnets are more self-consciously literary than the young-man sonnets and that they develop a novel account of subjectivity from this literariness. So "fully literary" (*Perjured Eye*, 300) is Fineman's focus that the tensions between poetry and theater in the sonnets never register for him; indeed, the theater is barely operative as a concept in his reading. Kernan, by contrast, claims that "the plot of the *Sonnets*" progresses "from an essentially lyric to an essentially dramatic conception of life" (36), and he calls the dark lady "the Muse of theater: illicit, darkly mysterious, sensual, infinitely complex, beautiful and ugly, common and public, the source of pleasure and pain" (46). But he does not follow through on the "new image of the poet" (48) that would correspond with this licentious new muse. Instead, he elevates what he has just de-idealized: "The *Son-*

nets justify the theater and the participation in it of professional writers with a high view of the importance of their art like Shakespeare" (48).

More recently, Patrick Cheney in *Shakespeare, National Poet-Playwright* (2004) has powerfully stressed the "conjunction of poetry and theater" as "twin forms of authorship" (236) in the sonnets. But he, too, overlooks the falling-off in Shakespeare's "self-representation" (209) as a poet after the theater sonnets because he, too, privileges Shakespeare's identity as a poet. More often than not, Cheney treats the role of "poet-playwright" as a "predicament" (208) or a "dilemma" (212) for "a speaker who quite literally speaks as a poet" (210). Poet and dramatist thus turn out to be "opposing representations" of authorial identity: where the dramatist experiences "public shame over the theater," the poet seeks "public fame through his poetry," and Shakespeare's references to himself as a poet are aimed at "offsetting a public infamy acquired through his role in the new English theater" (213). I am arguing the opposite: that the sonnets were intended to compromise Shakespeare's identity as poet by *insisting* on the infamy of his theatrical career.

24. The contradiction is noted by Neely, "Detachment," 88–89. For "motley" as signifying range, see, e.g., Sylvester's translation of du Bartas's *Weekes and Workes* (1605) on God at work in Eden: "with thousand Dyes he motleys all the mead" (274; cited in *OED* "motley" v.).

25. That link is nevertheless *suggested* in the very first sonnet to characterize the speaker as a poet. In sonnet 15, which is also the first to propose that the speaker's verse can immortalize the young man, the speaker calls the world a "huge stage" that "presenteth nought but shows." But this stage is merely a figure of speech. By the same token, sonnet 23 merely *compares* the speaker to "an unperfect actor on the stage," but it *declares* that the speaker is a writer: "let my books be then the eloquence"; "learn to read what silent love hath writ." For more on the conjunction of poetry and theater in the early sonnets, see Cheney, *Shakespeare*, 216ff. For the early sonnets as implying what the later sonnets state more emphatically, see above all Fineman, *Perjured Eye*.

26. Shakespeare, *Sonnets*, 29, 150, 78, 151.

27. For a particularly suggestive account of the Will sonnets, see de Grazia, "Babbling Will."

28. The 1609 text of the sonnets indicates that readers should pay special attention to the word "will" by italicizing it seven times in sonnet 135 and three times in sonnet 136. Only thirty-five words are italicized in the entire sonnet sequence, so the italicized instances of "will"

in 135 and 136 account for more than a quarter of all italicized words in the sonnets.

29. For a contemporaneous reference to the short form of a Christian name as a "Nickname" or "Nursename," see Camden, *Remaines,* 114.

30. Heywood, *Hierarchie,* 205–6; Shakespeare, incidentally, is the only dramatist whom Heywood describes as succeeding at both comedy and tragedy. Actors, too, were known by their nicknames, as in the second part of *The Return from Parnassus* (acted c. 1601–2), where the clown Kemp declares that "for honor, who of more report than *Dick Burbage* & *Will Kemp?*" (4.4.1791–92).

31. *HS,* 8.392. The comically generic first name in "Johannes fac-totum" is another part of Greene's assault on the proper name "Shakespeare."

32. According to E. G. Withycombe, parish baptismal records from the second half of the sixteenth century show that 22.5 percent of males were given the name "William," compared with 15.5 percent for the next most popular first name, "John." "William" and "John" each averaged about 20 percent of masculine first names from that time to the nineteenth century (*Oxford Dictionary,* xxviii and 280; cited in Ramsey, *Fickle Glass,* 23).

33. Shakespeare, *Sonnets,* 135, 136, 149, 113, 136. De Grazia comments that in sonnet 136 "every word could be said to signal his desire, homonymically or synonymically," which results in "the tautological deadlock of 'Will wills will'" ("Scandal," 47).

34. Shakespeare, *Sonnets,* 137, 7, 136. My argument here is influenced by Catherine Gallagher's famous discussion of how and why the Restoration playwright Aphra Behn used "the prostitute and the monarch as her most frequent authorial metaphors"; see Gallagher, *Nobody's Story,* 1–87. But Behn as Gallagher understands her deployed the tropes of prostitute and monarch differently from Shakespeare as I understand him. Although "literalizing and embracing the playwright-prostitute metaphor" (27), Behn in Gallagher's account hoped that "selling bawdiness and then complaining of the necessity to do so" would assure "her female readers that there is an innocent self above the exchange" (16). Such innocence is hard to find in Shakespeare's dark-lady sonnets. According to Gallagher, moreover, Behn used the authorial tropes of prostitute and monarch in different phases of her career: Behn's identifications of the prostitute with "theatrical representation," and of "sovereign authorial selfhood" (56) with print, were so strong that "shortly after Behn started using the monarch-author metaphor, she stopped

being a prolific playwright" (56). In Shakespeare's sonnets, by contrast, the prostitute and the monarch are mutually constitutive authorial roles.

For powerful accounts of the link between prostitution and authorship in classical poetry, see Kurke, *Traffic* and "Pindar."

35. In *BF,* D2v. Published in 1647, this poem by the playwright-turned-preacher William Cartwright was written after Fletcher's death in 1625 and before Cartwright's own death in 1643.

36. Coleridge, *Biographia,* 2.13; Keats, Letter to Richard Woodhouse, 27 October 1818 (*Selected Letters,* 194–95); Beard, *Theatre,* 147; Gosson, *Schoole,* in *Markets,* A6v. For a modern critique of this license in Shakespeare, see Bristol, *Big-time Shakespeare:* "Shakespeare has been censured repeatedly for indiscriminate pandering to the vulgar taste of the groundlings. He has also been denounced for complicity with patriarchy, oppressive state power, and class domination. It might make more sense, however, to follow the lead of Samuel Johnson in condemning Shakespeare as morally unprincipled and opportunistic. The complexity of the plays might then be described not as an artistic achievement but rather as a shrewd strategy to curry favor with as many sectors as possible within a complex multi-cultural market" (50). This last sentence of Bristol's seems too austere: why can't Shakespearean complexity count as both a shrewd business strategy *and* an artistic achievement?

37. I quote the 1599 *Idea,* P2v.

38. I am counting from Bernard Newdigate's list in his *Michael Drayton,* 104.

39. E.g., "there is in the new sonnets a marked tendency to view the world through the eyes of a dramatist rather than through those of a lyric poet" (St. Clair, "Drayton's First Revision," 46).

40. Drayton, *Idea* (1599), P2v.

41. To explain Drayton's self-characterization as "libertine," Louise Westling surveys the various meanings of *libertine* in the period, but then ignores the moral connotations of the term altogether, defining it instead as the stylistic "irregularity" of Drayton's "satiric personality" ("Pose," 132–37, 141–42, and 118; cf. Davis, "'Fantastickly'"). In a sense, Westling's partial reading accurately reflects Drayton's own pullback from the implications of his posturing. Westling also dismisses Drayton's involvement in the theater as a "naive" explanation for his change of style in *Idea* (6), pointing instead to Sir Thomas Wyatt's emphasis on his own "diverseness" as a model for Drayton's persona in *Idea* ("Pose,"

82ff.). But why must we choose between one influence or the other? The traditional representation of sonnet speakers as ranging through moods and passions seems to me a primary reason for Shakespeare's interest in writing sonnets.

42. A character in the second part of *The Return from Parnassus* says of Drayton that "he wants one true note of a Poet of our times, and that is this, he cannot swagger it well in a Tavern, nor domineer in a hot-house" (249–51).

43. Drayton, *Poems* (1605), Cc4v.

44. Drayton, *Works*, 2.358. For more on Drayton's disenchantment with the stage, see Newdigate, *Michael Drayton*, 109–10.

45. I am not claiming that Shakespeare's stress on the disgracefulness of his love was new to English sonnets. For instance, sonnet 19 of *Astrophil and Stella* begins:

> On *Cupid's* bow how are my heart-strings bent,
> That see my wrack, and yet embrace the same?
> When most I glory, then I feel most shame:
> I willing run, yet while I run, repent.
> My best wits still their own disgrace invent.

The difference in Shakespeare's sonnets was the linkage of his erotic disgrace with his professional circumstances, with the vileness of his beloved, and with his own vulgarity.

46. This one-for-many-ness is again a revision of earlier praise for the young man, whom the speaker said in sonnet 31 was "endeared with all hearts / Which I by lacking have supposed dead": "Their images I loved I view in thee, / And *thou, all they,* hast all the all of me" (my emphasis).

47. *1H4* 3.2.86–87 and 2.3.92. In *1H4*, the future Henry V is called "Harry" twenty times; Hotspur is given the name fifteen times, and Henry IV is called "Harry" once. For an indication that "Harry" was understood to be a more formal name than "Hal," see the dueling scene of *Richard II*, where the Lord Marshal begins the action with the ceremonial question, "My Lord Aumerle, is Harry Herford arm'd?" (1.3.1). Bullingbrook declares himself to be "Harry of Herford, Lancaster, and Derby" (35), which is how the Lord Marshal (100) and the first Herald (104) also address him. The interchangeability of "Harry" and "Henry" is suggested by the second Herald's substitution of "Henry" for "Harry" in the ceremonial formula (113). Finally, there are plenty of references to kings named "Harry" in other drama of the time, but so far as I can

tell, *1H4* was the first play of the English Renaissance to call a future king "Hal."

Only once in the three plays where Henry V appears is he called "Henry," by himself in *H5* 5.2.240; his father is "Henry" in *1H4* 3.1.63 and *2H4* 4.1.115, Hotspur is "Henry" in *1H4* 5.1.87, and Lord Scroop is "Henry" in *H5* 2.chorus.24.

48. Shakespeare, *Sonnets,* 154, 153; Boswell quoted in de Grazia, "Scandal," 39.

49. Auden "Introduction," xxxv–xxxvi. Auden adds, "It is impossible to believe either that Shakespeare wished them to be published or that he can have shown most of them to the young man and woman, whoever they were, to whom they are addressed" (xxxv).

50. Shakespeare, *Sonnets,* 72, 88, 89 (my emphasis).

51. Shakespeare, *Sonnets,* 121, 84, 121, 144, 141, 147, and 150.

52. Shakespeare, *Sonnets,* 88. Lars Engle treats Shakespeare's stake in shame more philosophically: he argues that the sonnets present shame as a "necessary" personal and social "resource" ("'I Am That I Am,'" 196).

53. Shakespeare, *Sonnets,* 62, 146, 142; Knapp, *Shakespeare's Tribe;* Bernard, *Faithfull,* 72.

54. Shakespeare, *Sonnets,* 19 and 49; for Paul, see 1 Tim. 1:12–16 (I quote the King James Version).

55. Shakespeare, *Sonnets,* 96, 95, and 149. For the marginal comment, see Rollins's *Variorum* edition of the sonnets, 2.348; for the manuscript count, see Beal, comp., *Index,* 1.2.452–54, cited in Roberts, *Reading,* 174.

56. *MFM* 1.1.21, 1.4.50, 4.4.1–3, 2.4.1–7 and 20–23, 2.1.31, 2.4.20–29.

57. Davies, *Poems,* 135–36; for the evidence that the sonnet had to have been written by November 1594, see 381.

58. *MFM* 1.1.67–68, 1.3.8, 4.5.2, 5.1.366–69, 4.3.143, and 5.1.367–73, 519, and 538–39. For a seminal analysis of the relation between politics and theater in *Measure for Measure,* see Tennenhouse, who somewhat overstates the consolidation of the duke's power through theatricality—for example, when he claims that the duke brings "purity where there had been obscenity and pollution" (*Power,* 159).

CHAPTER TWO

1. Gosson, *Playes Confuted,* D3v–D4r. "Author's pen" and "actor's voice," the most famous instance of this distinction, from the prologue to Shakespeare's *Troilus and Cressida,* was standard shorthand that

Gosson, too, employed: in his version, "a *Poet's* inkhorn" and "a Player's tongue" (Dɪᴠ; cf. D3ᴠ–D4r and Fɪᴠ).

2. Udall[?], *Respublica*, p. 1; W. Wager[?], *Triall of Treasure*, A2ᴠ. So, too, does the epilogue to the early 1580s play *Fedele and Fortunio* beg "pardon" of the spectators for both "our Writer" and "our selves" (Munday, *Fedele and Fortunio*, Hɪᴠ).

3. *2 Return from Parnassus* 1927–28, 1920–21, 1918–19; Greene, *Groatsworth*, 85.

4. Webster, in *ES*, 4.258; Moryson, in Hughes, ed., *Shakespeare's Europe*, 304, 373, and 476; cited in *ES*, 1.343.

5. Gosson, *Playes Confuted*, Dɪr and D2ᴠ; Dekker, *If It Be Not Good*, A4ᴠ.

6. Helgerson, *Forms of Nationhood*, 203, 200, 202, 216, 218, 199, 200, 199, 204. While endorsing the idea of this shift, Masten maintains that "a contestation of author/ity between actors and authors" was only "nascent" as late as 1609 (*Textual Intercourse*, 112).

7. Helgerson, *Forms of Nationhood*, 213; Nashe, *Works*, 3.311, 3.324, 1.215; *HS*, 8.57.

8. Kastan, *Shakespeare*, 48; Erne, *Shakespeare*, 43; Marcus, *Puzzling Shakespeare*, 26.

9. Saeger and Fassler, "London Professional Theater," 69 and fig. 7 on 108; Farmer, "Title Page Attributions," in "Shakespeare and the Book"; Saeger and Fassler, "London," 68. Saeger and Fassler claim that the percentage of company attributions decreases when "large collections" of plays "that made no explicit attributions of company" are included in the calculations. But the collections they mention, "the Shakespeare First Folio, 1623, and the Beaumont and Fletcher folio of 1647" (68), are clearly associated with the King's Men in the front matter to both volumes. Saeger and Fassler acknowledge this, but they add that they are concerned with "specific and direct attributions" (109 n. 12) on title pages only—which highlights, I think, the limited usefulness of title pages as markers of conceptual or even promotional developments during the period.

10. Farmer and Lesser, "'Vile Arts,'" 82. While Farmer and Lesser agree with Saeger and Fassler "that, in print, authors came to supersede companies as the sole producers of the dramatic text" (note the seemingly inevitable ambiguity in "producers"), they mean that references to authors alone became more numerous than references to companies

alone. In general, however, companies were cited just as often at the end of the period as they were at the start.

11. Farmer and Lesser, "'Vile Arts,'" 81.

12. Farmer and Lesser, "'Vile Arts,'" 82; Bentley, *Profession*, 10.

13. For Masten, the sentiment in favor of collaboration is sexual as well as economic: he describes coauthorship as "a mode of homoerotic textual production existing prior to and eventually alongside the more familiar mode of singular authorship" (*Textual Intercourse*, 60). As Radel points out in his review of *Textual Intercourse*, however, Masten does not provide "adequate evidence to demonstrate anything like a consistent discursive paradigm linking homoerotic desire and authorial collaboration" (526). Cf. Paulina Kewes's review, 162 and 164.

14. *ES*, 4.206, 3.497; Nashe, *Works*, 1.304–5. The title page of *The Coblers Prophesie* (London, 1594) attributed the play to "Robert Wilson. Gent." For Wilson's playwriting career, which seems to have spanned the 1580s and 1590s, see *ES*, 3.515–17.

15. Baker, *Chronicle*, 120.

16. Weimann, *Author's Pen*, 9–10, 3, 65; *2 Return from Parnassus*, 1846; *Witts Recreations*, B8v.

17. Dekker, *Satiro-Mastix*, "To the World," 7; Jonson, *Poetaster*, Apology "To the Reader," 3–4, 13, 20, 237–40.

18. Stallybrass and White, *Politics*, 77, 66–67, 61. Masten claims that "representations of authors" did not figure in Renaissance drama until the seventeenth century, when authors supposedly began to take the stage by storm. "Perhaps the earliest explicit appearance of the *playwright*-author on the English stage," he believes, occurred in Jonson's *Bartholomew Fair*, which "explicitly stages the intrusion of an author into the theater" (*Textual Intercourse*, 74 and 108). But the "Author" had already appeared in Jonson's Apology, not to mention other, earlier productions that I will shortly cite. Conversely, the author never does appear on stage in *Bartholomew Fair*.

19. The two plays are *Candlemas Day and the Killing of the Children of Israel* (dated 1512 in the text) and *The Conversion of St. Paul*, which its recent editors date to "the first quarter of the sixteenth century" (Baker et al., eds., *Late Medieval Religious Plays*, xviii, xxii). For evidence that the plays were revived in Chelmsford in 1562, see Coldewey, "Digby Plays."

20. *Terens in Englysh*, A1v; Udall?, *Jacob and Esau*, G4r.

21. Day, *Isle*, A2r.

22. Stallybrass and White, *Politics*, 67.

23. *HS*, 1.140; Dekker, *Satiro-Mastix* 2.2.s.d., 5.2.262, 5.2.253, 4.3.93–94, 5.2.258–59, 1.2.367 and 364, 4.3.99, 1.2.138–39, and 4.3.157–58.

24. Dekker, *Satiro-Mastix* 4.2.61–62 and 4.3.202–5, 4.1.128–31, 4.1.123, 4.1.131–32, 1.2.356–57, 5.2.300–7, 1.2.s.d. and 9–14.

25. Ovid speaks of the "difference 'twixt those jaded wits / That run a broken pace for common hire, / And the high raptures of a happy Muse" (*Poetaster*,1.2.241–43) such as his own.

26. Jonson, *Poetaster* 1.2.12, 1.2.63–64 and 67. For Ovid as the prototypical poet-playwright, see Cheney, *Shakespeare*, especially chap. 2.

27. Jonson, *Poetaster* 3.4.323 and 5.3.372–74.

28. *Poetaster* 5.2.47, 62, 75, 88–89, 78. The word *stalk* and its variants appear in 3.4.116, 123, 162, 169, 277, and 361; 5.3.47–49; 5.1.105–6; 4.3.122–23; 3.1.

29. Jonson, Apology, 226–28; Dekker, *Satiro-Mastix* 1.2.142; Jonson, *Every Man Out* 4.8.164 (although "actors" here may mean "characters"). The idea preceded Jonson nevertheless: e.g., Erasmus in his *First Tome or Volume of the Paraphrase* (1548) states that "the setter forth of interludes appointeth time for his players to come and go" (EEE2v). Cromwell made payments to "Bale and his fellows" in September 1538 and early 1539 (Happé, *John Bale*, 10).

30. Jonson, *Bartholomew Fair* Induction.60, 64, 75–76, 82–83. Stallybrass and White themselves note that the contract cannot be taken seriously as an expression of elitist authorial will. They describe it as "a mock-version" of "critical positions" that Jonson had previously espoused. "Even in the Induction," they acknowledge, "Jonson seems aware that here, for once, he may have produced a play which is in keeping with the grotesque, saturnalian traditions of the Elizabethan theater" (*Politics*, 69–71). For a suggestive account of Jonson's feeling torn between his own "ludic impulses" and his desire for "authorial control" in *Bartholomew Fair*, see Marcus, "Of Mire."

31. Jonson, *Bartholomew Fair* Induction.26, 28–30. This is a reversal from Jonson's earlier self-characterization in the Induction to *Cynthia's Revels*, which insists that Jonson is *not* in the tiring house (160–66).

32. The *Staple*'s "Prologue for the Court" highlights this shift by describing the play as "a Work not smelling of the Lamp" (1).

33. Jonson, *Staple of News* Induction.60–74. For an extremely suggestive account of Jonson's basing his authorship on the figure of the fool, see Preiss, "Finite Jest."

34. *Staple of News* Induction.71–72, 60. Ian Donaldson observes that

"competition and collaboration are the central and conflicting impulses in many of Jonson's plays, in which teams of collaborators—Volpone and Mosca, Tiberius and Sejanus, Dol and Face and Subtle—are torn asunder by the irresistible and at times inexplicable need to compete against one another" ("Looking Sideways," 246). For a fine reading of *Volpone* along these lines, see Chaplin, "Divided."

35. Jonson also wrote additions to *The Spanish Tragedy* for a new run of the play in 1601–2.

36. Kyd, *Spanish Tragedy* 1.4.135–41. The first stage direction begins, "Enter Hieronimo with a drum," so it is possible that Hieronimo is the drummer.

37. Kyd, *Spanish Tragedy* 4.1.157–61, 4.4.146–47.

38. Kyd, *Spanish Tragedy* 3.13.132; Dekker, *Satiro-Mastix* 1.2.355–56; Kyd, *Spanish Tragedy* 4.3.1–4, 4.4.149–50.

39. *Hamlet* 3.2.38-45; Helgerson, *Forms*, 223–26; Shapiro, *Year*, 37.

Hamlet is attributed to Shakespeare not only in the First Folio and on the title pages of three quarto editions published during his lifetime but also in various contemporary references to the play, some of which I will shortly consider. In my view, there is currently no compelling evidence that significant portions of the 1604 Second Quarto and 1623 Folio texts were written by someone other than Shakespeare or that these two texts represent significantly different conceptions of the play. Therefore, I cite the collated version of *Hamlet* in *The Riverside Shakespeare*.

I agree with the majority of scholars who regard the 1603 First Quarto as a memorial reconstruction of the play. (Although Erne is somewhat vague about this, he challenges a particular account of Q1 as a memorial reconstruction, not the broader claim of memorial reconstruction per se: see *Shakespeare as Literary Dramatist*, chap. 8.) For the most vigorous defense of Q1 as a coherent play in its own right, see Marcus, *Unediting the Renaissance*, 132-76. Marcus associates scholarly dismissals of Q1 with a preference for the literate, authorial, and elite over the oral, collaborative, and popular. I am arguing that the Q2 and F *Hamlet*s undercut these oppositions.

40. Kemp was a restless man: he toured the Continent at least three times, and his most famous venture was his 130-mile morris dance from London to Norwich shortly after he left Shakespeare's company. See Wiles, *Shakespeare's Clown*.

In support of his claim that Shakespeare needed to rid himself of

Kemp in order to assert his own authority over the stage, Shapiro notes that Kemp is twice named in the surviving stage directions of Shakespeare's plays. "What's so striking," Shapiro adds, "is that [Shakespeare] rarely does this for other actors in the company" (*Year,* 40). Shapiro draws a stronger conclusion a few pages later: that "as Shakespeare's characters became more real and as Shakespeare's name figured more and more prominently on printed editions of his plays, his fellow players, with the exception of Burbage, became increasingly anonymous" (42). It does seem striking evidence of Kemp's fame or charisma that his name should appear in stage directions, but two namings is not a lot, and the non-naming of other actors in the stage directions does not make them "anonymous" in anything but the text.

41. *2 Return from Parnassus,* 1766-69; Helgerson, *Forms,* 216.

42. Jonson, *Poetaster,* Apology, 226-28; *Hamlet* 3.2.277–78 and 25–28.

43. *Hamlet* 2.2.328–44; *Cynthia's Revels* Induction.182.

44. *Hamlet* 2.2.345–62.

45. *Hamlet* 2.2.466–67 and 541–42, 3.2.1; Helgerson, *Forms of Nationhood,* 224. Greenblatt anticipates this point about Hamlet as reviser in his "General Introduction" to *The Norton Shakespeare,* 67.

46. *Hamlet* 5.2.31, 51; Helgerson, *Forms of Nationhood,* 224; *Hamlet* 3.2.125. Leah Marcus, among others, makes this point about Hamlet's clowning during the play: see *Puzzling Shakespeare,* 47.

47. *Hamlet* 1.5.97–104; 2.2.142; 1.2.36–38, 131–32; 1.5.13–14, 105–10, 116, 172.

48. *Hamlet* 5.1.184–91, 2.2.561–62, 1.2.129, 5.1.190; I have substituted the better known Folio reading of "solid" for the quartos' "sullied," although Elizabethan pronunciation made the choice between them almost moot.

49. Scoloker, *Daiphantus,* A2r. As Charles Nicholl notes, the name "Anthony Scoloker" is "a bibliographic convenience": *Daiphantus* is actually signed by "An. Sc." (*Lodger,* 312n.35).

50. Sidney, *Defence of Poesie,* 121–24. Helgerson himself places Sidney on the side of an authors' theater (Helgerson, *Forms of Nationhood,* 201) and the mingling of kings and clowns on the side of "a popular theater" (227). Acknowledging the existence of a few classical tragicomedies, Sidney insists that "if we mark them well, we shall find, that they never or very daintily, match Horn-pipes and Funerals" (*Defence,* 123). Shakespeare seems to allude to this passage when he has Claudius euphuisti-

cally defend "mirth in funeral" and "dirge in marriage" (*Hamlet* 1.2.12), a theme upon which Hamlet famously obsesses.

51. Scoloker, *Daiphantus*, A2r.

52. *Hamlet* 2.2.435–39. In Hamlet's memory, the play was as homogeneous in tone as it was select in admirers, with "no sallets in the lines to make the matter savory, nor no matter in the phrase that might indict the author of affection" (441–43).

53. *Hamlet* 3.2.25–28, 1.2.160–63, 2.2.222–24, 2.2.537 and 546; 4.3.4, 4.7.18.

54. Harvey, *Marginalia*, 232–33. With customary brilliance, A. C. Bradley comments on the inseparability of the popular and arcane aspects of the play: "Into this most mysterious and inward of his works, it would seem, the poet flung, as if in derision of his cultured critics, well-nigh every stimulant of popular excitement he could collect: 'carnal, bloody, and unnatural acts'; five deaths on the open stage, three appearances of a ghost, two of a mad woman, a dumb-show, two men raving and fighting in a grave at a funeral, the skulls and bones of the dead, a clown bandying jests with a prince, songs at once indecent and pathetic, marching soldiers, a fencing-match, then a litter of corpses, and explosions in the first Act and explosions in the last. And yet out of this sensational material—not in spite of it, but out of it—he made the most mysterious and inward of his dramas" ("Shakespeare's Theater," 372).

55. Fulwell, *Like Will to Like*, A2r. The title page states that the play was "made by Ulpian Fulwell," and the name "Ulpian Fulwell" (F1v) appears at the end of the play as well.

56. For Gascoigne's letter, see *A Hundreth Sundrie Flowres*, 369. Gascoigne thinks that the heterogeneity of a play is in any case inevitable: "I am of opinion, that in every thing which is written (the holy scriptures excepted) there are to be found wisdom, folly, emulation, and detraction. For as I never yet saw any thing so clerkly handled, but that therein might be found some imperfections: So could I never yet read fable so ridiculous but that therein some morality might be gathered" (370).

57. Coleridge, *Biographia*, 2.13. On Pauline accommodationism in the theater, see my *Shakespeare's Tribe*.

58. *Hamlet* 2.2.500–1, 3.2.10–12, 2.2.396–99, 5.2.107 and 113, 3.1.151, 5.1.76 and 160–61, 5.1.140–41.

59. *Hamlet* 3.2.149, 1.5.143–64; Empson, "Hamlet" (1953), 85. Gurr

cites a further instance of a strangely improvisational moment in *Hamlet* that spotlights the actors as actors. When Hamlet and Polonius discuss how Polonius once played the part of Julius Caesar "i' the university" and was "kill'd" by Brutus (3.2.98–106), they seem to be alluding to Shakespeare's own *Julius Caesar*, in which the original actor of Hamlet's part, Richard Burbage, must have played Brutus, and the original actor of Polonius's part must have played Caesar. Gurr treats this illusion-breaking as a final remnant of a bygone clownish theatrics: while "Richard Burbage as Hamlet could still step outside his role" in the manner of Tarlton "to joke" with the audience, contemporary praise for Burbage's ability to "convince his audiences of the reality of the roles he played" shows "how fully the power of dramatic illusion in the self-contained play took over from Tarltonizing" (*Playgoing*, 127–28). But Gurr distinguishes improvisational comedy from scripted tragedy too sharply. The illusion-breaking in this scene is characteristic of the play, and its effect is as tragic as comic: by alluding to these past roles of "Hamlet" and "Polonius," Shakespeare eerily forecasts that Hamlet will kill Polonius.

60. Nicholas Rowe (1709) claimed to have been told that the "top" of Shakespeare's "Performance was the Ghost in his own *Hamlet*" (quoted in *WS*, 2.265).

61. In his exhilarating reading of *Hamlet*, Weimann similarly emphasizes how the bifold authority of players and dramatists "pervasively informs what is most enigmatic, but for all that highly effective, in the characterization of Hamlet" (*Author's Pen*, 151–79 [161]).

62. Helgerson, *Forms of Nationhood*, 224; *Hamlet* 2.2.401; my emphasis.

63. Gee, *New Shreds*, 21; *HS*, 8.57. Thomas Lorkins refers to "Burbage his company" in a 1613 letter (quoted in Foakes, ed., *Henry VIII*, 179), while the title page to the 1594 edition of *A Knack to Knowe a Knave* states that the comedy has "sundrie tymes bene played by ED. ALLEN and his Companie." Drant, *Art*, B1r (my emphasis); in Thomas North's 1579 translation, Plutarch mentions that Thespis "played a part himself, as the old fashion of the Poets was" (*Lives*, 104).

64. "But oh! what praise more powerful can we give / The dead, than that by him the King's Men live, / His Players" (Digges, quoted in *WS*, 2.232).

65. Sonnets 31 and 29; *Midsummer* 1.2.1, 3.1.1, 3.1.23–24 and 47, and 1.2.106.

66. *Midsummer* 1.2.85 and 4.2.9–12. Quince is the only one who gets two parts—the Prologue, and Thisby's father—although the father never actually appears in the performance.

67. *Midsummer* 4.2.35–38 and 5.1.186–87; *Hamlet* 3.2.240 and 263. Bottom is competitive with Quince from their first scene, where he feels the need to speak nearly every time after Quince has spoken. In the scene when Bottom returns, Quince has two short lines and Bottom does all the rest of the talking. It is not often remarked, however, that the unlearned Bottom does not aspire to become a writer as well as an actor: after he awakes from his fairy-induced sleep, he decides that "I will get Peter Quince to write a ballet of this dream" (4.1.214–15).

68. *Midsummer* 1.2.2–3 and 5.1.357–61.

69. *Hamlet* 1.2.125; 3.3.22–23; 2.2.474–75; 1.2.3-4, 3, 14–15; 1.1.48; 1.2.6–7, 25–26, 11–12, and 122.

70. *Hamlet* 1.3.20–24, 3.1.5, 1.2.20, 5.2.230, 1.5.97, and 2.2.252–62, where Rosencrantz tells Hamlet that his "ambition" makes Denmark seem "too narrow for your mind."

71. *Hamlet* 3.2.44–45.

72. *Hamlet* 3.1.150 and 154; Earle, *Micro-cosmographie*, E3r–v; Davies, *Humours Heav'n on Earth*, 208, cited (with incorrect date) in *WS*, 2.214. Davies offers the initials "W. S." and "R. B."—presumably, William Shakespeare and Richard Burbage—for players whom Fortune had not "guerdoned . . . to their deserts."

73. Gentili, *Commentatio*, 234/256.

74. *Hamlet* 4.7.43. When Ophelia describes Hamlet as the courtier, the soldier, and the scholar all rolled into one, and Osric calls Laertes "the card or calendar of gentry" (5.2.109–10), they both view a single person as many. Yet neither can imagine this comprehensive self as incorporating more than a high-class variety. Cf. Gabriel Harvey's characterization of Sidney in *Pierces Supererogation* (1593) as "the Secretary of Eloquence; the breath of the Muses; the honey-bee of the daintiest flowers of Wit, and Art; the Pith of moral, & intellectual Virtues; the arm of Bellona in the field; the tongue of Suada in the chamber; the spirit of Practice in esse; and the Paragon of Excellency in print" (53).

75. *Hamlet* 3.2.384; J. Cocke, in John Stephens, *Satyrical Essayes*, quoted in *ES*, 4.255–57.

76. *HS*, 1.140; *Staple of News*, "Prologue for the Stage," 22–24, induct.11–12, prol. 1.

77. *Julius Caesar* 1.2.236–66, 1.1.70, 2.1.166 and 173; *1H4* 3.2.41. For the

politics of "the people" in *Julius Caesar*, see Oliver Arnold's superb *Third Citizen*, chap. 4.

CHAPTER THREE

1. For a useful collection of documents on the suppression of the cycles, see Wickham et al., eds., *English Professional Theatre*, 64–69.

2. Shakespeare was not the first English playwright to attempt a radical revision of the Corpus Christi plays. In the 1530s John Bale wrote a now-lost cycle of Protestant plays on the life of Christ, although it is unclear whether this cycle was ever presented commercially; see Happé, *John Bale*, 5–6. Bale was also the author of the early English history play *King Johan*.

3. See, e.g., Barber, "Family"; Kernan, "Henriad"; Montrose, "Purpose"; and Greenblatt, *Shakespearean Negotiations*.

4. Barber, "Family," 29. For these critics, religion is always already secularized, which is why they call it "ritual." Kernan describes secularization in the history cycle as "a movement from ceremony and ritual to history" ("Henriad," 270), while Barber characterizes the Renaissance theater generally as "an agency in the historical shift of the Renaissance and Reformation from a ritual and ceremonial view of life . . . toward a psychological and historical view" ("Family," 19).

5. Nashe, *Works*, 1.212; Barber, "Family," 24. In *Shakespearean Negotiations*, Greenblatt famously speaks of the "exchange of social energy" (94) between church and theater.

6. See Knapp, *Shakespeare's Tribe;* Barber, "Family," 38. It is important to stress that the English church never eliminated the image of Christ's sacrifice from its worship. Rather, church polemicists insisted on the *internalization* of that image through a contemplation inspired by communion as well as by preaching. When, for example, Thomas Becon (1564) tells communicants that they should worship Christ "in mind," he means that they "should not too much fix and set their minds or eyes upon the bread and cup, that is set upon the holy table, but rather they should lift up their minds and hearts, and consider, behold, honor, and worship Christ, . . . which . . . sitteth on the right hand of the heavenly Father" (*Works*, 3.360). As Becon's exhortation demonstrates, the established church regarded the Eucharist as effectively an image of an image, a limited version of the fuller picture that a worshipper should "behold" internally.

7. For Smith and the lawsuit in which he appears, see Raylor, *Cava-*

liers, 59–65. Raylor transcribes some of the court case from Public Record Office manuscripts, but I quote from a fuller transcription that Alan Nelson has generously provided me.

8. I draw this information from Raylor. Like so many clerical theater lovers during the English Renaissance, Smith was an Oxford graduate and a Christ Church man.

9. Erne, *Shakespeare,* 76.

10. *2 Henry IV* epil.27–30; *Henry V* epil.1–2.

11. *Richard II* 1.2.37–38.

12. Honigmann, *John Weever,* 33, 90.

13. Here is the relevant passage from *The Whipping of the Satyre:*

I dare here speak it, and my speech maintain,
That Sir John Falstaff was not any way
More gross in body, than you are in brain.
But whether should I (help me now, I pray)
For your gross brain, you like J. Falstaff graunt,
Or for small wit, suppose you John of Gaunt?
(D3r)

14. *2 Henry IV* epil.27–32; Weever, *Mirror,* A2r.

15. Weever, *Mirror,* A3v. How do we know that Weever had Shakespeare's *Julius Caesar* specifically in mind? As F. J. Furnivall notes in *The Shakspere Allusion-Book,* "there is no speech by Brutus on Caesar's ambition" in Plutarch (Ingleby et al., eds., *Shakspere,* 1.94).

16. *Julius Caesar* 3.2.159, 225, 130–33.

17. Weever, *Agnus Dei,* O1r, L8v, M2v, N1r. By contrast, the Corpus Christi plays insist that the Crucifixion is a mass spectacle: "I pray you pepyll that passe me by," exclaims Jesus on the cross in the Towneley Crucifixion play (*Towneley Plays,* 1.23.233), while in the York version he speaks to "al men pat walkis by waye or strete" (*York Plays,* 35.253).

18. In this light, it is revealing to compare Weever's *Agnus Dei* to the Passion poem of another Shakespeare admirer, John Davies of Hereford. Davies's poem, *The Holy Roode* (1609), called a "Speaking Picture" on its title page, manifests none of Weever's competitive edge toward playwrights. On the contrary, *The Holy Roode* narrows the gap between theatrical and literary art by insisting on the visuality of the reading experience. Like the Chorus in *Henry V,* Davies continually exhorts his readers to "look" and "see": "Now think, O think, thou seest" (B2r); "Now, Eye of Sp'rite, behold this Spectacle" (D4v); "Now let a sacred

Trance transport thy Spirit / O Man, to that unholy-holy Mount" (E2r). In Davies's account, Christ's Passion was indeed a spectacle for the masses—he lay "nail'd amidst the Throng" (E3v)—and Christ himself had insisted on the visuality of his suffering: "You that pass by this place, behold me" (F2r). For Davies, Christ crucified remains an image *as* a "Book": "when we read him over, see we shall / His Head with Thorns, his Ears with Blasphemies; / His Eyes, with Tears; his honied Mouth with Gall; / With Wounds his Flesh; his Bones with Agonies / All full" (G1r). Thus Davies begins his poem by asking Christ to allow a kind of transubstantiation of the Passion into Davies's poetry: "Vouchsafe, sweet *Christ,* my *Paper,* be thy *Cross:* / My *Pen,* that *Nail,* that *Nail'd* thine holy Hand: / Mine *Ink,* thy *Blood*" (A4r). Tellingly, Davies thinks that the gap between reading and beholding can be narrowed only if he offers himself as a sacrifice, too, with a "Heart" able to "bleed" "through my Pen" (A3v).

19. Beard, *Theatre,* 192.

20. F[ord]., *Christes Bloodie Sweat,* 889–94, 985–86.

21. Ingleby et al., eds., *Shakspere,* 1.237; *The Merchant of Venice* 4.1.278–81.

22. [Kyd], *Spanish Tragedy,* 4.4.76–82; I retain the parentheses of the 1592 text.

23. Vickers, *'Counterfeiting' Shakespeare,* 276. To my mind, Vickers definitively settles the question of Ford's authorship.

24. Goffe, *Careless Shepherdess,* 72–73; Goffe, *Deliverance.* During his lifetime, Goffe also published two pious Latin eulogies that he delivered while a student at Oxford. For doubts about Goffe's authorship of *The Careless Shepherdess,* see *JCS,* 4.501–5. No such questions surround Goffe's tragedies, which were published posthumously. All of them end with "murd'red Trunks" on the stage, as the final speaker of *Orestes* puts it (I3v). Yet even one of these tragedies resists the finality of death, if only to envision more bleeding. In *The Raging Turk* (written c. 1618, published 1631), the emperor Soliman refuses to bury his father, whose "corpse" he mentions three times in his closing speech. Rather than let "Religion . . . cloak" his loss, Soliman vows to make the "world" his father's "tomb," particularly at the expense of "Christians": "thy Epitaph I'll carve / In Funerals, destruction is the book / In which we'll write thy annals, blood's the Ink, / Our sword the Pen" (O2r–v).

25. *Richard II* 1.1.103–4; *1 Henry IV* 1.1.24–27; *Richard II* 4.1.240–41; *2 Henry IV* 4.5.210–12; *Richard II* 5.6.49–50.

26. *1 Henry IV* 2.4.383–84; 1.2.114–16; 5.4.133–34, 110 s.d., and 115–19.

27. *Richard II* 5.6.45–46; *1 Henry IV* 1.2.113 and 95–96; *Henry V* 2.3.18–22.

28. *1 Henry IV* 3.3.9–10; *Henry V* 2.3.16–17 and 22–23.

29. *Henry V* 1.1.22–23, 32–33, and 53.

30. *Henry V* 1.1.54-55 and 64. In his 1817 *Characters of Shakespeare's Plays,* Hazlitt writes, "It has sometimes occurred to us that Shakespeare, in describing 'the reformation' of the Prince, might have had an eye to himself" (*Complete Works,* 4.287).

31. *Henry V* 4.1.304.

32. *Henry V* epil.1–8.

33. *Henry V* epil.9–13.

34. *Henry V* 5.ch.28, 1.2.224. Shakespeare's reference to his "mangling" pen recalls Pistol's threat to a French soldier that he shall be "mangled . . . by this my sword" (*1 Henry V* 4.4.39; cf. 2.4.60 and 5.2.34).

35. *Henry V* epil.9–14, 4.1.135–37, 4.8.120; *Richard II* 3.3.94.

36. *Henry V* 5.2.353–55; 1.1.79–81, 1–11, 20, 71; prol. 9. I address these eucharistic questions in *Henry V* more fully in chapter 4 of *Shakespeare's Tribe.*

37. Phil. 1.18. I quote the 1568 Bishops' Bible; the 1587 Geneva Bible reads, "Christ is preached all manner ways, whether it be under a pretence, or sincerely: and I therein joy: yea and will joy." Calvin in his *Commentarie . . . Uppon . . . Philippians* (1548; trans. 1584) paraphrases, "they promoted the Gospel notwithstanding, whatsoever their intent was: for God by evil and wicked instruments sometime bringeth to pass an excellent work." Calvin is, however, careful to add that we should not therefore ordain "the ungodly" as "lawful ministers of Christ" (17).

38. Letter of Sir Walter Cope to Robert Cecil, quoted in *WS,* 2.332. The *OED* is seriously off the mark when it cites an 1823 text as the earliest usage of *revive* meaning "to put (an old play) upon the stage again." The entries for *revive* as a noun and for *revival* do better, citing examples from 1663 and 1664, respectively. But Cope's letter suggests a conversational ease with the usage in Shakespeare's lifetime. For other pre-Restoration instances, see, e.g., Sir Henry Herbert on collecting the receipts for "a revived play" in 1628 (quoted in *JCS,* 1.23), and Thomas Heywood's "Prologue to the Play of Queen *Elizabeth* as it was last revived at the Cock-pit" in his 1637 *Pleasant Dialogues and Dramma's* (248).

39. *Cynthia's Revels,* Ind. 194–96; Gardiner, *BF,* C2r; C.G. in Brome, *Antipodes,* A3r; *FF,* A7r, in *Riverside Shakespeare,* 103. Cf. John Warren in the 1640 edition of Shakespeare's *Poems:* "What, lofty *Shakespeare,* art again reviv'd?" (*4v).

40. *Pericles* 5.1.207–8.

CHAPTER FOUR

1. See *PD,* chap. 8, especially 198–99, 220–24, and 209–10. Bentley tightens the focus even further when he notes that different theater companies compiled different records of coauthorship. Over the lifespan of the King's Men, for instance, coauthorship appears to have *succeeded* single authorship in importance. While the first principal dramatist of the King's Men, Shakespeare, seems to have preferred writing singly, the next principal dramatist, Fletcher, greatly preferred writing with others. And Bentley adds that, from 1616 to 1642, the King's Men performed far more coauthored than single-authored plays at court. McGuire also stresses that the King's Men became relatively more interested in collaborative plays later in their history ("Collaboration," 543–45), but he fails to acknowledge the trouble this causes for a timeline in which authorship takes the place of collaboration.

2. Day, Rowley, and Wilkins, *Travailes,* H4v, A2r. There are two ambiguous possessives in manuscripts dating from around 1599: "our Authors intent" in the epilogue to *Club Law* (p. 105), and "our Authors pen" in the chorus ending the first act of *The Thracian Wonder* (although the play may have been written a decade or so later: see *Thracian,* xlix–lvii). *The Little French Lawyer,* performed c.1620 but not printed till the 1647 Beaumont and Fletcher folio, refers in prologue to "the writers and our selves," in epilogue to "us and our Poets" (*BF,* 75). The prologue to *Arviragus and Philicia* (1639) speaks in general of "our Poets" but more ambiguously of "the Authors judgment" (A3r-v).

3. Vickers, *Shakespeare,* 10–18. Vickers notes that his figures document "only the first publication of acknowledged coauthored plays, not their reprintings (often considerable). Nor have I attempted to list the many collaborations of which we have evidence in Henslowe's Diary, the Stationers' Register, the licensing records of Sir Henry Herbert, and other contemporary sources" (15). With the different cutoff dates of 1584 and 1623, Erne finds "multiple authorship" acknowledged in "13 of the 111 plays attributed," or "less than 12 percent" (*Shakespeare,* 44).

4. Vickers, *Shakespeare*, 10. The exceptional decade, according to Vickers's chart, is the 1620s, when 28 single authorships and 5 coauthorships were acknowledged—a ratio of less than 6 to 1.

5. Masten, *Textual Intercourse*, 131. Cf. Brooks: "The phrase 'collaborative authorship' did not exist in 1647, but the Beaumont-Fletcher folio . . . suggests that it would have already been an oxymoron," because "collaboration was incompatible with emergent notions of authorship as an individualized activity" (*From Playhouse to Printing House*, 152 and xiv).

6. Vickers, *Shakespeare*, 18; *PD*, 232n.29; *JCS*, 4.753.

7. This is not to say that coauthorship was difficult to *admit*. For instance, Jonson told Drummond that after writing *Eastward Ho!* he "voluntarily imprisoned himself with Chapman and Marston, who had written it amongst them." Bentley comments: "Jonson evidently took collaboration for granted as a common method of composition in his time and felt no shame or hesitancy in acknowledging his participation to Drummond" (*PD*, 206–7). When I claim that coauthorship was hard to *notice*, I mean that it seemed relatively insignificant.

8. Barroll, *Politics*, 19. For skepticism about Barroll's argument, see Honigmann, "Plague." In particular, Honigmann casts doubt on Barroll's claim that "Shakespeare did not write plays if he had no stage readily available for public performance" (*Politics*, 208).

9. *Hamlet* 5.2.30–31 and 10–11; for the sake of clarity, I have substituted "ere" for its older form in the text, "or."

10. Greenblatt, *Will*, 369; Duncan-Jones, *Ungentle*, 209. For the best introduction to Wilkins, see Nicholl, *Lodger*, 197–226.

11. *Pericles* 1.1.149, 5.3.3. Nicholl speculates that Shakespeare turned to Wilkins for help in "keeping up with the new brash fashion of the city comedies" (*Lodger*, 220), although none of the city comedy in *Pericles* occurs in the scenes attributed to Wilkins.

12. The 1609 *Pimlyco or Runne Red-Cap* complains of a "Crowd" so "loud" and "swarm"ing that it reminds the speaker of the audience at "*Shore*, or *Pericles*" (C1r, cited in *WS*, 2.217). Erne notes that "in the fifteen years prior to the publication of the First Folio, *Pericles* was, in fact, printed more often than any other of Shakespeare's plays" (*Shakespeare*, 192n.1).

13. *Pericles* 5.1.241. The last words of Pericles' wife Thaisa in the play—"My father's dead"—are followed by Pericles' decree that "ourselves / Will in that kingdom spend our following days. / Our son and daughter shall in Tyrus reign" (5.3.78–82).

14. Shakespeare, *Sonnets*, 1, 16, and 2.

15. These were *A Plaine and Familiar Exposition of the Ninth and Tenth Chapters of the Proverbs of Salomon* (1st ed., 1606); *A Plaine and Familiar Exposition of the Eleventh and Twelfth Chapters of the Proverbs* (1607); *A Plaine and Familiar Exposition of the Thirteenth and Fourteenth Chapters of the Proverbs* (1608); *Two Sermons* (1608); *Ten Sermons . . . of the Lords Supper* (1609); *A Plaine and Familiar Exposition of the Fifteenth, Sixteenth, and Seventeenth Chapters of the Proverbs* (1609); *A Plaine and Familiar Exposition: of the Eighteenth, Nineteenth, and Twentieth Chapters of the Proverbs* (1610); *Foure Godlie and Fruitfull Sermons* (1610); *Three Godlie and Fruitful Sermons* (1610); and *Ten Godly and Fruitfull Sermons* (1610).

16. "Three copies [of the *Travailes*] exist in which a leaf has been inserted with a dedication to the Sherley family signed by the authors, 'Iohn Day. William Rowley. George Wilkins'" (Vickers, *Shakespeare*, 11; for an image of the page, see 14). Not all copies of *The Dumbe Knight* cite Markham on their title page, though all include the dedication by Machin.

17. The novelty of the Dod and Cleaver publications is even more striking when one considers the evidence that these publications arose almost by accident. The letter to the reader in the second anonymous edition of the *Plaine and Familiar Exposition of the Ten Commandements* declared that the book had been "received" from the "mouth" of "a reverent faithful Pastor," although it was "neither penned nor perused by himself, nor published with his consent or knowledge"; instead, an unnamed "godly ingenious young man" had "collected" it (A2r), presumably by shorthand, during the pastor's sermons. The next year, Dod and Cleaver acknowledged the *Ten Commandements* in a dedicatory letter explaining that "when these Sermons were first preached, it was never once intended that they should come to the press. . . . But since some of the ordinary hearers had published their notes . . . without our knowledge or consent, and many faults were escaped in writing & printing, . . . therefore both for our clearing, and the better satisfying of the Christian reader, we were compelled to review and refine the whole treatise. Wherein we have jointly labored (as near as we could) to set down everything, without addition or detraction, as it was first delivered in the public ministry" (A2r). Circumstances had changed by the time Dod and Cleaver published their next work, *A Plaine and Familiar Exposition of the Ninth and Tenth Chapters of the Proverbs of Salomon* (1606).

Puritan stalwarts, they had both been suspended from preaching, and, as they declared in the dedicatory letter to their commentary on Proverbs, they were "now more willing to make some work for the Press, because we have no employment in the Pulpit" (A3r). This enforced leisure resulted in the nine other titles published by 1610.

18. Outside of the theater, the only coauthors to have more than one living partner were Dod and Cleaver: Cleaver and Richard Webb are named as the authors of *Foure Sermons* (1613), and Dod and William Hinde are named as the authors of *Bathshebaes Instructions* (1614).

19. Day, Rowley, and Wilkins, *Travailes*, 55–56.

20. I quote the title page of *The Tragedies of Tancred and Gismund, Compiled By the Gentlemen of the Inner Temple* (1591); Greene, *Groatsworth*, 82. A gentlemanly sense of corporate identity is also stressed in Spenser and Harvey's *Three Proper, and Wittie, Familiar Letters: Lately Passed Betweene Two Universitie Men* (1580).

21. Deacon and Walker, *Summarie Answere*, *2r, *3v, *5r. Dod and Cleaver preached together at Banbury as part of a "combination" of godly clergymen. The title page of Preston and Green's *Appellatio* (1620) anounces that the coauthors were "Benedictini," brothers of the same religious order. For both clergymen and theater people, the language of fraternity often bespoke ties that were literally familial. Dod married Ann Bownd, the sister of the preacher Nicholas Bownd, who was also the step-daughter of the preacher Richard Greenham, and two of John and Ann's children went on to become preachers themselves. Likewise, theater people often "married into each other's families," and "the leading theatrical families intermarried repeatedly" (Honigmann and Brock, eds., *Playhouse Wills*, 5–6).

22. On the practice of portioning out the writing of plays, see *PD*, 228–34; and Vickers, *Shakespeare*, 27–28 and 33–34. As Neil Carson points out, a play might have been divided among coauthors "in a variety of ways: the allocation of scenes might be entirely mechanical (for example by act); one author might supply the plot and another carry out its execution; one writer might take the main action, another the underplot; or one playwright might undertake farcical scenes while another wrote the serious episodes" (*Companion*, 58). Masten is right to emphasize that theater scholars are often highly speculative in their attempts "to make collaborative playtexts conform to an authorial model by separating them into smaller units ostensibly identified with particular single playwrights" ("Playwrighting," 372), but he is too quick

to dismiss the evidence that the writing of plays by units was both a common practice and a common hypothesis about the practice during the Renaissance.

23. I cite the dates of first editions only. *Ten Sermons* had eleven editions between 1609 and 1634.

24. See also the *Cantiones . . . Sacrae . . . Autoribus Thoma Tallisio & Guilielmo Birdo* (1575), which interweaves sets of songs by each composer, attributing the songs (seventeen to each composer) at the top of the page.

25. Holinshed, *Chronicles*, ¶2v. Harrison's *Historicall Description of the Islande of Britayne* required separate pagination, too; he signs his dedicatory epistle "W. H." (*2v). Stanyhurst's name appears on the title page of *The Historie of Irelande* as the author who "continued" Holinshed's history to 1547; Stanyhurst's portion begins with a dedicatory letter to Sir Henry Sidney (76). In his own dedicatory letter to the *Historie of Irelande*, Holinshed emphasizes that he has followed the order of Edmund Campion's history and used Campion's "own words" as much as possible: "this I thought good to signify, the rather for that I esteem it good dealing in no wise to defraud him of his deserved praise" (B2r). For interesting reflections on the "syndicate" that wrote the *Chronicles*, see Patterson, *Reading Holinshed's Chronicles*, especially chaps. 1–3.

26. Baldwin et al., *Myrroure*, ed. Campbell, 68–69. John Higgins added *The First Part of the Mirour for Magistrates* in 1574, and Thomas Blenerhasset added *The Second Part* in 1578; see Campbell, *Parts*. In each of the 1573, 1575, and 1587 editions of Gascoigne's collected works, the internal title page of *Jocasta* states that the play was written by "George Gascoigne and Francis Kinwelmershe of Grays Inn, and there by them presented." The notation "done by F. Kinwelmarshe" appears after acts 1 and 4; "done by G. Gascoigne" appears after acts 2, 3, and 5; while "done by Chr. Yelverton" appears after the epilogue. Similarly, the 1591 text of *The Tragedies of Tancred and Gismund, Compiled By the Gentlemen of the Inner Temple* adds "Exegit Rod. Staff." after act 1, "Per Hen. No." after act 2, "G. Al." after act 3, "Composuit Chr. Hat." after act 4, and "R. W." after the epilogue, which Chambers takes to mean that Wilmot wrote act 5, too (*ES*, 3.514). Although Thomas Hughes claims that he was the sole reviser of the Inns of Court play *The Misfortunes of Arthur* (1587), he takes pains to note that the "Introduction" was "penned by Nicholas Trotte Gentleman," that he has omitted two speeches "penned by William *Fulbecke gentleman*" and also "a *Chorus* for the first act, and

another for the second act, by Master *Frauncis Flower*," and finally that "the dumb shows were partly devised by Master *Christopher Yelverton*, Master *Francis Bacon*, Master *John Lancaster* and others, partly by the said Master *Flower*" (*Certain Devises*, G1r–G2r).

27. In his letter to the reader of the Beaumont and Fletcher folio, the printer Humphrey Moseley apologizes for his inability to find a picture of Beaumont (unpag.), but the fact remains that he chose to include a picture of Fletcher rather than drop the idea of pictures altogether.

28. Cf. Brooks, *From Playhouse*, 185–87; and Masten, *Textual Intercourse*, 132–38. The twenty-one poems on Fletcher are by Howard, Mody, Peyton, Cockaine, Stapylton, Denham, Waller, Lovelace, Habington, Howell, Stanley, Gardiner, Buc, I. M., Herrick, Powell, Hills, Harris, Harington, Richard Brome, and Shirley. The five on both authors are by Pettus, Lisle, Web, Mayne, and Berkenhead. Three further poems (by Earle, Corbet, and Jonson) are addressed to Beaumont only, although the editor stresses that these were written at least "thirty years since" (*BF*, C3v), when Beaumont was alive or else shortly after his death. The remaining six poems (by L'Estrange, Howe, Palmer, Alexander Brome, and Cartwright, who wrote two) mention both playwrights but are torn between thinking about the plays as single-authored or coauthored. L'Estrange shifts uneasily between Beaumont and Fletcher, and Fletcher alone; Brome addresses his poem to "those renowned Twins of Poetry BEAUMONT & FLETCHER" (F3r) but spends most of his time talking about Fletcher. Howe, Palmer, and Cartwright all seem irritated by the idea that Fletcher needed Beaumont in any way: as Howe puts it in extolling Fletcher's "alone self," "his wit with wit he did not twist / to be Assist'd, but to Assist" (F2r).

29. Among the "Protestants' Helps for *Devotion*" that John Brinsley lists at the end of his *Fourth Part of the True Watch* (1624) are "M. Dod on the Commandments. M. Dod on the Lords Supper. M. Dod's household government" (V2v), even though all three books were published as coauthorships of Dod and Cleaver. The coauthorship of the *Ten Commandements* is haphazardly noted in the text itself. While retaining the cosigned dedicatory epistle with its multiple references to coauthorship, the 1606 edition claims that the text has been "Newly corrected by the Author," and the next document after the epistle is titled "A Friendly Counsel to the Christian reader, touching the Author and his book" (A3r).

The *Ten Commaundements* went through 18 editions between 1604 and 1635. The best introduction to Dod remains William Haller's *The Rise of Puritanism*, esp. 56–62. Haller mentions Cleaver only once in his entire book (120).

30. Gamage, *Linsi-Woolsie*, D1r–v.

31. I quote Mayne, in *BF*, D1r–v. Cf. Brooks on "the fantasy of an indivisible collaboration" in the commendatory poems, a "seamless univocality" of authorship (*From Playhouse*, 167 and 161). John Pettus refers to the two authors as "*Beaumont-Fletcher*" (*BF*, A4r); George Lisle says that their "fancies are so wov'n and knit,/'Twas *Francis-Fletcher*, or *John Beaumont* writ" (B1r); John Web thinks of the two as "two wits in growth/So just, as had one Soul informed both" (C2v); John Berkenhead calls them "Twins" (E1v). While scholars such as Masten have stressed the homoerotic charge in John Aubrey's famous assertion that Beaumont and Fletcher not only "lived together" but also "lay together; had one Wench in the house between them, which they did so admire; the same clothes and cloak, &c.; between them" (*Brief Lives*, 21), the stronger implication of Aubrey's account is that Beaumont and Fletcher were effectively one and the same.

32. Deacon and Walker, *Dialogicall Discourses*, A5r–v. Even books that showcased debates between writers could flirt with the notion that the two adversaries were somehow one, as in *Of Mariage and Wiving. An Excellent . . . Controversie, Betweene the Two Famous Tassi Now Living, the One Hercules the Philospher, the Other, Torquato the Poet* (1599), and *The Trying Out of the Truth . . . Between John Aynsworth and Henry Aynsworth* (1615). Neither the Tassos nor the Aynsworths were related, although in a prefatory letter to *The Trying Out* Henry claims that he has chosen to respond to John instead of several other possible "opposites" "for nation and for name (& I know not whither also for nearer alliance)" (A2r).

33. I am passing over the many books that presented themselves as compilations or anthologies of dead single authors, such as *The Workes of Geffrey Chaucer . . . With the Siege and Destruccion of the Worthy Citee of Thebes, Compiled by Jhon Lidgate* (1561), or *Epictetus Manuall. Cebes Table. Theophrastus Characters* (1616). Other clearly separable coauthorships include annotations or commentaries, such as *Annotationi di Scipio Gentili sopra La Gierusalemme Liberati di T. Tasso* (1586) and *Pub. Vergilii Maronis Opera. P. Mantutii Annotationes. G. Fabricii Annotationes* (1597). Translators, too, could be seen as coauthors—in his *Discourse of English Poetrie*, for instance, William Webbe (1586) refers to "the laudable Au-

thors of *Seneca* in English" (C4r)—and the language difference between original author and translator made it relatively easy to distinguish between them in theory.

34. Golding, trans., *Thabridgment,* *6r. Trogus is not mentioned in Wilkins's translation till Justinus' own preface beginning on A6r. After Justinus' history, Wilkins supplies "An Epitome of the Lives and Manners of the *Roman* Emperors. From the Reign of Caesar Augustus, to the Reign of *Rudolphus* the Emperor now living: *taken out of the books of Sext. Aurelius Victor*" (138r).

35. Jonson famously told readers of the 1616 Folio version of *Sejanus* "that this Book, in all numbers, is not the same with that which was acted on the public Stage, wherein a second Pen had good share: in place of which I have rather chosen, to put weaker (and no doubt less pleasing) of mine own, than to defraud so happy a *Genius* of his right, by my loathed *usurpation*" (*HS,* 4.351, my emphasis).

36. Meres, *Palladis,* 281v; Alexander in Drayton, *Englands* (1600 edition), A4r (my emphasis on "revives"); Harvey in Shirley's *Wedding,* A3v; May, quoted in Bradley and Adams, *Jonson Allusion-Book,* 141. Cf. Nicholas Downey's claim that, although "BEN is deceas'd," Samuel Harding's *Sicily and Naples* (1640) shows that Jonson is "*redivivus now*" (Harding, *Sicily,* 2v [*sic*]; cited in Bradley and Adams, *Jonson Allusion-Book,* 269). See also Robert Hills in Robert Baron's *Mirza* (1647), A4r, cited in Bradley and Adams, *Jonson Allusion-Book,* 285.

37. Cockaigne in Massinger, *Emperour,* A3r. John Jacson's commendatory poem to Shirley's *Royal Master* (1638) similarly ends, "Therefore will I hereafter cease to mourn / For those great wits, commended to the Urn, / And if't be true, that transmigrations be / They are in *Shirley* all, for aught I see" (B1v). Cf. George Lynn on John Tatham's *The Fancies Theater* (1640), (*)7v, cited in Bradley and Adams, *Jonson Allusion-Book,* 270.

38. Habington in Shirley, *Grateful Servant,* A5r, cited in Bradley and Adams, *Jonson Allusion-Book,* 143; Cooper in Shirley, *Royal Master,* A3v; W. Markham in the same volume states that Apollo "doth deign / (His darling Ben deceased) thou should'st be / Declar'd the heir apparent to his tree" (A4v, cited in Bradley and Adams, *Jonson Allusion-Book,* 258). See also Richard Doddridge in Harding, *Sicily and Naples,* A1v, cited in Bradley and Adams, *Jonson Allusion-Book,* 268.

39. Stow, Munday et al., *Survey of London* (London, 1633), A3r (a 1618 edition of the *Survey* contains a slightly different version of Munday's account).

40. Holinshed et al., *Chronicles*, ¶2v. The 1574 will of Wolfe's widow does indeed state that "Raphael Holinshed shall have and enjoy all such benefit profit and commodity as was promised unto him by my said late husband Reginald Wolfe for or concerning the translating or printing of a certain Chronicle which my said husband before his decease did prepare and intend to have printed"; see Plomer, ed., *Abstracts*, 20; cited by Pettegree, "Reyner Wolfe."

41. Estienne and Liebault, *Maison Rustique*, B2r.

42. *Pericles* 1.0.1–2, 12 (my emphasis), and 20.

43. For an excellent summary of the evidence, see Vickers, *Shakespeare;* for the fullest recent case, see Jackson, *Defining.*

44. As Steven Mullaney notes in *The Place of the Stage*, "Gower in fact conceals as much as he reveals, especially where the genealogical entanglements of Shakespeare's sources are concerned" (148). Mullaney does not mention Wilkins. For more on the instability of Gower as a figure for authorship, see also Masten, *Textual Intercourse*, 77–78.

45. See *PD*, 228–34. Again, a parceling out by acts was not the only available method of dramatic coauthorship, nor would it have prevented authors from consulting with each other and possibly editing each other's contributions to the play. In a letter to the theatrical impresario Philip Henslowe, the actor-playwright Nathan Field asserts that he and another playwright, Robert Daborne, "have spent a great deal of time in conference" about the "plot" of a play they are cowriting (*Henslowe Papers*, 84).

46. As Suzanne Gossett observes in her Arden edition of the play, "Almost all readers of *Pericles* note a striking change in the quality of the poetry at the beginning of the third act" (62). For the evidence that Wilkins composed the first two acts of *Pericles* and Shakespeare the last three, see especially Vickers's and Gossett's detailed accounts of such scholars as Dugdale Sykes, who underscored the "frequent omission of the relative pronoun in the nominative case" in the first two acts, which happens often in Wilkins's other writings but rarely in Shakespeare's (Sykes, quoted in Vickers, *Shakespeare*, 300); MacDonald Jackson, who isolated three rhyme pairs—"consist/resist," "him/sin," and "impudence/offence"—that appear in the first two acts of *Pericles* and in Wilkins's play *The Miseries of Inforct Marriage* but nowhere else in Shakespeare's attributed works; David Lake, who drew our attention to the presence in the first two acts of *Pericles* and in the *Miseries* of "rifts—a series of couplets broken by an unrhymed line, aabcc—and

rafts, or couplets appearing sporadically in passages of blank verse" (as paraphrased by Gossett, ed., *Pericles,* 64); and Ernst Honigmann, who discovered that "beginning a phrase with 'which' or 'to which' or 'of which' (the so-called Latin resumptive) and . . . beginning a sentence or phrase with 'this' or 'by this' or 'to this'" (as paraphrased by Gossett, 64) happens twenty times in the first two acts of *Pericles* yet not at all in the last three.

47. *Pericles* 1.0.2 and 11.

48. *Pericles* 1.1.26 and 1.0.22. Although most scholars agree that these tragedies were written between 1604 and 1608, the chronological order of Shakespeare's plays is speculative. Some have argued that *Measure for Measure* and *All's Well That Ends Well* were written after *Othello* and that *Timon* was written two or three years before *Pericles.* Even with this rearrangement, however, the clustering of tragedies remains striking.

49. *Coriolanus* 5.6.116; *Timon* 4.3.100; *Pericles* 5.3.102.

50. Pericles immediately decides to "leave" (3.1.79) the baby at Tharsus, although he does stay with her awhile before departing from Tharsus without her.

51. *Pericles* 1.1.69 and 1.0.18. Cf. Masten: "the incest . . . figures a particularly totalizing version of the (dangerous) control the author-function is said to exert" (*Textual Intercourse,* 80).

52. *Pericles* 2.5.19, 73, 81–82, 76, 90, and 18.

53. I quote the title page of the book. In his epistle dedicatory, Cleaver explains that "I durst not be too confident of my self, nor lean too hard on mine own judgment, but entreated, and obtained the assistance of that worthy and judicious Baronet, Sir *Erasmus Dryden,* and of the reverend learned, and eminent Divine, Master *John Dod,* with others of good note" (*Patrimony,* A4r). Thomas Nashe (1599) asserts the value of consensual coauthorship in its absence: attempting to excuse his part in the controversial *Isle of Dogs,* he calls the play "an imperfit Embrion," "for I having begun but the induction and first act of it, the other four acts without my consent, or the least guess of my drift or scope, by the players were supplied, which bred both their trouble and mine too" (*Works,* 3.153–54).

54. While Pericles is thrilled to recover a suit of armor that "my dead father did bequeath to me" (2.1.124), this is presented as so superficial an inheritance that Simonides can warn observers not to undervalue the armored Pericles by mistaking "the outward habit" for "the inward man" (2.2.57).

55. *Pericles* 2.3.3, 1.0.22 and 3.1.20. My thinking here depends, of course, on Stanley Cavell's *Disowning Knowledge*. For the suppression of motherhood in the play, see especially Adelman, *Suffocating Mothers*, 193–99; and Kahn, "Providential Tempest." Jennifer Panek shows how Dod and Cleaver, among other writers, habitually turn parents into one parent, the father: see her "Mother as Bawd."

56. Forty years later, Berkenhead ends his poem on Beaumont and Fletcher with a celebration of such marriage: "What strange Production is at last display'd,/(Got by two Fathers, without Female aid)/Behold, two *Masculines* espous'd each other,/*Wit* and the World were born without a *Mother*" (*BF,* E2v). But, as "strange" is meant to underscore, Berkenhead presents the analogy as strained, uncanny, and therefore sublime. Interestingly, *Pericles* has little to say about homosocial friendship as a model of unity. The loyal Helicanus serves as Pericles' "substitute" (5.3.51) at Tyre, and Pericles calls him "mine own" (5.1.214), but he is also "ancient" (5.3.51) like Gower, and he therefore seems less a friend than another nonbiological father-figure for Pericles. To Shakespeare's mind, as I'll shortly explain, the problem with friendship is not so much the possible sexual dimension of its unity (on which see Masten, *Textual Intercourse,* especially chap 2) as its lack of biologically generative power.

57. Adelman claims that "the play exorcizes sexuality itself and remakes the sexual family by nonsexual means, permitting it to escape its origin in the problematic maternal body" (*Suffocating Mothers,* 196), but Caroline Bicks rightly points to Thaisa's implicit promise at the end of the play that her "sanctity" will "bend" a "licentious ear" to her "sense" upon the recovery of her husband ("Backsliding," 222).

58. "Supremacy" is what Pericles attributes to his father after Simonides has reminded him of his father: "In that glory once he was;/Had princes sit like stars about his throne,/And he the sun for them to reverence;/None that beheld him but, like lesser lights,/Did vail their crowns to his supremacy" (2.3.38–42).

59. *Pericles* 1.2.17 and 5.1.195; at Ephesus, Pericles proclaims Marina "my daughter" (5.3.13) and Thaisa calls her "mine own" (48). Steevens was the first to add a comma to Pericles's "mine own Helicanus" (5.1.214) and thus change it into the statement that Marina is "mine own, Helicanus," but the emendation is uncertain.

60. *Cymbeline* 5.5.120 and 452–58.

61. *Winter's Tale* 5.2.29 and 5.3.128; *Tempest* 5.1.195. Prospero also as-

sures Miranda that, when they were both left for dead on the high seas, she "did preserve me" (1.2.153).

62. Brome, in *BF,* G1r; Randolph, *Poems* (written c. 1632, published 1638), 97, in *HS,* 11.392.

63. *HS,* 1.137; Chapman in Field, *Woman,* A4r; *Henslowe Papers,* 67 and 84; all these references are cited in Brinkley, *Nathan Field.* Child actors were often apprenticed to adult actors as their "boys": see *ES,* 1.362. And adult actors were capable of viewing younger actors as their heirs: one of the jests in *Tarltons Jests* (1613) is entitled "How *Tarlton* made *Armin* his adopted son to succeed him" (C2r).

64. Aubrey MS quoted in *WS* 2.254; *Venus and Adonis,* ded. letter; *Sonnets,* 1 and 18.

65. *TNK* 2.2.32–34 and 78–83, 1.2.1, and 2.2.18.

66. *TNK* 2.2.154, 5.1.17, 3.6.46, 2.1.26 and 30, 2.5.28–29.

67. The best account of the play as allegorizing the coauthorship that produced it is Donald Hedrick's "'Be Rough With Me,'" which argues that "the play thematically explores the nature of artistic rivalry" (46). See also Frey, "Collaborating."

68. *TNK* 5.3.20; prol. 10, 13, 28, 18–20, 23–24. For example, Arcite assures Palamon that in a previous battle "you outwent me,/Nor could my wishes reach you," while Palamon counters that "still before" him "flew/The lightning" of Arcite's "valor" (3.6.79–85).

69. Waith, ed., *Two Noble Kinsmen,* 62. For a summary of the evidence, see Vickers, *Shakespeare,* 402–32.

70. *TNK* 2.1.53–54. As Hedrick observes, the play represents "collaborative labor" as "at once imitative and adversarial" ("'Be Rough with Me,'" 59).

71. *TNK* 3.1.97 and 5.3.123–28. Cf. Hedrick, "'Be Rough with Me,'" 69.

72. *TNK* 5.3.22. By keeping the battle offstage, however, Shakespeare and Fletcher do give the audience an aural rather than visual appreciation of the combat.

73. *TNK* 5.3.128–30. Singing is consistently opposed to virility in the play. *Two Noble Kinsmen* begins with a boy singing; the Jailer's Daughter sings, and she fantasizes about boys who "must be all gelt for musicians,/And sing the wars of Theseus" (4.1.131–34). Remembering the mutuality of her childhood love for another girl, Emilia declares that "Had mine ear/Stol'n some new air, or at adventure humm'd one/From

musical coinage, why, it was a note/Whereon her spirits would sojourn (rather dwell on)/And sing it in her slumbers" (1.3.74–78).

74. *TNK* prol.15 and 11, 1.1.64–70.

75. *TNK* 5.4.7, 2.2.107–10.

76. Hedrick finds the "professionalist subtext" so "odd for a retiring" rather than "aspiring" dramatist that he concludes Shakespeare did not coauthor the play ("'Be Rough with Me,'" 71).

77. *TNK* 5.4.114; Steevens, quoted in Vickers, *Shakespeare*, 404; Spencer, "*Two Noble Kinsmen*," 257.

78. *TNK* prol.14; 4.3.5; prol.17–18, 29; 1.1.45; 5.1.107–15.

79. *TNK* 5.1.115, 1.2.13 and 32, 5.4.1–3, 95, and 86. Marjorie Garber sensibly characterizes the ending of the play as "the melting of two (kinsmen, authors) into one" but only "at the price of a death" (Garber, *Shakespeare*, 906). I am arguing that, for Shakespeare, the price was as much a survival as a death.

80. Spencer, "*Two Noble Kinsmen*," 264.

81. According to Paul Bertram, "comparisons of one kind or another between the Daughter and Ophelia have in fact been commonplace since the time of [the eighteenth-century Shakespeare editor] Seward" (*Shakespeare*, 214–15). Coleridge blamed Fletcher for "the mad scenes of the Jailer's Daughter," which he believed Fletcher had "coarsely imitated from *Hamlet*" (*Coleridge on Shakespeare*, 133), while Hazlitt made Fletcher share the guilt of the "fantastic copy" with Beaumont (*Complete Works* 6.261). By contrast, Greenblatt notes of Shakespeare that "the ghosts of his past accomplishments haunt the late plays to an exceptional degree" (*Will*, 370).

82. *TNK* 4.2.26.

EPILOGUE

1. Aubrey (c. 1681) reports that Shakespeare "was not a company keeper[,] lived in Shoreditch, wouldn't be debauched, & if invited to[,] writ[,] he was in pain" (*WS*, 2.252).

2. In *Two Gentlemen of Verona* (c. 1591), a band of outlaws find the banished Valentine to be "a man of such perfection/As we do in our quality much want" (4.1.55–56) and demand that he be "king for our wild faction" (37), like "Robin Hood" (36). Only after his reign of outlawry does Valentine have his "unrivall'd merit" (5.4.144) confirmed, in the wild, by the duke who banished him from court.

3. *Tempest* 1.2.55, 3.3.21-24; Hakewill, *Apologie*, 8; *Tempest* 4.1.123.

4. In a fine reading of *The Tempest*, Masten makes the connection to Jonson but then rejects it (*Textual Intercourse*, 111–12).

5. *Tempest* 1.2.77; Prospero's magic is called his "art" four times in his first scene alone, at 1.2.1, 25, 291, and 372.

6. *Tempest* 1.2.89–90, 104, 167–68, and 107–8; 4.1.120–22; Hakewill, *Apologie*, 9; and *Tempest* 5.1.23 (my emphasis). For more on Prospero's kenosis, see my *Shakespeare's Tribe*, 54–55.

7. *Tempest*, epilogue; Marston, *Sophonisba* 5.4.4–46 and epilogue. Cf. William Fennor's more qualified acknowledgment of the playwright's weakness in his 1616 "Description of a Poet," where he characterizes a play as the author's baby:

> at first 'tis weak,
> Till by the life of Action it doth speak,
> In a square Theater: yet understand
> The Actor speaks but at the second hand.
> (*Fennors Descriptions*, B2v–B3r)

8. *Tempest* 4.1.3; *Winter's Tale* 2.3.96–100; *Tempest* 5.1.54–57.

9. Greene, *Groats-worth*, 76, 71, 76–77, 85-86.

10. Greene, *Groats-worth*, 43, 45, 46, 75, 90, 42, 84, 71. Greene's fascination with a single bombastic line of Shakespeare's—"O tiger's heart wrapp'd in a woman's hide!"—bespeaks his sense of a heritage that "the only Shake-scene" has stolen from him. By voicing that line, however satirically, Greene puts himself in the part of York in *3 Henry VI*, at the point in the story when Queen Margaret has just told York that his son Rutland has been murdered: "Look, York, I stain'd this napkin with the blood/That valiant Clifford with his rapier's point/Made issue from the bosom of the boy;/And if thine eyes can water for his death,/I give thee this to dry thy cheeks withal." "O tiger's heart wrapp'd in a woman's hide!" York replies to this horrific speech: "How couldst thou drain the life-blood of the child,/To bid the father wipe his eyes withal,/And yet be seen to wear a woman's face?" (*3 Henry VI* 1.4.79–83 and 137–40). In the melodramatically inflated vision of his life that Shakespeare's play allows him, Greene's lost feathers become the life's-blood that Shakespeare "made issue" from his issue.

11. Greene, *Groats-worth*, 80, 85, 69, and 68. The letter on Shakespeare has an interesting echo of Greene's earlier work that supports this connection between Greene's conception of authorial mastery and

Prospero's magical power. In characterizing actors as "Puppets" and "Antics" (83–84), the letter recalls the Induction to Greene's *James IV,* which refers to the "subjects" of the fairy king Oberon as his "puppets" and "antics" (12–14, 80–82; I can find no other Renaissance text that places "puppets" and "antics" in such close association). A spell-binder as well as ruler, Oberon magically prevents the Scotsman Bohan from lifting his sword, just as Prospero will later prevent Ferdinand in *The Tempest.*

12. For an indictment of Shakespeare's greed, among other vices, see Duncan-Jones's *Ungentle Shakespeare.*

13. *HS,* 8.583; cf. *FF,* A3r, reprinted in *Riverside Shakespeare,* 95. Gordon McMullan similarly maintains that *Henry VIII* and *Two Noble Kinsmen* "serve to question the redemptive life structure traditionally created for Shakespeare—moving from the bleakest of tragedies into a final phase of hope invested in the young—since the tone of the two extant collaborations (especially *The Two Noble Kinsmen*) does not fit comfortably into this narrative" ("John Fletcher").

14. *HS,* 11.397. For this and other, similar references, see Jennifer Brady's wonderfully suggestive essay, "'Noe fault, but Life,'" which also briefly envisions Jonson as "his own heir" (193). Theodore Spencer judges the Shakespearean portions of *Two Noble Kinsmen* to be so "dramatically stagnant" that he wonders whether Shakespeare's retirement from the stage "was entirely voluntary": "One can even imagine a deputation calling on Shakespeare—it is not an agreeable thought—to suggest that, all things considered, it would be wise to go home and write no more" ("*Two Noble Kinsmen,*" 276).

15. Shakespeare, *Sonnets,* 8, 6, 1, 4, and 2; *Lear* 2.4.250.

16. *FF,* A7r, in *Riverside Shakespeare,* 103; Dryden, *Essay,* 51, 55, and 72–73.

Works Cited

ABBREVIATIONS OF FREQUENTLY CITED WORKS

BF   Beaumont and Fletcher, et al., *Comedies and Tragedies*
ES   Chambers, *Elizabethan Stage*
FF   Shakespeare, *Mr. William Shakespeares Comedies, Histories, &*
       Tragedies
HS   Jonson, *Ben Jonson,* ed. Herford and Simpson
JCS Bentley, *Jacobean and Caroline Stage*
PD   Bentley, *Profession of Dramatist*
WS   Chambers, *William Shakespeare*

Unless otherwise noted, all citations of classical authors refer to Loeb Classical Library editions, and all publication dates refer to first editions.

Ackerman, Diane. "On the Bard's Brain." In *The Bard on the Brain: Understanding the Mind through the Art of Shakespeare and the Science of Brain Imaging,* ed. Paul M. Matthews and Jeffrey McQuain. New York: Dana Press, 2003. 1–12.
Acolastus. See Palsgrave, John.
Adams, Robert M. "New Bards for Old." *New York Review of Books* 33 (6 November 1986). Online edition.
———. Reply to Joel Fineman. *New York Review of Books* 34 (26 March 1987). Online edition.

Adelman, Janet. *Suffocating Mothers: Fantasies of Maternal Origin in Shakespeare's Plays*, Hamlet *to* The Tempest. New York: Routledge, 1992.

Aers, David. "A Whisper in the Ear of Early Modernists; or, Reflections on Literary Critics Writing the 'History of the Subject.'" In *Culture and History, 1350–1600*, ed. David Aers. Detroit: Wayne State Press, 1992. 177–202.

Ainsworth, Henry, and John Ainsworth. *The Trying Out of the Truth . . . between John Aynsworth and Henry Aynsworth.* [Amsterdam], 1615.

Alexander, William. *The Poetical Works of Sir William Alexander, Earl of Stirling.* Ed. L. E. Kastner and H. B. Charlton. 2 vols. Manchester: Manchester University Press, 1921–29.

All for Money. See Lupton, Thomas.

Altman, Joel. "The Practice of Shakespeare's Text." *Style* 23 (1989): 466–500.

Apius and Virginia. See Bower, Richard.

Arnold, Oliver. *The Third Citizen: Shakespeare's Theater, the Early Modern House of Commons, and the Tragedy of Political Representation.* Baltimore: Johns Hopkins University Press, 2007.

Arviragus and Philicia. [By Lodowick Carlell.] Acted 1635–36. London, 1639.

Aubrey, John. *Aubrey's Brief Lives.* Ed. Oliver Lawson Dick. 1957. 2d ed. Jaffrey, N.H.: David R. Godine, 1999.

Auden, William. "Introduction." *William Shakespeare: The Sonnets.* Ed. William Burto. New York: Signet, 1964. xvii–xxxviii.

Baker, Donald C., John L. Murphy, and Louis B. Hale Jr., eds. *The Late Medieval Religious Plays of Bodleian MSS Digby 133 and E Museo 160.* Oxford: Oxford University Press for the Early English Text Society, 1982.

Baker, Sir Richard. *A Chronicle of the Kings of England From the Time of the Romans Government, Unto the Reign of Our Soveraigne Lord King Charles.* London, 1643.

Baldwin, William, et al. *A Myrroure for Magistrates.* 1559. *See* Campbell, ed., *Mirror for Magistrates.*

Bale, John. *The Complete Plays of John Bale.* Ed. Peter Happé. 2 vols. Cambridge: D. S. Brewer, 1986.

Barber, C. L. "The Family in Shakespeare's Development: Tragedy and Sacredness." 1980. Revised version in C. L. Barber and Richard

Wheeler, *The Whole Journey: Shakespeare's Powers of Development*. Berkeley: University of California Press, 1986. 1–38.

Barker, Francis. *The Tremulous Private Body: Essays on Subjection*. 1984. 2d ed. Ann Arbor: University of Michigan Press, 1995.

Barker, Richard Hindry. *Thomas Middleton*. New York: Columbia University Press, 1958.

Barnet, Sylvan. "Shakespeare: Prefatory Remarks." 1963. In *Shakespeare: Narrative Poems*, ed. William Burto. New York: New American Library, 1968.

Barnfield, Richard. *The Encomion of Lady Pecunia*. London, 1598.

Barroll, J. Leeds. *Politics, Plague, and Shakespeare's Theater: The Stuart Years*. Ithaca, N.Y.: Cornell University Press, 1995.

Barthes, Roland. "The Death of the Author." 1968. Trans. Stephen Heath. In *The Norton Anthology of Theory and Criticism*, ed. Vincent Leitch et al. New York: W. W. Norton, 2001. 1466–70.

Beal, Peter. "Massinger at Bay: Unpublished Verses in a War of the Theatres." *Yearbook of English Studies* 10 (1980): 190–203.

Beal, Peter, comp. *Index of English Literary Manuscripts*. Vol. 1, part 2. London: Mansell, 1980.

Beard, Thomas. *The Theatre of Gods Judgements . . . Translated out of French [Histoires Mémorables by Jean Chassanion (1581)] and Augmented by More Than Three Hundred Examples*. London, 1597.

Beau-Chesne, Jehan de, and John Baildon. *A Booke Containing Divers Sortes of Hands*. London, 1571.

Beaumont, Francis, and John Fletcher [et al.]. *Comedies and Tragedies Written by Francis Beaumont and John Fletcher Gentlemen*. London, 1647. [Cited as *BF*.]

Becon, Thomas. *Works*. Ed. John Ayre. 3 vols. [Vol. 1: *Early Works*. Vol. 2: *The Catechism*. Vol. 3: *Prayers*.] Cambridge, 1844.

Bednarz, James P. *Shakespeare and the Poets' War*. New York: Columbia University Press, 2001.

Belsey, Catherine. *The Subject of Tragedy: Identity and Difference in Renaissance Drama*. London: Methuen, 1985.

Bentley, G. E. *The Jacobean and Caroline Stage*. 7 vols. Oxford: Clarendon Press, 1941–68. [Cited as *JCS*.]

———. *The Profession of Dramatist in Shakespeare's Time, 1590–1642*. 1971. Rev. ed. Princeton: Princeton University Press, 1986. [Cited as *PD*.]

―――. *The Profession of Player in Shakespeare's Time, 1590–1642.* 1984. Princeton: Princeton University Press, 1986.

―――. *Shakespeare: A Biographical Handbook.* New Haven: Yale University Press, 1961.

―――. *Shakespeare and Jonson: Their Reputations in the Seventeenth Century Compared.* 1945. Rpt. Chicago: University of Chicago Press, 1969.

Berger, Thomas L., and Jesse M. Lander. "Shakespeare in Print, 1593–1640." In Kastan, ed., *Companion*, 395–413.

Bernard, Richard. *The Faithfull Shepheard.* London, 1607.

Bertram, Paul. *Shakespeare and Two Noble Kinsmen.* New Brunswick, N.J.: Rutgers University Press, 1965.

Bicks, Caroline. "Backsliding at Ephesus: Shakespeare's Diana and the Churching of Women." In *Pericles: Critical Essays,* ed. David Skeele. New York: Garland, 2000. 205–27.

[Bishops' Bible.] *The. Holie. Bible.* London, 1568.

Blayney, Peter. "The Publication of Playbooks." In *New History of Early English Drama,* ed. Cox and Kastan, 383–422.

Blenerhasset, Thomas. *The Second Part of the Mirrour for Magistrates.* 1578. In Campbell, ed., *Parts Added,* 361–496.

Bloom, Harold. *The Western Canon: The Books and School of the Ages.* New York: Harcourt Brace, 1994.

Booth, Stephen, ed. *Shakespeare's Sonnets.* New Haven, Conn.: Yale University Press, 1977.

B[ower?]., R[ichard?]. *Apius and Virginia.* Acted 1559–67, pub. 1575. Ed. W. W. Greg. London: Oxford University Press, 1911.

Bradley, A. C. "Shakespeare's Theatre and Audience." In *Oxford Lectures on Poetry.* Originally published 1902; 2d ed., 1909. Rpt. London: Macmillan, 1962. 361–93.

Bradley, Jesse Franklin, and Joseph Quincy Adams, eds. *The Jonson Allusion-Book: A Collection of Allusions to Ben Jonson from 1597 to 1700.* New Haven, Conn.: Yale University Press, 1922.

Brady, Jennifer. "'Noe Fault, But Life': Jonson's Folio as Monument and Barrier." In *Ben Jonson's 1616 Folio,* ed. Jennifer Brady and W. H. Herendeen. Newark: University of Delaware Press, 1991. 192–216.

Brandon, Samuel. *The Tragicomoedi of the Vertuous Octavia.* London, 1598.

Brinkley, Roberta Florence. *Nathan Field, the Actor-Playwright.* 1928. Rpt. Hamden, Conn.: Archon Press, 1973.

Brinsley, John. *The Fourth Part of the True Watch.* London, 1624.

Bristol, Michael. *Big-time Shakespeare.* New York: Routledge, 1996.

———. "*The Two Noble Kinsmen:* Shakespeare and the Problem of Authority." In Frey, ed., *Shakespeare, Fletcher, and* The Two Noble Kinsmen, 78–92.

Brome, Richard. *The Antipodes.* Acted 1638. London, 1640.

Brooks, Douglas. *From Playhouse to Printing House: Drama and Authorship in Early Modern England.* Cambridge: Cambridge University Press, 2000.

Burckhardt, Jacob. *The Civilization of the Renaissance in Italy.* 1860. Trans. S. G. C. Middlemore. 1878. 2 vols. New York: Harper & Row, 1958.

Burns, Raymond S., ed. *The Isle of Guls: A Critical Edition.* By John Day. New York: Garland, 1980.

Burrow, Colin, ed. *The Oxford Shakespeare: The Complete Sonnets and Poems.* Oxford: Oxford University Press, 2002.

Butler, Martin. *Theatre and Crisis, 1632–1642.* Cambridge: Cambridge University Press, 1984.

Byrd, William, and Thomas Tallis. *Cantiones . . . Sacrae . . . Autoribus Thoma Tallisio & Guilielmo Birdo.* 1575. Fascimile. Leeds: Boethius Press, 1976.

Calvin, Jean. *A Commentarie . . . Uppon the Epistle to the Philippians.* From *Commentarii in Quatuor Pauli Epistolas.* 1548. Trans. William Becket. London, 1584.

Cambises. See Preston, Thomas.

Camden, William. *Remaines of a Greater Worke, Concerning Britaine.* London, 1605.

Campbell, Lily B., ed. *The Mirror for Magistrates, Edited from Original Texts in the Huntington* Library. Cambridge: Cambridge University Press, 1938.

———. *Parts Added to* The Mirror for Magistrates. Cambridge: Cambridge University Press, 1946.

Carson, Neil. "Collaborative Playwriting: The Chettle, Dekker, Heywood Syndicate." *Theatre Research International* 14 (1989): 13–23.

———. *A Companion to Henslowe's Diary.* Cambridge: Cambridge University Press, 1988.

Cavell, Stanley. *Disowning Knowledge in Seven Plays of Shakespeare.* Cambridge: Cambridge University Press, 1987.

Cerasano, S. P. "Edward Alleyn's 'Retirement,' 1597–1600." *Medieval and Renaissance Drama in England* 10 (1998): 98–112.

Chambers, E. K. *The Elizabethan Stage.* 4 vols. Oxford: Oxford University Press, 1923. [Cited as *ES.*]

———. *William Shakespeare.* 2 vols. Oxford: Oxford University Press, 1930. [Cited as *WS.*]

Chapman, George, trans. *Homer Prince of Poets: . . . His Iliads.* London, [1609].

Chapman, George, and Christopher Marlowe. *See* Marlowe and Chapman, *Hero and Leander.*

Chaplin, Gregory. "'Divided amongst Themselves': Collaboration and Anxiety in Jonson's *Volpone.*" *ELH* 69 (2002): 57–81.

Chaucer, Geoffrey. *The Workes of Geffrey Chaucer . . . With the Siege and Destruccion of the Worthy Citee of Thebes, Compiled by Jhon Lidgate.* [London], 1561.

Cheney, Patrick. *Shakespeare, National Poet-Playwright.* Cambridge: Cambridge University Press, 2004.

Cicero. *Letters to His Friends.* Vol. 2. Trans. W. Glynn Williams. Loeb Classical Library. Cambridge, Mass.: Harvard University Press, 1959.

Cleaver, Robert. *The Patrimony of Christian Children . . . With the Joynt Consent of Mr. John Dod.* London, 1624.

Cleaver, Robert, and John Dod. *See* Dod and Cleaver.

Cleaver, Robert, and Richard Webb. *Foure Sermons. The Two First . . . By Robert Cleaver. The Two Last . . . By Richard Webb.* London, 1613.

Club Law. MS acted c. 1599. Ed. G. C. Moore Smith. Cambridge: Cambridge University Press, 1907.

Clyomon and Clamydes. Acted c. 1570–83. London, 1599.

Coblers Prophesie, The. See Wilson, Robert.

Coldewey, John C. "The Digby Plays and the Chelmsford Records." *Research Opportunities in Renaissance Drama* 18 (1975): 103–21.

Coleridge, Samuel Taylor. *Biographia Literaria.* 1817. Ed. J. Shawcross. Oxford: Clarendon Press, 1907.

———. *Coleridge on Shakespeare: The Text of the Lectures of 1811–12.* Ed. R. A. Foakes. Charlottesville: University Press of Virgina, 1971.

Common Conditions. Acted 1576. [London, c. 1577.]

Conflict of Conscience, The. See Woodes, Nathaniel.

Cooper, Thomas, and Thomas Lanquet. *See* Lanquet and Cooper.

Cox, John D., and David Scott Kastan. "Introduction: Demanding History." In Cox and Kastan, eds., *A New History,* 1–5.

Cox, John D., and David Scott Kastan, eds. *A New History of Early English Drama.* New York: Columbia University Press, 1997.

Craig, D. H., ed. *Ben Jonson: The Critical Heritage, 1599–1798.* London: Routledge, 1990.

Crosse, Henry. *Vertues Common-wealth.* London, 1603.

Daniel, Samuel. *Musophilus.* 1599. In *Poems and* A Defence of Ryme, ed. Arthur C. Sprague. Chicago: University of Chicago Press, 1930. 65–98.

———. *The Whole Workes of Samuel Daniel.* London, 1623.

Davies, John, of Hereford. *The Holy Roode.* London, 1609.

———. *Humours Heav'n on Earth.* London, 1609.

———. *Microcosmos.* Oxford, 1603.

———. *The Scourge of Folly.* London, 1611.

Davies, Sir John. *The Poems of Sir John Davies.* Ed. Robert Krueger. Oxford: Clarendon Press, 1975.

Davis, Walter R. "'Fantasticlly I Sing': Drayton's *Idea* of 1619." *Studies in Philology* 66, no. 2 (1969): 204–16.

Davison, Francis. *A Poetical Rapsodie.* London, 1611.

Day, John. *The Isle of Guls.* Acted and pub. 1606. Ed. Raymond S. Burns. New York: Garland, 1980.

Day, John, William Rowley, and George Wilkins. *The Travailes of the Three English Brothers.* Acted and pub. 1607. In *Three Renaissance Travel Plays:* The Travels of The Three English Brothers, The Sea Voyage, The Antipodes, ed. Anthony Parr. Manchester: Manchester University Press, 1995. 55–134.

Deacon, John, and John Walker. *Dialogicall Discourses of Spirits and Divels . . . By John Deacon. John Walker. Preachers.* London, 1601.

———. *A Summarie Answere . . . By John Deacon. John Walker. Preachers.* London, 1601.

de Grazia, Margreta. "Babbling Will in *Shake-speares Sonnets* 127 to 154." *Spenser Studies* 1 (1980): 121–34.

———. "The Scandal of Shakespeare's Sonnets." *Shakespeare Survey* 46 (1993): 35–49.

———. *Shakespeare Verbatim: The Reproduction of Authenticity and the 1790 Apparatus.* Oxford: Oxford University Press, 1991.

de Grazia, Margreta, and Peter Stallybrass. "The Materiality of the Shakespearean Text." *Shakespeare Quarterly* 44 (1993): 255–83.

Dekker, Thomas. *The Dramatic Works of Thomas Dekker.* Ed. Fredson Bowers. 4 vols. Cambridge: Cambridge University Press, 1953–62.

————. *If It Be Not Good, The Devil Is In It.* [Running title: *If This Be Not a Good Play, the Devil Is in It.*] Acted 1611–12, pub. 1612. In *Dramatic Works*, ed. Bowers, 3:113–223.

————. *Satiro-mastix. Or The Untrussing of the Humourous Poet.* Acted 1601, pub. 1602. In *Dramatic Works*, ed. Bowers, 1:299–395.

DiGangi, Mario. "Review of *Textual Intercourse: Collaboration, Authorship, and Sexualities in Renaissance Drama.*" *Journal of English and Germanic Philology* 98 (1999): 91–93.

Dobson, Michael. *The Making of the National Poet: Shakespeare, Adaptation and Authorship, 1660–1792.* Oxford: Clarendon Press, 1992.

Dod, John, and Robert Cleaver. *A Briefe Dialogue, Preparation for the Worthy Receiving of the Lords Supper.* London, 1614.

————. *Foure Godlie and Fruitfull Sermons.* London, 1610.

————. *A Godly Forme of Houshold Government.* London, 1612.

————. *A Plaine and Familiar Exposition of the Ninth and Tenth Chapters of the Proverbs of Salomon.* London, 1606.

————. *A Plaine and Familiar Exposition of the Eleventh and Twelfth Chapters of the Proverbs of Salomon.* London, 1607.

————. *A Plaine and Familiar Exposition of the Thirteenth and Fourteenth Chapters of the Proverbs of Salomon.* London, 1608.

————. *A Plaine and Familiar Exposition of the Fifteenth, Sixteenth, and Seventeenth Chapters of the Proverbs of Salomon.* London, 1609.

————. *A Plaine and Familiar Exposition: of the Eighteenth, Nineteenth, and Twentieth Chapters of the Proverbs of Salomon.* London, 1610.

————. *A Plaine and Familiar Exposition of the Ten Commandements.* London, 1604.

————. *Seven Godlie and Fruitfull Sermons.* London, 1614.

————. *Ten Godly and Fruitfull Sermons Preached Upon Several Places of Scripture.* London, 1610.

————. *Ten Sermons Tending Chiefly to the Sitting of Men for the Worthy Receiving of the Lords Supper.* London, 1609.

————. *Three Godlie and Fruitful Sermons.* London, 1610.

————. *Two Sermons on the Third of the Lamentations of Jeremie.* London, 1608.

Dod, John, and William Hinde. *Bathshebaes Instructions to her Sonne Lemuel.* London, 1614.

Donaldson, Ian. "Looking Sideways: Jonson, Shakespeare, and the Myths of Envy." In *Shakespeare, Marlowe, Jonson: New Directions in Biography*, ed. Takashi Kozuka and J. R. Mulryne. Aldershot: Ashgate, 2006. 241–57.

Donne, John. *The Complete English Poems.* Ed. A. J. Smith. New York: St. Martin's Press, 1971.

Drant, Thomas, trans. *Horace His Arte of Poetrie.* London, 1567.

Drayton, Michael. *Englands Heroicall Epistles.* London, 1600.

———. *Idea.* In *Englands Heroicall Epistles.* London, 1599. P2r–Q8v.

———. *Ideas Mirrour. Amours in Quatorzains.* London, 1594.

———. *Poems.* London, 1605.

Dryden, John. *An Essay of Dramatick Poesie.* 1668. In *The Works of John Dryden*, gen. eds. Edward Niles Hooker and H. T. Swedenberg, Jr. 20 vols. Vol. 17, *Prose, 1668–1691,* ed. Samuel Holt Monk et al. Berkeley: University of California Press, 1971. 1–81.

Duncan-Jones, Katherine. *Ungentle Shakespeare: Scenes from His Life.* London: Arden Shakespeare, 2001.

Dutton, Richard. "Shakespeare: The Birth of the Author." In *Licensing, Censorship and Authorship in Early Modern England: Buggeswords.* Basingstoke: Palgrave, 2000. 90–113.

Earle, John. *Micro-cosmographie.* London, 1628.

Edwardes, Richard. *Damon and Pithias.* Acted c. 1565, pub. 1571. In *The Works of Richard Edwardes*, ed. Ros King. Manchester: Manchester University Press, 2001. 108–84.

Elliott, John R., Jr., and Alan H. Nelson, eds. *Oxford: Records of Early English Drama.* 2 vols. Toronto: University of Toronto Press, 2004.

Elyot, Thomas. *The Dictionary of Syr Thomas Eliot Knyght.* London, [1538].

Empson, William. "Hamlet." 1953. Revised version in *Essays on Shakespeare*, ed. David B. Pirie. Cambridge: Cambridge University Press, 1986. 79–136.

Engle, Lars. "'I Am That I Am': Shakespeare's Sonnets and the Economy of Shame." In *Shakespeare's Sonnets: Critical Essays.* Ed. James Schiffer. New York: Garland, 1999. 185–97.

Epictetus Manuall. Cebes Table. Theophrastus Characters. London, 1616.

Erasmus, Desiderius. *The First Tome or Volume of the Paraphrase of Erasmus.* [Ed. Nicholas Udall, trans. Udall et al.] London, 1548.

Erne, Lukas. *Shakespeare as Literary Dramatist.* Cambridge: Cambridge University Press, 2003.

Estienne, Charles, and Jean Liebault. *Maison Rustique, or The Country Farme. Compiled in the French Tongue by Charles Stevens and John*

Liebault Doctors of Physicke. And Translated into English by Richard Surflet Practitioner in Physicke. London, 1600.

Farmer, Alan. "Shakespeare and the Book: A Companion Study Environment to David Kastan's Book." Available online: http://ccnmtl .columbia.edu/projects/shakespeareandthebook/studyenv/index .html

Farmer, Alan, and Zachary Lesser. "'Vile Arts': The Marketing of English Printed Drama, 1512–1660." *Research Opportunities in Renaissance Drama* 39 (2000): 77–165.

Fedele and Fortunio. See Munday, Anthony.

Fennor, William. *Fennors Descriptions.* London, 1616.

Field, Nathaniel. *A Woman is a Weather-cocke.* Acted c. 1609–10, pub. 1612. In *Plays,* ed. William Peery. Austin: University of Texas Press, 1950. 55–139.

Fineman, Joel. *Shakespeare's Perjured Eye: The Invention of Poetic Subjectivity in the Sonnets.* Berkeley: University of California Press, 1986.

Finkelpearl, Philip J. *John Marston of the Middle Temple: An Elizabethan Dramatist in His Social Setting.* Cambridge, Mass.: Harvard University Press, 1969.

F[leming]., A[lexander]., trans. *The Bucoliks of Publius Virgilius Maro, Prince of All Latine Poets . . . Together With His Georgiks.* London, 1589.

Fletcher, John and Francis Beaumont. *See* Beaumont and Fletcher, *Comedies and Tragedies.*

Fletcher, John [and Philip Massinger]. *The Little French Lawyer.* Acted c. 1620, pub. 1647. In Beaumont and Fletcher, *Comedies and Tragedies,* 51–75.

Fletcher, John, and William Shakespeare. *See* Shakespeare and Fletcher, *Two Noble Kinsmen.*

Foakes, R. A., ed. *King Henry VIII.* By William Shakespeare. London: Methuen, 1957.

F[ord]., I[ohn]. *Christes Bloodie Sweat, or the Sonne of God in his Agonie.* 1613. In *The Nondramatic Works of John Ford,* ed. L. E. Stock et al. Binghamton, N.Y.: Medieval and Renaissance Texts and Studies, in conjunction with Renaissance English Text Society, 1991. 135–216.

Foucault, Michel. "What Is an Author?" 1969. Revised version, trans. Josue V. Harari. In *Textual Strategies: Perspectives in Post-*

Structuralist Criticism, ed. Harari. Ithaca, N.Y.: Cornell University Press, 1979. 141–60.

Foxe, John. *Two Latin Comedies.* Ed. and trans. John Hazel Smith. Ithaca, N.Y.: Cornell University Press, 1973.

Frey, Charles. "Collaborating with Shakespeare: After the Final Play." In Frey, ed., *Shakespeare, Fletcher, and* The Two Noble Kinsmen, 31–44.

Frey, Charles, ed. *Shakespeare, Fletcher, and* The Two Noble Kinsmen. Columbia: University of Missouri Press, 1989.

Fulwell, Ulpian. *Like Will to Like.* Acted 1563–69. London, 1568.

Gallagher, Catherine. *Nobody's Story: The Vanishing Acts of Women Writers in the Marketplace, 1670–1820.* Berkeley: University of California Press, 1994.

Gamage, William. *Linsi-Woolsie. Or Two Centuries of Epigrammes.* Oxford, 1613.

Garber, Marjorie. *Shakespeare after All.* New York: Anchor Books, 2004.

Garter, Thomas. *Susanna, The Commody of the Most Vertuous and Godly.* Acted 1563–69. London, 1578.

Gascoigne, George. *A Hundreth Sundrie Flowres.* 1573. Ed. G. W. Pigman III. Oxford: Oxford University Press, 2000.

Gee, John. *New Shreds of the Old Snare.* London, 1624.

[Geneva Bible (with Tomson's revisions).] *The Bible.* London, 1587.

Gentili, Alberico. *Commentatio ad Legem III Codicis de Professoribus et Medicis.* 1593. Ed. and trans. J. W. Binns. In "Alberico Gentili in Defense of Poetry and Acting." *Studies in the Renaissance* 19 (1972): 224–72.

Goffe, Thomas. *The Careless Shepherdess.* Acted c. 1618–29; rev. c. 1638; pub. London, 1656.

———. *Deliverance From the Grave.* London, 1627.

———. *The Raging Turk.* Acted c. 1613–18. London, 1631.

———. *The Tragedy of Orestes.* Acted c. 1613–18. London, 1633.

Golding, Arthur, trans. *Thabridgment of the Histories of Trogus Pompeius. [Iustini ex Trogii Pompeii Historia.]* London, 1564.

Googe, Barnabe. *Eglogs[,] Epytaphes, and Sonettes.* London, 1563.

Gossett, Suzanne, ed. *Pericles, by William Shakespeare.* London: Thomson Learning, 2004.

Gosson, Stephen. *Markets of Bawdrie: The Dramatic Criticism of Stephen Gosson.* [Contains *The Schoole of Abuse* (1579), *An Apologie of the*

Schoole of Abuse (1579), and *Playes Confuted in Five Actions* (1582).]
Ed. Arthur F. Kinney. Salzburg: Institut für Englische Sprache und
Literatur, Universität Salzburg, 1974.

Greenblatt, Stephen. "Foreword." In Cox and Kastan, eds., *A New
History*, xiii–xiv.

———. "General Introduction." In Greenblatt et al., eds., *Norton
Shakespeare*, 1–76.

———. *Renaissance Self-Fashioning: From More to Shakespeare*. Chicago: University of Chicago Press, 1980.

———. *Shakespearean Negotiations: The Circulation of Social Energy in
Renaissance England*. Berkeley: University of California Press, 1998.

———. *Will in the World: How Shakespeare Became Shakespeare*. New
York: W. W. Norton, 2004.

Greenblatt, Stephen, Walter Cohen, Jean Howard, and Katharine
Eisaman Maus. "Preface." In Greenblatt et al., eds., *Norton Shakespeare*, ix–xiv.

Greenblatt, Stephen, Walter Cohen, Jean Howard, and Katharine
Eisaman Maus, eds. *The Norton Shakespeare*. New York: W. W.
Norton, 1997.

Greene, Robert. *The Scottish Historie of James the Fourth*. Acted c.
1588–92, pub. 1598. Ed. Norman Sanders. London: Methuen, 1970.

Greene, Robert [and Henry Chettle?]. *Greenes, Groats-Worth of Witte*.
1592. Ed. D. Allen Carroll. Binghamton, N.Y.: Medieval and Renaissance Texts and Studies, 1994.

Greene, Robert, and Thomas Lodge. *A Looking Glasse for London and
England*. Acted c. 1587–91. London, 1594.

Greene, Thomas M. "Pitiful Thrivers: Failed Husbandry in the Sonnets." In *Shakespeare and the Question of Theory*, ed. Patricia Parker
and Geoffrey Hartman. New York: Methuen, 1985. 230–44.

Gurr, Andrew. "Maximal and Minimal Texts: Shakespeare v. The
Globe." *Shakespeare Survey* 52 (1999): 68–87.

———. *Playgoing in Shakespeare's London*. Cambridge: Cambridge
University Press, 1987.

———. *The Shakespearian Playing Companies*. Oxford: Oxford University Press, 1996.

Hakewill, George. *An Apologie of the Power and Providence of God in
the Government of the World*. Oxford, 1627.

Hall, Joseph. *Virgidemiarum, Sixe Bookes*. 1597. In *The Collected Poems
of Joseph Hall, Bishop of Exeter and Norwich*, ed. Arnold Davenport.
Liverpool: Liverpool University Press, 1949. 5–99.

Haller, William. *The Rise of Puritanism.* New York: Columbia University Press, 1938.

Happé, Peter. *John Bale.* New York: Twayne Publishers, 1996.

Harbage, Alfred. *Annals of English Drama: 975–1700.* 1940. Revised by Samuel Schoenbaum. Philadelphia: University of Pennsylvania Press, 1964.

H[arding]., S[amuel]. *Sicily and Naples, or, The Fatall Union.* Acted and pub. 1640. Ed. Joan Warthling Roberts. New York: Garland, 1986.

Harvey, Gabriel. *Foure Letters, and Certain Sonnets.* London, 1592.

———. *Marginalia.* Ed. G. C. Moore Smith. Stratford-upon-Avon: Shakespeare Head Press, 1913.

———. *Pierces Supererogation.* London, 1593.

Harvey, Gabriel, and Edmund Spenser. *See* Spenser and Harvey, *Three . . . Letters.*

Hazlitt, William. *The Complete Works of William Hazlitt.* Ed. P. P. Howe. 21 vols. London: J. M. Dent and Sons, 1930–34.

Hedrick, Donald K. "'Be Rough with Me': The Collaborative Arenas of *The Two Noble Kinsmen.*" In Frey, ed. *Shakespeare, Fletcher, and The Two Noble Kinsmen,* 45–77.

Helgerson, Richard. *Forms of Nationhood: The Elizabethan Writing of England.* Chicago: University of Chicago Press, 1992.

Henslowe Papers, Being Documents Supplementary to Henslowe's Diary. Ed. Walter W. Greg. London: A. H. Bullen, 1907.

Heywood, Thomas. *The Foure Prentises of London.* Acted c. 1594. London, 1615.

———. *The Hierarchie of the Blessed Angells.* London, 1635.

———. *Pleasant Dialogues and Dramma's.* London, 1637.

Higgins, John. *The First Part of the Mirour for Magistrates.* London, 1574.

Hirschfeld, Heather. "Early Modern Collaboration and Theories of Authorship." *PMLA* 116 (2001): 609–22.

Holinshed, Raphael, et al. *The First Volume of the Chronciles of England, Scotlande, and Irelande.* London, 1577.

———. *The First and Second Volumes of Chronicles.* London, 1587.

Honigmann, E. A. J. *John Weever. See* Weever, *Epigrammes.*

———. "Plague on the Globe?" *New York Review of Books* 39, no. 19 (19 November 1992). Online edition.

———. *The Stability of Shakespeare's Text.* Lincoln: University of Nebraska Press, 1965.

Honigmann, E. A. J., and Susan Brock, eds. *Playhouse Wills, 1558–1642: An Edition of Wills by Shakespeare and His Contemporaries.* Manchester: Manchester University Press, 1993.

Hooker, Richard. *Two Sermons Upon Part of S. Judes Epistle.* Written c. 1583, pub. 1614. In *The Folger Library Edition of the Works of Richard Hooker,* ed. W. Speed Hill. 5 vols. Cambridge, Mass.: Harvard University Press, 1977. 5:1–57.

Hooks, Adam G. "'At the Signe of the White Greyhound': Shakespeare, Poetry, and Print in the 1590s." Unpublished.

Hosley, Richard, ed. *Fedele and Fortunio. See* Munday, Anthony.

Hughes, Charles, ed. *Shakespeare's Europe: A Survey of the Condition of Europe at the End of the 16th Century, Being Unpublished Chapters of Fynes Moryson's Itinerary (1617).* 1903. 2d. ed. New York: Benjamin Blom, 1967.

Hughes, Thomas, et al. *Certain Dev[is]es and Shewes Presented to Her Majestie by the Gentlemen of Grayes-Inne at her Highnesse Court in Greenewich* [*The Misfortunes of Arthur*]. London, 1587.

Hutson, Lorna. *The Invention of Suspicion: Law and Mimesis in Shakespeare and Renaissance Drama.* Oxford: Oxford University Press, 2007.

Ingleby, C. M. (1874), L. Toulmin Smith (1879), F. J. Furnivall (1886), and John Munro (1909), eds. *The Shakspere Allusion-Book.* Reprint. Ed. E. K. Chambers. 2 vols. London: Oxford University Press, 1932.

Ioppolo, Grace. *Dramatists and Their Manuscripts in the Age of Shakespeare, Jonson, Middleton and Heywood: Authorship, Authority, and the Playhouse.* London: Routledge, 2006.

Jackson, MacDonald P. *Defining Shakespeare: Pericles as Test Case.* Oxford: Oxford University Press, 2003.

Jonson, Ben. *Ben Jonson.* Ed. C. H. Herford, Percy Simpson, and Evelyn Simpson. 11 vols. Oxford: Oxford University Press, 1925–52. [Cited as *HS.*]

Jonsonus Virbius: or, The Memorie of Ben Johnson Revived by the Friends of the Muses. Compiled by Brian Duppa. 1638. In *HS,* 11:438–39.

Kahn, Coppélia. "The Providential Tempest and the Shakespearean Family." In *Representing Shakespeare,* ed. Murray Schwartz and Coppélia Kahn. Baltimore: Johns Hopkins University Press, 1980. 217–43.

Kastan, David Scott. *Shakespeare and the Book.* Cambridge: Cambridge University Press, 2001.

———. "Shakespeare and the 'Element' He Lived In." In Kastan, ed., *Companion*, 3–6.

Kastan, David Scott, ed. *A Companion to Shakespeare*. Oxford: Blackwell Press, 1999.

Keats, John. *Selected Letters*. Ed. Grant F. Scott. Rev. ed. Cambridge, Mass.: Harvard University Press, 2002.

Kernan, Alvin. "The Henriad: Shakespeare's Major History Plays." In *The Revels History of English Drama*, gen. eds. Clifford Leech and T. W. Craik. 8 vols. Vol. 3, *1576–1613*, ed. J. Leeds Barroll et al. London: Methuen, 1969; rev. 1975. 3:262–99.

———. *The Playwright as Magician: Shakespeare's Image of the Poet in the English Public Theater*. New Haven, Conn.: Yale University Press, 1979.

Kewes, Paulina. "Review of *Textual Intercourse: Collaboration, Authorship, and Sexualities in Renaissance Drama*." *Library* 21 (1999): 162–64.

King Darius, A Pretie New Enterlude of the Story of. Acted 1565. London, 1565.

[King James Bible.] *The Holy Bible*. London, 1611.

Knack to Knowe a Knave, A. Acted 1592. London, 1594.

Knapp, Jeffrey. *An Empire Nowhere: England, America, and Literature from* Utopia *to* The Tempest. Berkeley: University of California Press, 1992.

———. "'Sacred Songs Popular Prices': Secularization in *The Jazz Singer*." *Critical Inquiry* 34 (2008): 313–35.

———. *Shakespeare's Tribe: Church, Nation, and Theater in Renaissance England*. Chicago: University of Chicago Press, 2002.

Kurke, Leslie. "Pindar and the Prostitutes, or Reading Ancient 'Pornography.'" In *Constructions of the Classical Body*, ed. James I. Porter. Ann Arbor: University of Michigan Press, 1999. 101–25.

———. *The Traffic in Praise: Pindar and the Poetics of Social Economy*. Ithaca, N.Y.: Cornell University Press, 1991.

Kyd, Thomas. *The Spanish Tragedy*. Acted c. 1582–92, pub. c. 1592. Ed. Philip Edwards. Manchester: Manchester University Press, 1959; rpt., 1988.

Laird, Holly A. "'A Hand Spills from the Book's Threshold': Coauthorship's Readers." *PMLA* 116 (2001): 344–53.

Lake, David. "Rhymes in *Pericles*." *Notes and Queries* 214 (1969): 139–43.

———. "Wilkins and *Pericles*—Vocabulary (I)." *Notes and Queries* 214 (1969): 288–91.

Lanquet, Thomas, and Thomas Cooper. *Coopers Chronicle . . . by Me Thomas Cooper.* London, 1560.

[————.] *An Epitome of Chronicles . . . First, by Thomas Lanquet . . . and Now Finished and Continued . . . by Thomas Cooper.* [London], 1549.

Lavater, Ludwig. *Of Ghostes and Spirites Walking By Nyght.* [*De Spectris.* 1570.] Trans. Robert Harrison. London, 1572.

Like Will to Like. See Fulwell, Ulpian.

Lodge, Thomas. *Scillaes Metamorphosis.* London, 1589.

Lodge, Thomas, and Robert Greene. *See* Greene and Lodge, *Looking Glasse.*

Loewenstein, Joseph. *The Author's Due: Printing and the Prehistory of Copyright.* Chicago: University of Chicago Press, 2002.

————. *Ben Jonson and Possessive Authorship.* Cambridge: Cambridge University Press, 2002.

————. "The Script in the Marketplace." *Representations* 12 (1985): 101–14.

Lupton, T[homas]. *All for Money.* Acted 1559–77. London, 1578.

Lyly, John. *Midas.* Acted 1589–90, pub. 1592. In *Galatea; Midas,* ed. George K. Hunter and David Bevington. Manchester: Manchester University Press, 2000.

————. *The Woman in the Moon.* Acted 1590–95, pub. 1597. Ed. Leah Scragg. New York: Palgrave, 2006.

Marcus, Leah. "Of Mire and Authorship." In *The Theatrical City: Culture, Theatre, and Politics in London, 1576–1649,* ed. David L. Smith, Richard Strier, and David Bevington. Cambridge: Cambridge University Press, 1995. 170–82.

————. *Puzzling Shakespeare: Local Reading and Its Discontents.* Berkeley: University of California Press, 1988.

————. *Unediting the Renaissance: Shakespeare, Marlowe, Milton.* New York: Routledge, 1996.

Markham, Gervase, and Lewis Machin. *The Dumbe Knight.* Acted c. 1607–8. London, 1608.

Markham, Gervase, and William Sampson. *True Tragedy of Herod and Antipater.* Acted 1619–22. London, 1622.

[Marlowe, Christopher.] *Tamburlaine the Great.* [Part 2.] Acted c. 1588. London, 1590.

Marlowe, Christopher, and George Chapman. *Hero and Leander: Begun by Christopher Marloe, and Finished by George Chapman.* London, 1598.

Marlowe, Christopher, and Thomas Nash[e]. *The Tragedie of Dido Queene of Carthage.* Acted c. 1587–93. London, 1594.

Marston, John. *The Plays of John Marston.* Ed. H. Harvey Wood. 3 vols. Edinburgh: Oliver and Boyd, 1934–39.

———. *The Workes of Mr. John Marston, Being Tragedies and Comedies, Collected into One Volume.* London, 1633.

Marston, John, and John Webster. *The Malcontent, Augmented by Marston. With the Additions Played by the Kinges Majesties Servants. Written by John Webster.* Acted 1600–1604, pub. 1604. Ed. W. David Kay. 2d ed. New York: W. W. Norton, 1998.

Massinger, Philip. *The Plays and Poems of Philip Massinger.* Ed. Philip Edwards and Colin Gibson. 5 vols. Oxford: Clarendon Press, 1976.

Masten, Jeffrey. "Playwrighting: Authorship and Collaboration." In Cox and Kastan, eds., *A New History,* 357–82.

———. *Textual Intercourse: Collaboration, Authorship, and Sexualities in Renaissance Drama.* Cambridge: Cambridge University Press, 1997.

Maus, Katharine Eisaman. *Inwardness and Theater in the English Renaissance.* Chicago: University of Chicago Press, 1995.

Maus, Katharine Eisaman, and David Bevington. "General Introduction." In *English Renaissance Drama: A Norton Anthology,* ed. David Bevington et al. New York: W. W. Norton, 2002. xiii–lvii.

McGuire, Philip C. "Collaboration." In *A Companion to Renaissance Drama,* ed. Arthur F. Kinney. Oxford: Blackwell, 2002. 540–52.

McMillin, Scott. "Professional Playwrighting." In Kastan, ed., *Companion,* 225–38.

McMullan, Gordon. "John Fletcher (1579–1625)." In *The Oxford Dictionary of National Biography.* Online edition. Oxford University Press, 2004–8. s.v.

Medwall, Henry. *Fulgens . . . [and] Lucres.* Acted c. 1490–1501, pub. c. 1512. In *The Plays of Henry Medwall: A Critical Edition.* Ed. M. E. Moeslein. New York: Garland, 1981. 57–243.

———. *Nature.* Acted c. 1490–1501, pub. c. 1534. In *The Plays of Henry Medwall: A Critical Edition.* Ed. M. E. Moeslein. New York: Garland, 1981. 245–451.

Menaecmi. See Plautus.

Meres, Francis. *Palladis Tamia.* London, 1598.

Midas. See Lyly, John.

Middleton, Thomas. *No {Wit Help} Like a Womans.* Acted 1611, pub. 1657. Ed. John Jowett. In Middleton, *Thomas Middleton,* 779–832.

————. *Thomas Middleton: The Collected Works.* Ed. Gary Taylor, John Lavagnino et al. Oxford: Oxford University Press, 2007.

[Middleton, Thomas], and William Shakespeare. *See* Shakespeare and Middleton, *Timon of Athens.*

Misogonus. Acted c. 1560–77. Ed. Lester E. Barber. New York: Garland, 1979.

Montrose, Louis. "The Purpose of Playing: Reflections on a Shakespearean Anthropology." *Helios* n.s. 7 (1980): 51–74.

————. *The Purpose of Playing: Shakespeare and the Cultural Politics of the Elizabethan Theatre.* Chicago: University of Chicago Press, 1996.

Mucedorus. Acted c. 1590, pub. 1598. *A Contextual Study and Modern-Spelling Edition of Mucedorus.* Ed. Arvin H. Jupin. New York: Garland, 1987.

Mullaney, Steven. *The Place of the Stage: License, Play, and Power in Renaissance England.* Chicago: University of Chicago Press, 1988.

M[unday]., A[nthony]. *Fedele and Fortunio.* Acted 1579–84, pub. 1585. Ed. Richard Hosley. New York: Garland, 1981.

Munday, Anthony[?], and Salvianus. *A Second and Third Blast of Retrait from Plaies and Theaters.* 1580. Ed. Arthur Freeman. New York: Garland, 1973.

Munday, Anthony, John Stow et al. *See* Stow and Munday et al., *Survey.*

Nabbes, Thomas. *Playes, Maskes, Epigrams, Elegies, and Epithalamiums.* London, 1639.

Nashe, Thomas. *The Works of Thomas Nashe.* Ed. R. B. McKerrow. 5 vols. 1903–10. Rpt. Ed. F. P. Wilson. Oxford: Basil Blackwell, 1958.

Nashe, Thomas, and Christopher Marlowe. *See* Marlowe and Nashe, *Tragedie of Dido.*

Nature of the .iiii. Elementes. [By John Rastell.] Acted c. 1517. [London, c. 1520.]

Neely, Carol. "Detachment and Engagement in Shakespeare's Sonnets: 94, 116, 129." *PMLA* 92 (1977): 83–95.

New Custom. Acted c. 1570–73. London, 1573.

Newdigate, Bernard H. *Michael Drayton and His Circle.* 1941. Oxford: Blackwell, 1961.

Nicholl, Charles. *The Lodger Shakespeare: His Life on Silver Street.* New York: Viking, 2007.

North, Thomas, trans. *The Lives of the Noble Grecians and Romanes.* By Plutarch. London, 1579.

Northbrooke, John. *A Treatise Wherein Dicing, Dauncing, Vaine Playes or Enterluds With Other Idle Pastimes etc. Commonly Used on the Sabboth Day, Are Reproved.* 1577[?] Ed. Arthur Freeman. New York: Garland, 1974.

Norton, Thomas, and Thomas Sackville. *The Tragedie of Gorboduc; Whereof Three Actes Were Wrytten by Thomas Nortone, and the Two Laste by Thomas Sackvyle.* Acted 1562. London, 1565.

Octavia. See Brandon, Samuel.

Of Gentylnes and Nobylyte. [By John Rastell.] Acted c. 1525. [London, c. 1525.]

Orgel, Stephen. *The Authentic Shakespeare, and Other Problems of the Early Modern Stage.* New York: Routledge, 2002.

———. *Imagining Shakespeare: A History of Texts and Visions.* New York: Palgrave, 2003.

———. "Shakespeare Imagines a Theater." *Poetics Today* 5 (1984): 549–61.

———. "What Is a Text?" 1981. In *The Authentic Shakespeare, and Other Problems of the Early Modern Stage.* New York: Routledge, 2002. 1–5.

Pacient and Meeke Grissill. See Phillips, John.

Palsgrave, John. *Acolastus.* Acted and pub. 1540. Ed. P. L. Carver. London: Oxford University Press, 1937.

Panek, Jennifer. "The Mother as Bawd in *The Revenger's Tragedy* and *A Mad World, My Masters.*" *Studies in English Literature 1500–1900* 43, no. 2 (2003): 415–37.

Parnassus Plays, The Three (1598–1601). [*The Pilgrimage to Parnassus; 1 The Return From Parnassus* (both acted c. 1599/1600); *2 The Return From Parnassus* (acted c. 1601–2; pub. 1606).] Ed. J. B. Leishman. London: Ivor Nicholson and Watson, 1949.

Patterson, Annabel. *Reading Holinshed's Chronicles.* Chicago: University of Chicago Press, 1994.

Petowe, Henry. *The Second Part of Hero and Leander.* London, 1598.

Pettegree, Andrew. "Reyner Wolfe." In *The Oxford Dictionary of National Biography.* Online edition. Oxford: Oxford University Press, 2004–8. s.v.

Phillips, John. *Pacient and Meeke Grissill.* Acted 1558–61. London, [1566?].

Pierce, William, ed. *The Marprelate Tracts: 1588, 1589.* London: James Clarke, 1911.

Pimlyco. Or, Runne Red-Cap. London, 1609.

Plautus, Titus Maccius. *Menaecmi.* Trans. William Warner. London, 1595.

Plomer, Henry R., ed. *Abstracts from the Wills of English Printers and Stationers, from 1492 to 1630.* London: Blades, East and Blades, 1903.

Preiss, Richard. "Finite Jest: Authorship and the Assimilations of the Stage Clown in Early Modern English Theater, 1588–1673." Ph.D. diss., Stanford University, 2006.

Preston, Thomas. *Cambises.* Acted c. 1558–69. [London, 1570?].

Preston, Thomas, and Thomas Green. *Appelatio.* Augustae [i.e., London], 1620.

———. *Reverendorum Patrum D. Thomae Prestoni . . . & Fr. Thomae Greenaei . . . Ad Sanctissimum . . . Pontificem . . . Humillima Supplicatio.* Augustae [i.e., London], 1621.

Public Record Office. State Papers 2 Charles I. Vol. 240 (25), fols. 58–75.

[Puttenham, George.] *The Art of English Poesy.* 1589. Ed. Frank Whigham and Wayne A. Rebhorn. Ithaca, N.Y.: Cornell University Press, 2007.

Radel, Nicholas. "Review of *Textual Intercourse: Collaboration, Authorship, and Sexualities in Renaissance Drama.*" *Shakespeare Quarterly* 52 (2001): 524–27.

Ramsey, Paul. *The Fickle Glass: A Study of Shakespeare's Sonnets.* New York: AMS Press, 1979.

Randolph, Thomas. *Poems.* 1638. Ed. G. Thorn-Drury. London: F. Etchells and H. MacDonald, 1929.

Rastell. *Three Rastell Plays:* Four Elements, Calisto and Melebea, Gentleness and Nobility. Ed. Richard Axton. Cambridge: D. S. Brewer, 1979.

Raylor, Timothy. *Cavaliers, Clubs, and Literary Culture: Sir John Mennes, James Smith, and the Order of the Fancy.* Newark: University of Delaware Press, 1994.

Respublica. See Udall, Nicholas.

Roberts, Sasha. *Reading Shakespeare's Poems in Early Modern England.* New York: Palgrave, 2003.

Rollins, Hyder, ed. *A New Variorum Edition of Shakespeare: The Sonnets.* 2 vols. Philadelphia: J. B. Lippincott, 1944.

Rose, Mark. *Authors and Owners: The Invention of Copyright.* Cambridge, Mass.: Harvard University Press, 1993.

Rowlands, Samuel. *The Letting of Humours Blood in the Head-Vaine.* London, 1600.

Ruggles, George[?]. *Club Law.* Acted c. 1599. Ed. G. C. Moore Smith. Cambridge: Cambridge University Press, 1907.

Sackville, Thomas, and Thomas Norton. *See* Norton and Sackville, *Tragedie of Gorboduc.*

Saeger, James P., and Christopher J. Fassler. "The London Professional Theater, 1576–1642: A Catalogue and Analysis of the Extant Printed Plays." *Research Opportunities in Renaissance Drama* 34 (1995): 63–109.

St. Clair, F. Y. "Drayton's First Revision of His Sonnets," *Studies in Philology* 36 (1939): 40–59.

Schoenbaum, Samuel. *William Shakespeare: A Compact Documentary Life.* New York: Oxford University Press, 1977.

Sc[oloker?]., An[thony?]. *Daiphantus.* London, 1604.

Shakespeare, William. *Mr. William Shakespeares Comedies, Histories, & Tragedies.* Ed. William Heminges and Henry Condell. London, 1623. [Cited as *FF.*]

———. *Poems: Written by Wil. Shake-speare. Gent.* London, 1640.

———. *The Riverside Shakespeare.* 2d ed. Ed. G. Blakemore Evans et al. Boston: Houghton Mifflin, 1997.

———. *Shake-Speares Sonnets.* London, 1609.

———. *The Tragicall Historie of Hamlet, Prince of Denmarke.* London, 1604.

Shakespeare, William, and John Fletcher[?]. *Two Noble Kinsmen.* Acted c. 1613, pub. 1634. In *The Riverside Shakespeare,* 1689–1731.

Shakespeare, William, and Thomas Middleton[?]. *Timon of Athens.* Acted 1605–8, pub. 1623. In *The Riverside Shakespeare,* 1489–1525.

Shakespeare, William, and George Wilkins[?]. *Pericles.* Acted c. 1607–8, pub. 1609. In *The Riverside Shakespeare,* 1526–64.

Shapiro, James. *Rival Playwrights: Marlowe, Jonson, Shakespeare.* New York: Columbia University Press, 1991.

———. *A Year in the Life of William Shakespeare: 1599.* New York: HarperCollins, 2005.

Shirley, James. *The Gratefull Servant.* Acted 1629. London, 1630.

———. *The Royal Master.* Acted 1637. London, 1638.

———. *The Wedding.* Acted 1626–29. London, 1629.

Sidney, Philip. *Astrophil and Stella.* Written c. 1582, pub. 1591. In *Defence of Poesie,* ed. Watson. 23–82.

———. *The Countess of Pembroke's Arcadia.* Written c. 1580–84, pub.

1593. Ed. Maurice Evans. Harmondsworth, Middlesex, England: Penguin, 1977.

————. *The Defence of Poesie*. Written c. 1580–82, pub. 1595. In *Defence of Poesie*, ed. Watson. 83–130.

————. *Defence of Poesie, Astrophil and Stella, and Other Writings*. Ed. Elizabeth Porges Watson. London: Everyman, 1997.

Sinfield, Alan. "*Poetaster*, the Author, and the Perils of Cultural Production." In *Material London, ca. 1600*, ed. Lena Cowen Orlin. Philadelphia: University of Pennsylvania Press, 2000. 75–89.

Smith, Thomas. *Sir Thomas Smithes Voiage and Entertainment in Rushia*. London, 1605.

Spanish Tragedie, The. See Kyd, Thomas.

Spencer, Theodore. "*The Two Noble Kinsmen*." *Modern Philology* 36 (1939): 255–76.

Spenser, Edmund. *The Yale Edition of the Shorter Poems of Edmund Spenser*. Ed. William A. Oram et al. New Haven: Yale University Press, 1989.

[Spenser, Edmund, and Gabriel Harvey.] *Three Proper, and Wittie, Familiar Letters: Lately Passed Betweene Two Universitie Men* London, 1580.

Stallybrass, Peter. "Shakespeare, the Individual, and the Text." In *Cultural Studies*, ed. Lawrence Grossberg et al. New York: Routledge, 1992. 593–612.

Stallybrass, Peter, and Allon White. *The Politics and Poetics of Transgression*. London: Methuen, 1986.

Stow, John. *A Summarye of the Chronicles of Englande*. London, 1570.

Stow, John, Anthony Munday et al. *The Survey of London*. London, 1633.

Susanna. See Garter, Thomas.

Sykes, Henry Dugdale. *Sidelights on Shakespeare*. 1919. Rpt. Folcroft: Folcroft Library Editions, 1972.

Tallis, Thomas, and William Byrd. See Byrd and Tallis, *Cantiones*.

II Tamburlaine. See Marlowe, Christopher.

Tancred and Gismund, The Tragedies of, Compiled By the Gentlemen of the Inner Temple . . . By R[obert]. W[ilmot]. Acted 1566–68. London, 1591.

Tarltons Jests. London, 1613.

Tasso, Ercole, and Torquato Tasso. *Of Mariage and Wiving. An Excellent . . . Controversie, Betweene the Two Famous Tassi Now Living,* the One Hercules the Philospher, the Other, Torquato the Poet. London, 1599.

Tatham, John. *The Fancies Theater.* London, 1640.

Taylor, Gary. "Thomas Middleton: Lives and Afterlives." In Middleton, *Thomas Middleton.* 25–58.

Tennenhouse, Leonard. *Power on Display: The Politics of Shakespeare's Genres.* New York: Methuen, 1986.

Terence. *Andria.* Trans. Maurice Kyffin. London, 1588.

———. [*Comœdæ Sex.*] [London, 1497.]

———. *Terence in English.* Trans. R[ichard]. B[ernard]. Cambridge, 1598.

———. *Terens in Englysh.* [Paris, c. 1520.]

Thomson, Peter. *Shakespeare's Professional Career.* Cambridge: Cambridge University Press, 1992.

Thracian Wonder, The. Acted c. 1590–1611. By John Webster[?], William Rowley[?], Thomas Heywood[?]. Ed. Michael Nolan. Salzburg: Institut für Anglistik und Amerikanistik, Universität Salzburg, 1997.

Towneley Plays, The. Ed. Martin Stevens and A. C. Cawley. 2 vols. Oxford: Oxford University Press, 1994.

Triall of Treasure, The. See Wager, W.

Turberville, George. *Epitaphes, Epigrams, Songs and Sonets.* London, 1567.

Tyde Taryeth No Man, The. See Wapull, George.

Udall, Nicholas. *Floures for Latine Spekynge Selected and Gathered Oute of Terence.* [London], 1534.

———.[?] *Iacob and Esau.* Acted c. 1550–57. London, 1568.

———.[?] *Respublica.* Acted 1553. Ed. W. W. Greg. London: Oxford University Press, 1952.

Vergil, Polydore. *An Abridgement of the Notable Woorke of Polidore Vergile.* By Thomas Langley. London, 1546.

Vickers, Brian. *"Counterfeiting" Shakespeare: Evidence, Authorship, and John Ford's* Funerall Elegye. Cambridge: Cambridge University Press, 2002.

———. *Shakespeare, Co-Author: A Historical Study of Five Collaborative Plays.* Oxford: Oxford University Press, 2002.

[Wager?, W.] *A New and Mery Enterlude, Called the Triall of Treasure.* Acted 1567. London, 1567.

Waith, Eugene M., ed. *The Two Noble Kinsmen by William Shakespeare.* Oxford: Oxford University Press, 1989.

Wall, Wendy. "Authorship and the Material Conditions of Writing." In *The Cambridge Companion to English Literature 1500–1600,* ed. Arthur F. Kinney. Cambridge: Cambridge University Press, 2000. 64–89.

———. "Dramatic Authorship and Print." In *Early Modern English Drama: A Critical Companion,* ed. Garrett A. Sullivan Jr., Patrick Cheney, and Andrew Hadfield. Oxford: Oxford University Press, 2006. 1–11.

Wapull, George. *The Tyde Taryeth No Man.* Acted 1576. London, 1576.

Webbe, William. *Discourse of English Poetrie.* London, 1586.

Weever, John. *Epigrammes.* 1599. In *John Weever: A Biography of a Literary Associate of Shakespeare and Jonson, Together with a Photographic Facsimile of Weever's Epigrammes (1599),* ed. E. A. J. Honigmann. New York: St. Martin's Press, 1987. 86–131.

W[eever]. I[ohn]. *An Agnus Dei.* London, 1601.

[———.] *The Mirror of Martyrs, or The Life and Death of that Thrice Valiant Capitaine, and Most Godly Martyre Sir John Old-castle Knight, Lord Cobham.* London, 1601.

[———.] *The Whipping of the Satyre.* 1601. In *The Whipper Pamphlets,* ed. Arnold Davenport. 2 parts. Liverpool: University Press of Liverpool, 1951. Part 1.

Weimann, Robert. *Author's Pen and Actor's Voice: Playing and Writing in Shakespeare's Theater.* Cambridge: Cambridge University Press, 2000.

Westling, Louise. "The Pose of the Libertine in Michael Drayton's *Idea.*" Ph.D. diss., University of Oregon, 1974.

Wickham, Glynne, et al., eds. *English Professional Theatre, 1530–1660.* Cambridge: Cambridge University Press, 2000.

Wiles, David. *Shakespeare's Clown: Actor and Text in the Elizabethan Playhouse.* Cambridge: Cambridge University Press, 1987.

Wilkins, George. *The Historie of Iustine . . . First Written in Latine by That Famous Historiographer IUSTINE, and Now Again Newly Translated into English, by G. W.* London, 1606.

[Wilkins, George,] and William Shakespeare. *See* Shakespeare and Wilkins, *Pericles.*

Wilson, Robert. *The Coblers Prophesie.* Acted c. 1589–93. London, 1594.

[———?.] *The Pedlers Prophecie.* Acted c. 1561–63. London, 1595.

Withycombe, E. G. *The Oxford Dictionary of English Christian Names.* 2d ed. Oxford: Clarendon Press, 1950; corrected through 1963.

Witts Recreations. London, 1640.

Woman in the Moone. See Lyly, John.

Woodes, Nathaniel. *The Conflict of Conscience.* Acted 1570–81. London, 1581.

Woodmansee, Martha. "On the Author Effect: Recovering Collectivity." In *The Construction of Authorship: Textual Appropriation in Law and Literature,* ed. Martha Woodmansee and Peter Jazi. Durham, N.C.: Duke University Press, 1994. 15–28.

York Plays, The. Ed. Richard Beadle. London: Edward Arnold, 1982.

Index